Beardie Basics

Also by
Barbara Rieseberg and B. J. McKinney:
Sheltie Talk, Alpine Publications, 1976.

Dedicated to

Mrs. Olive Willison
for her tireless work
to revive the Bearded Collie
as a show breed,

and to

Miss Margaret Osborne
for introducing us to the breed,
and for her generous help and hospitality
while we were doing research.

Should you,
while wandering in the wild sheep land,
happen on moor or in market
upon a very perfect gentley knight,
clothed in dark grey habit,
splashed here and there with rays of moon;

free by right divine
of the guild of gentlemen,
strenous as a prince,
lithe as a rowan,
graceful as a girl,
with high king carriage,
motions and manners of a fairy queen;
should he have a noble breadth of brow,
an air of still strength
born of right confidence, all anassuming;

last and most unfailing test of all,
should you look into two snow-clad eyes,
calm, wistful, inscrutable,
their soft depths clothed on with eternal sadness—
yearning, as is said,
for the soul that is not theirs—

know then,
that you look upon
one of the line of the most illustrious
sheepdogs of the North.

Alfred Ollivant

Ch. Rich-Lins Royal Shag, ROM. Richard and Linda Nootbar, Richlin.

Beardie Basics

by Barbara Rieseberg and B. J. McKinney

Revised by B. J. McKinney and Freedo Rieseberg

Revised 1983
Alpine Publications
214 19th Street S.W.
Loveland, Colorado 80537

viii

Library of Congress Card No. 83-73606
International Standard Book Number: 0-931866-16-2

Third edition 1983.
Printed in the United States of America.

Contents

Foreword

When I was asked to do the foreword for "Beardie Basics," my first thought was, "Yes, it's easy." But when I picked up my pen, suddenly I realized this was not going to be a simple task.

It's fifteen years since our first Beardie entered my life. Alas, she left us in December, but it's entirely due to Bluebelle that I am in a position to write today.

Beardies first caught my eye because of their shaggy appearance. They looked, and are, rather mischievious, friendly, family dogs that really steal your heart.

When I first entered the show ring there didn't seem to be two Beardies who looked alike. Some, in fact, were filthy, ungroomed animals who looked as if they had just come in from a hard day's work in muddy fields. There was a wide range of sizes; coats varied from short to floor length and from straight to tight curls. In fact, at that time you could virtually fit the Standard to any shaggy dog.

I am often asked how Beardies have changed over the years. Size is still a problem in the breed, and coats still vary in length and texture, but now at least the Bearded Collies do look like a breed. They are shown well groomed and clean. But how I deplore the habit of parting the hair down the spine, and then draping it like curtains over the dog's sides! Coats are straighter, but many are soft and far too long. Eyes seem to be getting lighter, and nasal pigmentation is often lacking. Now, some dogs are very obviously being trimmed.

The Beardie is comparatively new to your country. Now is the time for you to decide if you want a glamorous show-stopper, or if you prefer an elegant, yet workmanlike dog who could, with training, still do the job for which he was destined. Fashion is fickle. Here in England, to my joy, the judges are again ignoring the "pretty long-coated dog with the hackney action" and reverting to his elegant, yet workmanlike, ground-covering brother whose coat, though thick and abundant, does not obscure his outline.

Like me, you must have been attracted to the Beardie for his handy size, adaptability, and of course his appearance. His future is in your hands. Search your consciences, examine the photos of the early winners (i.e. Benjie, Bravo, Beauty Queen, Bronze Penny, Blue Bonnie, etc.), then compare them with today's winners. Remember — it was these original Beardies that attracted you to the breed in the first place.

In conclusion, I wish the Beardie well in the country of his adoption. I hope this book will prove useful to experienced and novice breeders alike.

Jenny H. Osborne SRN

President, Bearded Collie Club
Osmart Kennels
Bacup
Lancashire OL13 8ND
England

ACKNOWLEDGEMENTS

We wish to thank all of the breeders and owners who supplied photographs for this book. Special thanks is due to Barbara Iremonger, Jennie Osborne, Jackie Tidsmarsh, and the many other English breeders who supplied priceless historic photos and assisted us with our research.

We are grateful for the help of the staff of the Valley Veterinary Clinic, Longmont, Colorado, and the Colorado State University Veterinary Medicine Clinic, Fort Collins, Colorado; as well as to Dr. Phyllis Holst, D.V.M., for assistance on the medical and breeding chapters.

xiv

Int. French, German, Luxembourg Ch., World Champion FCI 1981, VDH-Ch. Davealex Willy Wumpkins. Willy has sired more than 250 children, including American, English, German, Luxembourg and International champions. He has a son and a daughter who both were junior world champions. Willy is sired by Ch. Legal Aide from Davealex ex Davealex Gold Tang. Breeder, Mr. & Mrs. Stopforth, England. Owners, Jan and Rose DeWit, Holland.

Tandewis photo.

1 *The Beardie Charisma*

The Bearded Collie is a "super dog" to those of us who love him.[1] While not perfect for everyone, the breed is unique in its capabilities, endearing qualities, and timeless beauty. He is truly a gift from the past—with a heritage all but lost in many of today's breeds. The "Beardie" comes to us unchanged in beauty and spirit over the centuries. Today's breeder is faced with the awesome responsibility of preserving the Beardies' virtues—virtues which are beyond price and which, once lost, can never be recovered.

I first acquired a Bearded Collie because of a compromise and, in doing so, accidentally found a breed that has been infinitely more satisfactory and enjoyable than most of its numerous predecessors in our household. I had become disillusioned with showing and felt that we needed a "glamour dog"—something like an Afghan Hound or a Shih Tzu. My husband wanted a utility breed such as a German Shepherd or a Border Collie. A friend from England suggested a Bearded Collie, and for the first time both of our interests were sparked. We had never actually seen a Beardie, but the dogs checked out satisfactorily. They were virtually free of hereditary problems and were a "natural" breed that appealed to both of us. While Beardies appeared a bit more "common" on first glance than I liked, they proved on closer inspection to possess a certain nobility and charm. They were a convenient size, undoubtedly would possess the working dog temperament I preferred, and had a long coat. The excitement of finding and importing acceptable individuals, and the attention they would attract as a rare breed, would keep me interested until I acquired a working knowledge of the breed. But what if we couldn't show them because the breed was unrecognized by the AKC? Well, I was tired of shows anyway (I thought), and we could always vacation in Canada where the dogs could obtain championships. They were certainly a close descendant of the farm worker and were highly intelligent and trainable, which made the breed acceptable to my husband.

1

All of these generalizations were to prove true; and as a bonus, we are now able to show Beardies in the United States—sooner than we had dreamed possible. However, none of these reasons caused us to be won over to the breed. One has to live with a Beardie to appreciate his worth and character. I never intended Beardies to be more than a sideline to my thoroughly established dog activities, and yet with each new puppy I now behave as though it were my first pet. This undermining of my resistance was accomplished so completely that now, within just a few years, we are associated almost entirely with Beardies. I love each one with a passion reserved for only a very special few in other breeds.

This phenomenon seems to affect most new owners, from the pet owner to those "doggy folk" in other breeds who get a Beardie for fun. It is something indescribable which we call "the Beardie charisma." It has to do with the temperament and personality of each dog, but it is more. It is an interrelationship between person and dog which transcends mere ownership. It encompasses devotion, companionship, and, perhaps most of all, a mutual respect. It instills in the person lucky enough to feel this bond a sense of responsibility to a particular animal.

TEMPERAMENT AND PERSONALITY

Each individual Bearded Collie is different from all others, yet all possess some traits that are uniquely "Beardie"—characteristics shared by

2

others within the breed but which set Beardies apart from other breeds of dog. Beardies are usually happy. They forgive easily and never hold grudges, yet they never miss a lesson along the way. Their enthusiasm for life and all it offers can be contagious; they are often funny, sometimes without intending to be. Beardies bubble over with love for everyone. They assume that everyone welcomes them with equal abandon, and a visitor may be surprised by a bear hug and kiss from the family Beardie.

Temperament is inherited. It dictates if a Beardie will be timid or aggressive, boisterous or quiet, responsive or stubborn. These basics cannot be drastically changed, and they will be passed on to the offspring. Luckily, most Beardies are self-assured, steady, and sensible. To pick an individual that is anything less is to jeopardize your chance for a happy relationship with the dog. There is a wide range of acceptable temperaments, but neither a dog that is very timid nor one that is offensively aggressive should be considered "typical." Some Beardies are reserved with strangers and some are openly affectionate with everyone, but all must respond to their owners to be correct working dogs.

Temperament can be modified by the dog's environment. Proper socialization and training are beneficial, while abuse or neglect can create character flaws. Personality, on the other hand, is acquired by association with man. It is the full expression of individual characteristics developed within the limitations of the dog's inherited temperament. "Character," an important element in the Beardie charisma, is a combination of the

A litter of eight-week-old pups at Artisan. All three finished their championship as adults.

dog's temperament and personality. A dog with sound character is one that behaves predictably and intelligently in any circumstance and that has enough personality to be an interesting companion.

One Beardie owner was surprised to see how her male dog handled a small dog that kept snapping at him and yanking his whiskers. He ignored it as long as possible, then nonchalantly sauntered over and sat on the offender. The Beardie rolled his angelic eyes upward and simply didn't hear the raging, though somewhat muffled, insults being flung at him. In another instance my male, Kent, was sleeping peacefully in an exercise pen at a crowded show. A smooth collie in a neighboring pen spotted him and began barking shrilly through her bars. Kent got up and approached her in a friendly manner. Her barking turned slightly hysterical, then she lunged at him and ran backward, barking all the while. Kent stood quietly and wagged his tail at her for about a minute, but she showed no signs of relenting in her tirade. Kent deliberately lifted his leg, took careful aim, and sprinkled her papers without getting a drop in the aisle between their pens. He then turned his tail to her and purposefully lay down again, refusing to look at her for the entire day.

When selecting a Beardie, choose one whose temperament appeals to you as long as it falls within reasonable limits. One person may prefer a rambunctious animal, another may select a sweet, quiet individual. The most important requisite at any age is responsiveness to the owner. This determines trainability, the ability to communicate, and the "will to please."

Instinctive Behavior and Needs

In addition to temperament, any given individual inherits instinctive responses. In Beardies, the dominant instinct is to herd. This makes them extremely suitable as family dogs, but also causes them to have certain requirements. Any potential owner should be aware that Beardies can be rather independent, and the owner must exert enough dominance to maintain control. Herding dogs have an inborn will to please, yet a compulsion to complete a job with single-minded fanaticism. Beardies have been selected for centuries on the basis of intelligence balanced by responsiveness to people. They are also protective of their charges, which can include children, puppies, and other animals in place of a flock of sheep, and may try to bunch their charges

together. A mother dog will often worry her puppies until she has them snuggly grouped together. The Beardie is not a guard dog, but he makes an outstanding nursemaid. Do not expect him to attack an intruder; unless his people are actually threatened, such action would be contrary to a Beardie's nature.

Beardies are active and intelligent and are easily bored if neglected. Although they are well mannered and capable of amusing themselves, they crave a fair amount of personal contact and mental stimulation. A neglected Beardie may become unintentionally destructive. Beardies need owners who are consistent about training and who offer a firm, but fair, authority. Good parents usually make good Beardie owners.

House Dog or Kennel Dog?

Most Beardies make admirable house dogs. They are clean and require little conscious housebreaking, and of course their personalities flourish best when they are part of the family. Although exuberant outdoors, they settle down and are well mannered after the initial greeting in the house.

Beardies do well under kennel situations also, but they must be provided with adequate exercise and enough human contact for proper socialization. When selecting a dog, be sure that he shows evidence of proper socialization. A friendly, responsive Beardie will adjust well as a pet regardless of whether he has been raised in the house or in the kennel.

A wildly exuberant, hesitant, or destructive dog is likely showing signs of neglect and will need individual attention before he behaves more favorably. He will probably adjust well with patience on the part of the new owner, but more effort must be expended than with a properly socialized puppy. It is far easier to get control of an extrovert than to give confidence to a timid dog.

A NEW START FOR AN ANCIENT BREED

To appreciate the intricacies of the Beardie's nature, one must look to his heritage. Until very recent times he has been strictly a working stock dog. Most Beardies exhibit herding characteristics similar to those of the Border Collie—they circle and bunch the flock and often display "eye" while working. History credits them with being herders but also records their service in working behind herds of cattle while driving them to market. Apparently Beardies excelled at both functions. This is remarkable, as most breeds specialize in only one of these tasks and must be taught the other chore against their instinct. Many modern herding books reference the Beardie as a drover, but I question this classification. Beardies, in fact, seem to be the only breed capable of rivaling Border Collies at their own herding trials. Though fewer in number, and virtually unknown in most areas, Beardies command respect from everyone when they do compete.

The documentation of the breed's history is incomplete because Beardies belonged to the hill shepherd rather than catching the nobleman's fancy as a show breed. However, they are mentioned throughout several centuries and appear to be one of the oldest British breeds, tracing probably as far back as A.D. 1540 in recognizable form.

Records show that in about 1514 three Lowland Polish Sheepdogs—two bitches and one male—were traded to a Scottish shepherd for a valuable ram and ewe. These individuals probably founded the breed we know as the Bearded Collie. Some researchers believe that the breed was already established in Britain at the time of the Roman invasion.

It is universally accepted that the Bearded Collie, like the Puli and most other shaggy sheepdog breeds, is descended from the Kommondor of the Magyars in central Europe.

By the 1700s Beardies were showing up regularly in British portraits and writings. Prior to

1900 the breed was often called the "Highland Sheepdog" or "Highland Collie"—the word "Collie" being a misnomer for the Scottish word of "sheepdog." The breed was also mentioned occasionally under the name of "Mountain Collie" or "Hairy Moued Collie."

By 1800 the breed was quite popular, and some individuals were even later bred for showing in southern Scotland. There were two distinct varieties. The Border or Lowland type was a large, slate-colored dog with long, harsh, straight hair. He often measured as tall as 24 or 25 inches at the shoulder. The brown-colored Highland variety was smaller and more agile. He had a shorter, wavy coat. The two varieties were crossed to combine the best qualities of both in the modern Beardie. The curly coat has been bred out, and coat quality (either straight or slightly wavy) is now the same in all colors.

Although the Beardie was well established as a breed, no Standard or breed club existed until 1912. This led to the virtual extinction of the breed as a recognized entity. The breed was kept alive only by a few shepherds who raised Bearded Collies to work sheep. These dogs were kept pure in lineage, but no records or registrations were kept. The Beardies were saved only because of their working ability and their resistance to the cold, rainy Scottish climate. Beardies are believed to figure prominently in the background of the more recent Border Collie and Old English Sheepdog breeds, and indeed, a specimen with Beardie coat and characteristics still crops up now and then in registered Border Collie litters. The occasional smooth Beardie is

4

An early Bearded Collie, photo courtesy of Jackie Tidmarsh.

Top: Bailie of Bothkennar and son, Bruce of Bothkennar.

First registered litter (by Bailie ex Jeannie): left to right: Bravado, Buskie, Bruce and Bogle.

Bottom, Jeannie of Bothkennar.

5

proof that the Border Collie could have been bred down from the Beardie with careful selection and perhaps a few outcrosses. Since Border Collies have always been selected for working ability rather than for type, it is likely that both rough and smooth varieties will be tolerated for some time in that breed. In Beardies, however, where type has always been more uniform and distinctive, breeders choose to eliminate and not register the occasional smooth specimen.

Revival of the Show Beardie

In 1944 Mrs. G. O. Willison accidentally acquired a brown Beardie bitch puppy while searching for a working Shetland Sheepdog. It took her some time to realize that "Jeannie" was a Bearded Collie and not just a Sheepdog cross, and by that time Mrs. Willison had been thoroughly won over by the Beardie charm. From this bitch and from a few other Beardies of working lineage who became certified as purebred come all of the registered Beardies in the world today. Mrs. Willison engaged in a long and frustrating search for a suitable mate for Jeannie and eventually acquired a slate male whom she called "Bailie of Bothkennar." The breed made a cautious comeback under her fostering and in 1959 gained championship status in England. Thanks to Mrs. Willison, the Bearded Collie is once again a popular breed in England, though perhaps no longer in his traditional role as a worker.

Beardies quickly spread to other countries. The first litter whelped in the United States was bred by Mr. and Mrs. Lawrence Levy in 1967. The Bearded Collie Club of America was founded in 1969. The tireless efforts of a few early members resulted in the AKCs granting miscellaneous recognition to the breed in 1974 and entering the Bearded Collie in the stud book with full working breed status in October 1976. Beardies began their show career in the United States on February 1, 1977. Their existence was made obvious to all when Ch. Brambledale Blue Bonnet C.D. won an all-breed "Best In Show"— a remarkable feat for any bitch, especially for one of a new, rare breed. My own Ch. Shiel's Mogador Silverleaf C.D. put the males in the record by taking a second "Best In Show" during the first year of breed recognition. Several other notable dogs won group placements, and a number of champions finished during 1977. The Bearded Collie established his reputation as a sound, stable working dog by show definition as well as by his proven herding ability.

ENDNOTES

[1]The authors have chosen to use the male gender when referring to dogs or people of either sex. No discrimination is intended.

The first Bearded Collie champion, 1959, Eng. Ch. Beauty Queen of Bothkennar, owned by Mrs. G. O. Willison.

6

The first American champion, 1977, Brambledale Blue Bonnet C.D., owned by Mr. and Mrs. Robert Lachman.

2 Ideals and Interpretations

A subjective evaluation of any animal must involve comparing him to what he should be. In the show ring, the contender is judged against the other entrants. However, to the breeder, every individual must be compared to the ideal specimen of the breed. But what is ideal? Is this different to each person, or is there a common goal? Must a beginner be influenced by the opinion of only one established breeder? Where can one turn to find a *universal* concept of the perfect Beardie? The flawless Beardie does not exist, but the mental image of what he looks like is necessary for any breeder or fancier. It provides a goal to strive toward with every selection and breeding.

Each recognized breed of dog has a written description of the "ideal" for that breed. This word picture is known as the "Standard" and is the final authority to which all breeders, judges, and students of the breed must turn. The Standard is often referred to as the blueprint for the breed; it allows for individual interpretation while drawing boundaries of acceptable variation. Any changes in the Standard must be undertaken very seriously, and the final product must be worthy of representing the breed for generations to come. Even the most minute change in the Standard can influence the interpretation of that section by the breeders and therefore influence the direction of breed evolution. We have seen this happen in other breeds, where a slight difference in the wording of the standards can change the emphasis so that the same breed becomes almost unrecognizable from country to country. We do not want to see this happen to the Bearded Collie, but breeders and judges desperately need a clear, descriptive Standard in these formative days of the breed in our country. The AKC approved a revised Standard for the Bearded Collie and published it in September 1978. It stresses the importance of naturalness and obvious working heritage of this breed.

The original Standard was extremely vague and could actually have described a number of shaggy breeds. Once a person knew what a good Beardie was, the old Standard could be made to fit the dog. The new Standard clarifies the details of breed characteristics without changing the intent of the original Standard. It is now the final authority for evaluating the Bearded Collie. For those learning the breed, for judges needing a basis for evaluation, and as a factor in maintaining uniformity within the breed, this Standard is clear, accurate, and encompass most aspects of the dog. Breeders must never presume to make the Standard fit the dogs; the dogs should always be bred to conform to a well written Standard.

OFFICIAL BEARDED COLLIE STANDARD

CHARACTERISTICS: The Bearded Collie is hardy and active, with an aura of strength and agility characteristic of a real working dog. Bred for centuries as a companion and servant of man, the Bearded Collie is a devoted and intelligent member of the family. He is stable and self-confident, showing no signs of shyness or aggression. This is a natural and unspoiled breed.

GENERAL APPEARANCE: The Bearded Collie is a medium-sized shaggy dog with a medium length coat that follows the natural lines of the body and allows plenty of daylight under the body. The body is long and lean, and, though strongly made, does not appear heavy. A bright, inquiring expression is a distinctive feature of the breed. The Bearded Collie should be shown in a natural stance.

HEAD: The head is in proportion to the size of the dog. The skull is broad and flat; the stop is moderate; the cheeks are well filled beneath the eyes; the muzzle is strong and full; the foreface is equal in length to the distance between the stop and occiput. The nose is large and squareish. A snipey muzzle is to be penalized. (See Color section for pigmentation.)
Eyes: The eyes are large, expressive, soft and affectionate, but not round nor protruding, and are set widely apart. The eyebrows are arched to the sides to frame the eyes and are long enough to blend smoothly into the coat on the sides of the head. (See Color section for eye color.)
Ears: The ears are medium sized, hanging, and covered with long hair. They are set level with the eyes. When the dog is alert, the ears have a slight lift at the base.
Teeth: The teeth are strong and white, meeting in a scissors bite. Full dentition is desirable.

NECK: The neck is in proportion to the length of the body, strong and slightly arched, blending smoothly into the shoulders.

FOREQUARTERS: The shoulders are well laid back at an angle of approximately forty-five degrees; a line drawn from the highest point of the shoulder blade to the forward point of articulation approximates a right angle with a line from the forward point of articulation to the point of elbow. The top of the shoulder blades lie in against the withers, but they slope outwards from there sufficiently to accommodate the desired spring of ribs. The legs are straight and vertical with substantial, but not heavy, bone and are covered with shaggy hair all around. The pasterns are flexible without weakness.

BODY: The body is longer than it is high in an approximate ratio of five to four, length measured from point of chest to point of buttocks; height measured at the highest point of the withers. The length of the back comes from the length of the ribcage and not that of the loin. The back is level. The ribs are well-sprung from the spine but

8 Eng. Ch. Pepperland Lyric John at Potterdale, *Potterdale,* a male of outstanding type.

Multi-group placing Ch. Lochengar Never Surrender exhibits femininity in a bitch.

are flat at the sides. The chest is deep, reaching at least to the elbows. The loins are strong. The level back line blends smoothly into the curve of the rump. A flat croup or a steep croup is to be severely penalized.

HINDQUARTERS: The hind legs are powerful and muscular at the thighs with well-bent stifles. The hocks are low. In normal stance, the bones below the hocks are perpendicular to the ground and parallel to each other when viewed from the rear; the hind feet fall just behind a perpendicular line from the point of buttocks when viewed from the side. The legs are covered with shaggy hair all around.

Tail: The tail is set low and is long enough for the end of the bone to reach at least the point of the hocks. It is normally carried low with an upward swirl at the tip while the dog is standing. When the dog is excited or in motion, the curve is accentuated and the tail may be raised but is never carried beyond a vertical line. The tail is covered with abundant hair.

FEET: The feet are oval in shape with the soles well padded. The toes are arched and close together, and well-covered with hair including between the pads.

COAT: The coat is double with the undercoat soft, furry and close. The outercoat is flat, harsh, strong and shaggy, free from wooliness and curl, although a slight wave is permissible. The coat falls naturally to either side but must never be artificially parted. The length and density of the hair are sufficient to provide a protective coat and to enhance the shape of the dog, but not so profuse as to obscure the natural lines of the body. The dog should be shown as naturally as is consistent with good grooming, but the coat must not be trimmed in any way. On the head, the bridge of the nose is sparsely covered with hair which is slightly longer on the sides to cover the lips. From the cheeks, the lower lips and under the chin, the coat increases in length towards the chest, forming the typical beard. An excessively long, silky coat or one which has been trimmed in any way must be severely penalized.

COLOR:
Coat: All Bearded Collies are born either black, blue, brown or fawn, with or without white markings. With maturity, the color may lighten, so that a born black may become any shade of gray from black to slate to silver, a born brown from chocolate to sandy. Blues and fawns also show shades from dark to light. Where white occurs, it only appears on the foreface as a blaze, on the skull, on the tip of the tail, on the chest, legs and feet and around the neck. The white hair does not grow on the body behind the shoulder nor on the face to surround the eyes. Tan markings occasionally appear and are acceptable on the eyebrows, inside the ears, on the cheeks, under the root of the tail, and on the legs where white joins the main color.
Pigmentation: Pigmentation on the Bearded Collie follows the coat color. In a born black, the eye rims, nose and lips are black, whereas in the born blue, the pigmentation is a blue-gray color. A born brown dog has brown pigmentation and born fawns a correspondingly lighter brown. The pigmentation is completely filled in and shows no sign of spots.

Eyes: Eye color will generally tone with the coat color. In a born blue or fawn, the distinctively lighter eyes are correct and must not be penalized.

SIZE: The ideal height at the withers is 21-22 inches for adult dogs and 20-21 inches for adult bitches. Height over and under the ideal is to be severely penalized. The express objective of this criterion is to insure that the Bearded Collie remains a medium sized dog.

GAIT: Movement is free, supple and powerful. Balance combines good reach in forequarters with strong drive in hindquarters. The back remains firm and level. The feet are lifted only enough to clear the ground, giving the impression that the dog glides along making minimum contact. Movement is lithe and flexible to enable the dog to make the sharp turns and sudden stops required of the sheep dog. When viewed from the front or rear, the front and rear legs travel in the same plane from shoulder and hip joint to pads at all speeds. Legs remains straight, but feet move inward as speed increases until the edges of the feet converge on a center line at a fast trot.

SERIOUS FAULTS:
  Snipey muzzle
  Flat croup or steep croup
  Excessively long, silky coat
  Trimmed or sculptured coat
  Height over or under the ideal

The original draft of this Standard as voted overwhelmingly by the members of the Bearded Collie Club of America included two disqualifications which regrettably have since been tabled by AKC. They read: "A predominantly white dog (over fifty percent) must be disqualified" and "Height more than an inch over the ideal is to be disqualified." Since whites and oversize are considered by most experienced breeders to be a specific threat to Beardie breed character, dogs exhibiting these traits should be among the first to be eliminated from a breeding program and show string.

The two most prevalent discrepancies from the Standard seen in the show ring today are oversize dogs and, in a few areas, total disregard for the insistence on naturalness. Dogs are seen with obvious trimming (especially on the feet and legs) and artificially parted coats. These individuals often have soft, silky, and many times too long coats which must be presented artificially to look neat. Beardies with incorrect coat texture, quantity, and/or grooming do not exhibit the most distinctive Beardie characteristic, SHAGGI-NESS. These dogs, especially those presented artificially, should be severely faulted in the show ring. If they are allowed to win, they will encourage those few short-sighted exhibitors who wish to "improve" on the Standard.

9

Other common faults to watch for are "east-west" feet (especially fronts); long, narrow heads with the eyes too close together; and bite faults.

Although this Standard is a vast improvement over the old one, it still has a few discrepancies. The most serious error is the ear set. It should read, "The *orifice* of the ear is set level with the eyes." I feel that the current wording could encourage a houndlike ear. The original Standard called for a high-set ear, which is probably more functional for hearing in a working dog. Because the tendency for small, high-set ears has gone to an extreme in some lines, the reaction of breeders is to compensate for it in the Standard. Be aware that this can create problems in the opposite direction. Moderation is always best because breeders will exaggerate their interpretations to both sides anyway.

Eye shape is still omitted. A large, oval eye is preferred.

Length of the upper arm is omitted, although it is indirectly specified by the gait requirement. The upper arm should be equal in length to the shoulder blade.

Croups should be described more completely. The correct slope of croup for a Beardie is about twenty-five degrees, which is slightly flatter than the thirty degree slope common to most other working breeds. The Beardie developed this trait to be able to leap straight up to facilitate his sheep herding on the rough moorish countryside. Since the flatter croup

and correspondingly squared off topline are distinctive breed characteristics, I feel they should be mentioned.

Recent studies indicate that a well laid back shoulder may actually measure less than the accepted 45 degree angle. Dogs with ideal lay-back who were previously assumed to have 45 degree shoulder angulation probably measure closer to 39 degrees. This discrepancy is due strictly to methods of measurement. It is NOT intended to advocate straighter shoulder angulation.

Two minor comments concerning the color section are in order, but involve interpretation rather than any needed change in the Standard. The phrase, "The white does not grow . . . on the face to surround the eyes" should never, by any stretch of the imagination, be interpreted to fault a blaze which arches over the eyes as the hair lengthens. The unacceptable white is seen as a predominately white head or a blaze so wide it encompasses the eyes at the skin line.

The reference that pigmentation should have no spots means no flesh colored spots should appear on the nose leather, visible part of the lips, or eyerims. It does not refer to a pink spot on the bridge of the muzzle, a normal occurrence in any breed which has white markings on the face.

Measurement of height has been changed to reach to the withers rather than to the shoulder blade. Although this changes the effect of the ideal size slightly, it now conforms with the

10

Lovely head type. Eng. Ch. Bravo of Bothkennar, *Osmart*.

Parcana Possibility, *Silverleaf*, shows correct coat texture.

required method of measurement of all breeds by AKC.

The deletion of the level bite as correct may affect some breeders, but the scissors bite is stronger and less wearing on the teeth, and is structurally more sound, so should be encouraged.

On the whole, this Standard is a tribute to those who compiled it. It has become an excellent, workable blueprint for the Bearded Collie, and is the only authority by which a Beardie should be judged in this country.

The Bearded Collie Club in England is also working on a proposed clarification of their Standard. I hope that the final form of the British and BCCA Standards can be similar enough to assure uniformity of the Bearded Collie the world over. There is some disagreement between the Bearded Collie Club and the Standards Committee of the Kennel Club over proportions of the muzzle and backskull. However, the breeders prefer it remain as proposed here.

PROPOSED BRITISH STANDARD

CHARACTERISTICS: The Bearded Collie must be alert, and should be lively, self-confident and active. The temperament should be that of a steady, intelligent working dog, with no sign of nervousness or aggression.

GENERAL APPEARANCE: This is a lean active dog, longer than it is high in an approximate proportion of 5 to 4, measured from point of chest to point of buttock. Bitches may be slightly longer. The dog, though strongly made, should show plenty of daylight under the body and should not look too heavy. Movement should be supple, smooth and long reaching, covering the ground with the minimum of effort. A bright, enquiring expression is a distinctive feature of the breed.

HEAD: The head should be in proportion to the size of the dog. The skull is broad and flat, the distance between stop and occiput being equal to the width between the orifices of the ears. The muzzle is strong and equal in length to the distance between the stop and occiput, the whole effect being that of a dog with strength of muzzle and plenty of brain room. The stop should be moderate. The nose is large and square, generally black but will normally follow the coat colour in blues and browns. The nose and lips should be of solid colour without spots or patches. Pigmentation of lips and eye rims should follow nose colour.

Bites: left, correct scissors bite; right, overshot bite – incorrect for an adult, but may correct if seen in a puppy.

Bottom left: correct ear set; bottom right: ears set too high.

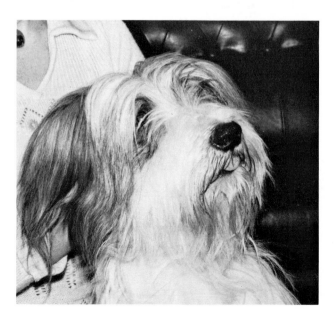

11

PARTS OF THE BEARDIE

1. Foreface or muzzle. Well filled below the eyes. Broad and blunt.
2. Stop. Nose to stop should be equal to or slightly shorter in length than stop to occiput. Stop should be well defined.
3. Occiput.
4. Line indicating center of gravity.
5. Withers. The point to which height is measured.
6. Back. Moderately long, strong, and level.
7. Loin. Close coupled and muscular. Loin is the area between last rib and hipbone.
8. Croup. Should have slight downward slope.
9. Tail. Must reach at least to the hock. Low carriage is preferred.
10. Thigh. Well muscled and long.
11. Hock. Low set and flexible.
12. Stifle. Should be long and well bent.
13. Flank. Slightly tucked-up.
14. Elbow. Depth of chest should reach at least to this point.
15. Pastern. Should be strong and moderately sloped.
16. Upper arm. Angle of upper arm is measured where a line from point of shoulder to point of elbow intersects the perpendicular.
17. Point of shoulder.
18. Throatlatch.
19. Underjaw. Should be of sufficient length to provide for correct bite and allow lips to meet evenly.
20. Nose. Should be large and square.
21. Length of body measured from point of shoulder to point of hip. Standard calls for five to four ratio of length to height. Much of this length is due to proper angulation and length of rib cage.

12

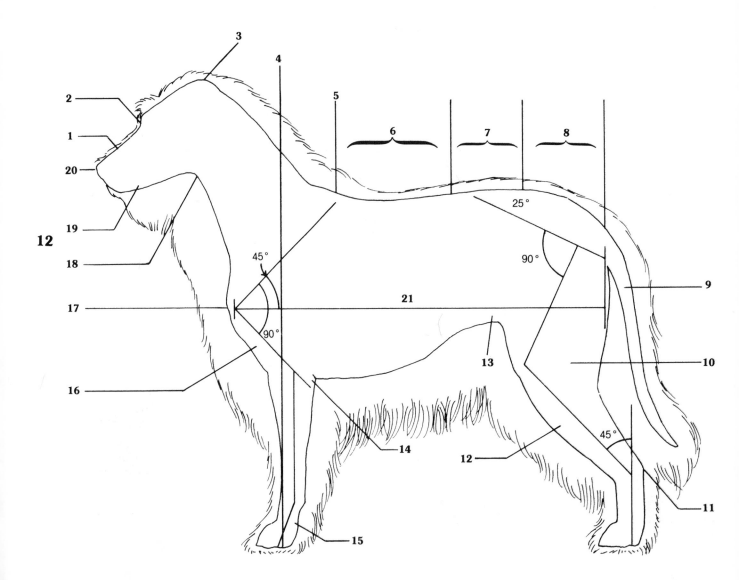

STRUCTURE OF THE BEARDIE

1. Skull. Should be broad and flat.
2. Neck. Moderately long and arched.
3. Rib cage. Long, sloping well back, with moderate spring flattened at the bottom.
4. Thoracic Vertibrae.
5. Lumbar Vertibrae.
6. Croup (Sacrum).
7. Pelvis (ilium).
8. Pelvis (ischium).
9. Upper thigh (femur). "Rear angulation" refers to the angle at which the upper thigh meets the pelvis. The ideal is ninety degrees.
10. Stifle joint (patella).
11. Stifle (tibia and fibula). Should be equal to or preferably longer than the thighbone.
12. Hock joint.
13. Metatarsus.
14. Elbow (olecranon).
15. Feet (phalanges).

16. Pastern (metacarpus).
17. Pastern joint.
18. Forearm (radius and ulna).
19. Upper arm (humerus). Should be equal in length to the shoulder blade. Actual length of bone is measured rather than to point of elbow.
20. Breastbone (prosternum). Projects slightly in front of point of shoulder, but should not be prominent.
21. Shoulder blade (scapula). "Front angulation" refers to the angle at which the scapula and humerus meet. Ideal angle is ninety degrees. Shoulder blade should be set at a 45-degree angle.
22. Cheekbones. Should be flat and merge smoothly with the skull without dips or ridges.

13

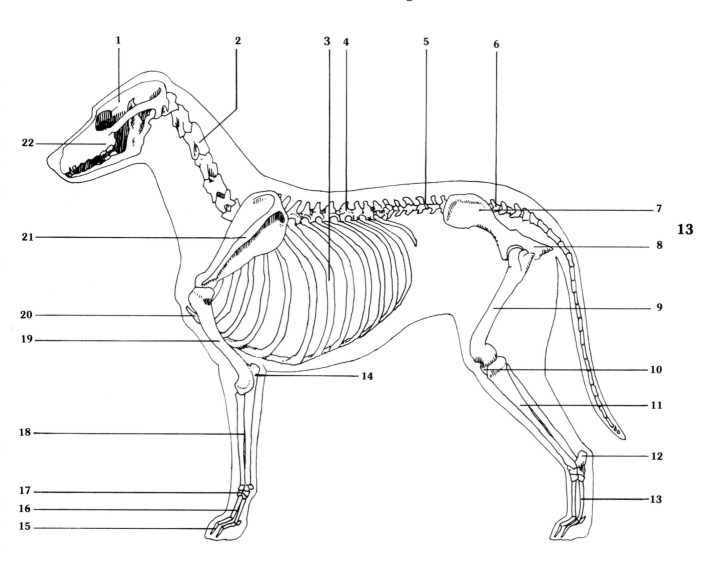

EYES: The eyes should tone with coat in colour, be set widely apart and be large, soft and affectionate, but not protruding. The eyebrows are arched up and forward but are not so long as to obscure the eyes.

EARS: The ears are of medium size and drooping. When the dog is alert, the ears lift at the base level with, but not above, the top of the skull, increasing the apparent breadth of the skull.

TEETH: The teeth are large and white, the incisors of the lower jaw fitting tightly behind those of the upper jaw. However a level bite is acceptable. A full set of forty-two teeth is desirable.

NECK: The neck must be of fair length, muscular and slightly arched.

FOREQUARTERS: The shoulders should slope well back, a line drawn through the centre of the shoulder blade should form a right angle (90°) with the humerus. The shoulder blades at the withers should only be separated by the vertebrae but must slope outwards from there sufficiently to accommodate the desired spring of rib. The legs are straight and vertical, with good bone, and covered with shaggy hair all round. The pasterns should be flexible without weakness.

BODY: The length of the back should come from the length of the ribcage and not that of the loin. The back must be level and the ribs well sprung but flat. The loins should be strong and the chest deep, giving plenty of heart and lung room.

HINDQUARTERS: The hindquarters are well muscled with good second thighs, well bent stifles and low hocks. The lower leg falls at a right angle to the ground and, in normal stance, will be just behind a line vertically below the point of the buttock.

FEET: The feet are oval in shape with the soles well padded. The toes are arched and close together, well covered with hair including between the pads.

TAIL: The tail is set low, without kink or twist, and is long enough for the end of the bone to reach at least the point of the hock. It is carried low with an upward swirl at the tip whilst standing or walking, but may be extended at speed. It is never carried curled over the back. The tail should be covered with abundant hair.

COAT: The coat must be double with the undercoat soft, furry and close. The outercoat should be flat, harsh, strong and shaggy, free from wooliness and curl, though a slight wave is permissible. The length and density of the hair should be sufficient to provide a protective coat and to enhance the shape of the dog, but not enough to obscure the natural lines of the body. The coat must not be trimmed in any way. On the head, the bridge of the nose should be sparsely covered with hair which should be slightly longer on the sides just to cover the lips. From the cheeks, the lower lips and under the chin, the coat increases in length towards the chest, forming the typical beard.

COLOUR: The colours are slate grey, reddish fawn, black, blue, all shades of grey, brown and sandy, with or without white markings. Where white occurs it should only appear in the foreface, as a blaze on the skull, on the tip of the tail, on the chest, legs and feet and, if round the collar, the roots of the white hair should not extend behind the shoulder. White should not appear above the hocks on the outside of the hind legs. Slight tan markings are acceptable on the eyebrows, inside the ears, on the cheeks, under the root of the tail, and on the legs where white joins the main colour.

SIZE: Ideal height at the shoulder:
Dogs 21"-22"
Bitches 20"-21"

14

Ch. Edenborough Parcana, Scothill.

Eng. Ch. Osmart Bonnie Blue Braid, *Doubletop.*

3 *Moving Out*

A Beardie's effectiveness as a working dog is primarily
determined by his physical ability. He must be swift, tireless, and
capable of sudden starts, stops, and turns. He has also developed the
unique ability to leap straight up from any position, a feat that is useful
in coping with the rough terrain and the half-wild sheep found in the
Beardie's native habitat.

While some aspects of structure influence efficiency of movement
more than others, a dog's conformation can be evaluated quickly and
relatively accurately by watching how he moves. Show ring evaluation of movement is made from three angles—as the dog approaches
the judge, as he gaits away from the judge, and from the side as the
dog circles the ring. Equal emphasis should be placed on each seg-
ment of gait. A dog that moves correctly is said to be "sound." (This
term can also refer to proper health and temperament but is usually
applied to gait.) When evaluating soundness, a judge looks for straight-
ness and strength of legs, ligamentation of the joints, and musculature.
These traits determine how well a dog will move within the limitations
of his skeletal structure. Evaluation is also made on strength of topline
and smoothness of motion, on where the feet hit the ground, and on
balance of the trot as determined by skeletal proportions and angles.
If everything is correct, the Beardie will exhibit a long, easy, effortless
stride which he can continue to use mile after mile. Conditioning the
muscles will enable a dog to exhibit his greatest potential (*see* ch. 7).

The natural working-dog gait is the trot. Since this is also the gait
at which structure can most easily be evaluated, it is the only gait used
in the show ring. The trot is achieved when the diagonal legs move in
unison (*see* fig. 1). It is a two-beat gait, with periods of suspension
between each beat in which all four legs are off the ground at once.
Length of stride is determined by the dog's "angulation." Front angulation is measured at the point of the shoulder; ideally, ninety degrees
between the shoulder blade and the upper arm, which should be of

equal length for maximum efficiency. Rear angulation is measured at the junction of the hip and thighbones—also a ninety-degree measurement in an ideal specimen. The thigh should be relatively long to allow for strong drive. In order for the trot to remain balanced, front and rear angulation must be the same. Therefore, if the ideal is not available, it is preferable to have a dog with a balanced front and rear angulation even though the angle is not perfect, rather than an individual that is well angulated at one end but poorly so at the other. The unbalanced dog cannot trot properly and must compensate in some aspect of his movement. Any gait deviation creates a weak point which, under prolonged stress or in old age, is subject to breakdown.

SIDE GAIT

The speed and endurance of the dog is determined by his side gait. To many breeders this is the most important aspect of gait because it has the greatest effect on the dog's efficiency. Unfortunately, it is also the most difficult for a beginner to recognize. It is imperative that any serious Beardie enthusiast learn to analyze side gait.

The correct trot viewed from the side is effortless and powerful (see fig. 2). The feet should be lifted only enough to clear the ground with a minimum of wasted vertical motion. This gives a Beardie the appearance of almost floating across the terrain. A bounce or roll to the topline is evidence of improper action. The topline should remain firm and level at all times.

The hindquarters provide the forward propulsion known as "drive." The front should be moving in line with and at the same efficiency as the rear in order to accept the drive and provide the primary balance and directional control. The front action is referred to as "reach" (see fig. 3).

The right hind leg and the left front leg move together, and the left hind leg and right foreleg move in unison. One set of diagonals hits the ground, completes the stride, and lifts for a period of suspension; then the second set of diagonals strikes the ground and propels the dog forward before another moment of suspension. Then the process repeats. As one set of diagonals is projecting the dog forward, the other is clearing the ground and stretching forward to start the next stride. The hind foot will usually strike the ground at the point where the front foot on the same side just left. Legs on the same side come together under the body in a "V," then extend fully to the front and rear as the legs on the other side come together. To recognize a correct trot, watch for the diagonals moving in unison and for good length of stride.

Breaking down the trot even further, let's examine the front alone. The shoulder lay-back, the length and angle of the upper arm, and the leg and pastern all contribute to proper reach.

16 Fig. 1. Diagonal legs move in unison during the trot.

Fig. 2. The correct trot. At full extension all four feet are off the ground.

The feet must be strong and resilient to absorb shock. The front leg reaches as far forward as possible (in a good mover it should extend as far forward as the tip of the nose or slightly farther) and strikes ground in unison with the hind diagonal. It then carries the dog forward until the front foot is under the body as far as possible, lifts just enough to clear the ground, and again reaches forward to accept the next stride. The hind foot follows a similar pattern. It reaches under the body and pushes the dog forward. Once it passes behind the vertical, it begins the portion of the stride known as "follow-through," which provides much of the forward push. The foot should remain on the ground until both stifle and hock joints are at full extension, then lift only enough to clear the ground as it again moves forward.

Croup, thigh, stifle, hock, and foot, plus muscling, all contribute to proper rear action. The Beardie has a slightly flatter croup than most working breeds. This allows for an extended follow-through in drive and, combined with the strong muscles and lighter frame, permits a Beardie the freedom for flat-footed leaps. When all this is put together, we see a graceful, startlingly agile dog in action. The longer and better balanced a trot, the longer and more effortlessly a dog can function.

Faults of Side Gait

Unbalanced Stride — The least severe side fault is one in which the dog is balanced but poorly angulated and must take more steps to keep up. With this fault, timing and cadence are still correct. More severe side faults are usually due to incorrect skeletal proportions. The cause of these faults can vary from unbalanced angulation to disproportionate length of individual bones.

A dog who has good rear angulation but inadequate shoulder lay-back is an all too common sight in many breeds, including Beardies. Although a dog with this fault has good drive, the front cannot keep up. The dog loses cadence in his trot and throws his front feet in an attempt to keep them away from the hind feet. Usually the front feet are lifted too high in a jerky motion (see fig. 4). In a severe case, the hind feet strike the front legs, and the dog looks as if he is trying to kick his chin. The shoulder is fairly rigid and lacks flexibility. Some individuals take short, picky steps and lift the rear feet very high in order to expend the extra drive. In any case, the back does not remain level, but instead bounces when the animal is in motion.

Likewise, a dog better in shoulder than in stifle angulation has problems. Probably he will appear to be running downhill when on the level because as he moves, his rear remains higher than his withers (see fig. 5). A dog that is straight in rear angulation usually has a kick-up, or at least inadequate follow-through (see fig. 6). His hind foot never reaches the print left by the front foot. Since the stride is shorter, power of the drive is severely reduced. Again, timing is thrown off and efficiency is below par.

17

Fig. 3. Maximum reach is limited by shoulder angulation.

Fig. 4. Front feet lifted too high due to straight shoulders.

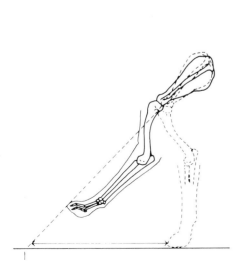

When synchronization of gait is disturbed, a dog may exhibit "pounding" or "dwelling." The front foot reaches full extension, hesitates in mid-air, then crashes down after the hind leg has begun the next stride (*see* fig. 7). This is extremely hard on the entire front assembly. It may be difficult to detect at first; watch for the diagonals moving together as an indication of correct gait.

Hocks set too high—An imperfection that often (but not always) accompanies straight stifles (*see* fig. 8). When both faults appear, the dog is usually high in rear. The hind leg lacks flexibility and the stride is shortened. Kick-up occurs sometimes and is quite noticeable in a dog with high hocks.

Sickle hocks—A condition in which the metatarsus curves slightly inward from hock to foot. Follow-through becomes virtually impossible,

and a stiff, stilted rear action results. Kick-up always occurs with sickle hocks. This condition is more common in Beardies than in many working breeds and should be severely faulted.

Short upper arm or stifle—The upper arm should be equal in length to the shoulder blade (*see* fig. 9). Regardless of angulation, a short upper arm throws off the gait. (Upper arm length is measured by the actual length of the bone, not to the point of the elbow.) A hackney or prancing action, with the front feet lifted high, is often indicative of a short upper arm. Less common is the proportionally shorter stifle. This results in a choppy rear action which again lacks in follow-through.

Incorrect pastern—The pastern is designed to absorb shock from the forequarters. It needs to be moderate in length and slope to perform its function efficiently (*see* fig. 10). Too much slope

Fig. 5. Downhill runner.   **Fig. 6. Kicking Up.**   **Fig. 7. Pounding or Dwelling.**

18

Fig. 8. Left to right: correct, high, and sickle hocks.

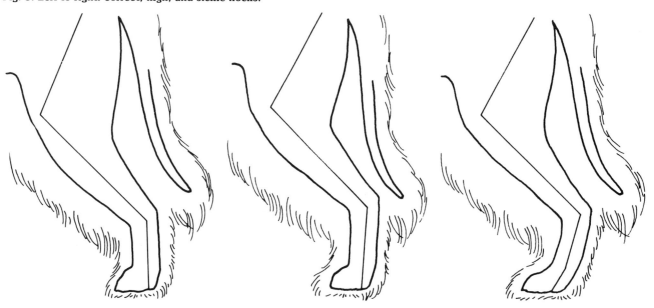

results in loose, extremely weak wrists, a very common problem in Beardies which is often accompanied by a crooked front. The other extreme is the too-steep pastern, which is usually short and often occurs in conjunction with a straight shoulder. Either condition is restrictive, and jarring strains the entire front assembly. The pastern is primarily a shock absorber, and under hard stress, a front assembly with poor pasterns will become sore and break down.

Pacing—An action similar to trotting, but one in which the legs on the same side (instead of the diagonals) move in unison (*see* fig. 11). Sometimes a dog will pace quite rapidly. Unless the handler is aware of the difference in gait, a dog may be allowed to remain in a pace in the show ring. Since structural analysis cannot be made from a pace, an individual that fails to trot readily will not be considered in a conformation class. The dog will often pace if the handler

moves too slowly or if the dog is tired. A quick jerk will usually put the animal into a trot.

Crabbing—The lack of alignment of the body in motion; the dog moves somewhat sideways, with the rear tracking to the left or right of the front (*see* fig. 12). This last consideration of side gait is more easily seen coming or going. In some instances, crabbing is a way to avoid striking the front legs with the hind feet—the result of too short a body. The same effect can be caused by more angulation in rear than in front. Crabbing is often simply a bad habit.

REAR OR "GOING" GAIT

The primary function of the dog's rear legs is to produce the drive which propels the body forward. However, the Standard also calls for the stance to be square and the gait true going away.

Fig. 9. Left: correct length of upper arm. Right: short upper arm causing foreleg to be set too far forward.

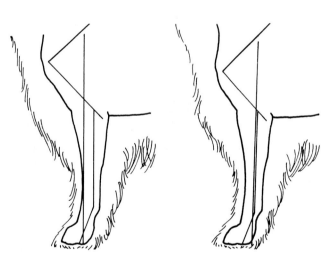

Fig. 10. Left to right: correct, weak, and short pasterns.

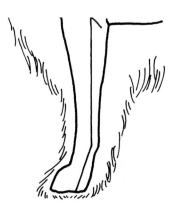 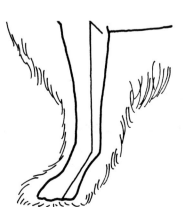 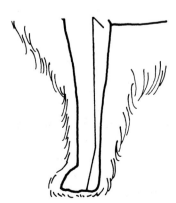

It is certainly more pleasing to the eye this way and also avoids encouraging weaknesses which may break down under stress. A dog with a less-than-perfect stance but that moves well is superior to an individual that stands correctly but cannot move properly. Stance can always be trained or "stacked," but movement is proof of structure.

To determine how well a dog is tracking in rear, draw an imaginary line down the center of each hind leg (as viewed from the rear), from hip to hock to foot. When the dog is standing, these lines should be straight, vertical, and parallel to each other (see fig. 13). A deviation at the hock or foot, either in or out, indicates a weakness. When the animal is moving, these lines should remain straight but come together in a "V" shape as speed increases (see fig. 14). The inside edges of the feet converge on a center line, thus, the term "singletrack" describing correct gait in a Beardie (see fig. 15). Beardies sometimes appear a bit narrow because of their long stifles and leaner builds. Also, the long coat can be deceptive. Brush the hocks thoroughly, or better yet, wet them down before evaluating rear action.

Rear Faults

Hocking out—Probably the most serious of the rear faults (see fig. 16) because it puts terrific stress on the ligaments and is likely to restrict the drive of the hindquarters. The condition is permissible in young puppies because it is likely to be caused by loose ligamentation which will tighten as the dog grows. Very slight hocking out is like any other fault—the severity is judged by its degree rather than by its nature.

Cow hocks, toeing out and close rears—The term "cow hocks" is used when the hocks turn in and the feet turn out (see fig. 17). If the legs are straight at the hocks but the feet turn outward, the dog is said to "toe out" (see fig. 18). True cow hocks exhibit both problems.

Among the first faults a novice learns to recognize are light eyes, wavy coats, gay tails,

Fig. 11. Legs on the same side move in unison during the pace.

Fig. 12. Bottom left: crabbing.

Fig. 13. Center: correct rear stance.

Fig. 14. Right: singletrack viewed from the rear.

20

and cow hocks. Since cow hocks are eventually determined to be the most serious of these faults, the novice will think of them as paramount among structural faults. But the truth is there are many worse and harder-to-detect faults than cow hocks. Cow hocks do not affect the rest of the dog unless they are so extreme as to constitute an actual deformity.

To a lesser degree than cow hocks, toeing out and close rears are undesirable. In both cases, the efficiency of gait is not badly restricted. Toeing out sometimes affects stance only, whereas a close parallel rear is also obvious in motion. A "close parallel rear" is one which, in motion, is parallel from hock to foot with an angle at the hock (see fig. 19). This condition is often accompanied by a narrow pelvis.

Crossing over— A fault in which feet overstep the center line to the center of the opposite side (see fig. 20). The feet actually cross when gaiting, and the entire rear of the dog usually bounces from side to side as the center of gravity is shifted with each step. This fault becomes more obvious with speed.

The wide parallel rear— A Beardie with this fault often (though not necessarily) stands perfectly; in fact, he is often touted as not being able to stand wrong. He is built like a table with unyielding vertical legs which remain the same distance apart at the feet in a swift trot as when standing (see fig. 21). The wide parallel gait is more obvious at a slow gait because the fast trot will force the legs toward a singletrack for balance. Wide rears are seldom seen in Beardies, and when this fault does occur it is usually accompanied by a short or straight stifle. Occasionally a wide mover, particularly one who is wide both front and rear, develops a characteristic "roll"

Fig. 15. Pawprints made when a Beardie singletracks. Dark and light prints represent opposing diagonals.

Fig. 16. Hocking out.

Fig. 17. Cow hocks.

Fig. 18. Toeing out.

21

Fig. 19. Close parallel.

Fig. 20. Crossing.

Fig. 21. Wide parallel.

from throwing his weight from side to side. This dog varies from the individual that hocks out in that the hocks of the wide mover remain in line and appear strong. Wide rears rarely affect side gait.

FRONT OR "COMING" GAIT

Beardies should also singletrack in front at a brisk trot (see fig. 22). When the dog stands the legs should be in straight parallel lines from elbows to pasterns to feet.

Correct front action is partially dependent on correct rib spring. Proper ribs are rounded at the top half to allow plenty of room for heart and lungs but are flattened on the bottom half to allow for unrestricted swing of the front leg backward along the side of the dog (see fig. 23). If the sides are too rounded (barrel-ribbed) or too flat (slab-sided), the plane in which the elbow moves is distorted, and some of the efficiency in gait is destroyed. Barrel ribs often lack depth, and their roundness causes the elbows to swing out to avoid interference. A slab-sided individual lacks substance and appears frail and narrow. Although a normal condition in a young dog, slab-sidedness usually causes a faulty front action because the front is not adequately supported.

Front Faults

Crooked front legs—Somewhat comparable to cow hocks in the rear. The legs bow outward at the top, inward at the pasterns, then out again at the foot (see fig. 24). A dog with a crooked front may move well, but he often possesses other front faults which complicate the issue. Carried to extreme, this fault is known as a "fiddle front." Narrow, crooked fronts are very prevalent in some lines of Beardies and should be eliminated from breeding wherever possible.

Out at elbows—Similar to hocking out. The elbows project out from the body rather than move smoothly straight back and forth when the dog trots (see fig. 25). This action can also be caused by excessive weight but is often a result of barrel ribs. Elbowing out is often found in conjunction with crooked legs, toeing in, short upper arm, or loose ligamentation.

Wide front—The dog does not move in a singletrack. The dog usually stands nicely, but the legs remain vertical and parallel when in motion (see fig. 26). A condition similar to the wide parallel rear.

Narrow or "tied-in" front—This refers to a dog that is narrow-chested and too close or pinched at the elbows. The legs may or may not be straight, but they lack adequate support from the rib cage and chest (see fig. 27). As a result, the front exhibits an eggbeater motion or is thrown randomly from side to side. This type of front in a young dog may improve as the chest broadens with maturity, provided the legs are straight. However, the feet often point outward. An individual that exhibits this fault should be considered a very questionable risk, even as a youngster.

22

Fig. 22. Singletrack viewed from the front.

Fig. 23. Ribspring: left to right: correct, barrel, and slab-sided.

Fig. 24. Crooked front.

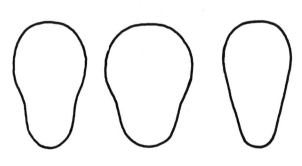

Paddling—When the dog throws the leg in an outward circle from the elbow as he moves (*see* fig. 28). A dog who paddles usually tracks wide.

Winging—Often erroneously called "paddling." While both faults involve throwing the feet outward, winging originates at the pastern rather than at the elbow (*see* fig. 29). Winging is seen more frequently than true paddling.

Crossing over—The same fault as crossing in the rear. The feet pass beyond the center line, and the center of gravity shifts, causing a choppy, bouncing appearance (*see* fig. 30). Crossing in front is usually due to a narrow chest.

Poor fronts have traditionally been a problem in all breeds and are particularly noticeable in a sound, working breed such as the Beardie. Once lost from a line, correct front structure is difficult to regain, but once obtained, it can be bred con-

sistently with a little effort. I encourage breeding for good fronts as a high priority in our breed.

Anything that interferes with the desired smooth-floating trot is faulty. The above are examples, but they do not cover every possibility for faults. The complex interrelationship between parts of the body can be easily disturbed, so one must be sure to breed only individuals that are correct in structure.

Fig. 25. Out at elbows.

Fig. 26. Wide.

Fig. 27. Narrow.

Fig. 28. Paddling.

Fig. 29. Winging.

Fig. 30. Crossing.

23

Fig. 31. Glennamoor Cayjen O' Glen Eire, *Glennamoor*.

4 *Love at First Sight*

Almost everyone loves to shop—especially when the object of their intention is a cuddly, loveable puppy. Before you get all wrapped up in the excitement of buying, we'd like to encourage you to make some practical deliberations. Your new Beardie will probably become a member of your household for a decade or more, and his selection deserves careful consideration.

As a potential dog owner, you may not have given any real thought to what type of dog will fit your needs. You may be attracted to a particular breed, such as the Beardie, because a friend has one or because you have seen pictures of the breed. However, you may not have stopped to assess the breed's suitability to your family or situation. Before you embark on a dog-shopping spree, we encourage you to take time to research a number of breeds. Learn about their temperament, care and space requirements, size, and hereditary strengths and weaknesses. Excellent sources for this information include books, veterinarians, the local kennel club breeder-referral service, and, of course, breeders themselves.

Will the breed you admire fit in with your home? Your lifestyle, the age of any children, and your own temperament should be considerations, as well as your space limitations. What will your dog be— a family pet, the foundation for a kennel, a working dog, an obedience dog for a 4-H project, a show dog, or a combination of these? Where will you keep him? Do you have the time and money to provide him with proper care and attention?

SOME OBVIOUS QUESTIONS

Three additional questions are of major importance and preferably will be made before you shop. They are: what sex, what age, and what quality of dog do you need?

He, She, or It?

There are many old wives' tales about which makes a better pet—a male or female Beardie. I believe that it is a matter of personal preference, because either sex makes a marvelous pet.

The pet-owner's ideal solution is a neutered Beardie of either sex. In fact, you will find that most reputable breeders require the neutering of a pet-quality Beardie when he is old enough. Neutering benefits both you *and* the breed by preventing unwanted litters and the perpetuation of mediocre-quality Beardies, and by doing away with the bothersome heat periods in a female or the tendency for a male to wander or fight. A neutered Beardie will be a more affectionate pet and a better worker less prone to being distracted. A neutered Beardie male is easier for most people to manage.

Today, neutering is safe, easy, and relatively inexpensive. Sluggishness, overweight, temperament change, or other side effects rarely occur provided neutering is performed when the dog is old enough to have an adequate supply of sex hormones (approximately eight months of age). *Nothing* is gained by allowing a bitch to whelp a litter or a male to sire puppies before they are neutered.

Of course, if you want to breed or show, a neutered dog is not for you. Neutered animals cannot be entered in conformation classes at any licensed show, but they can be shown in obedience. The foundation for a breeding kennel should be the best bitch you can find (*see* Ch. 11). It is usually not advisable to start with a male, because the best males in the country are readily available for your use. Never start a breeding kennel with a male/female pair. Even if you are lucky enough to find suitable mates, they may not produce well together, and if perchance they do, you will still have to go outside to continue your program after the first couple of litters.

Males are impressive and are apt to become top show winners; therefore, some exhibitors prefer to start with a male. Even if you do not plan to breed, a top winning male can be promoted at stud if you can take the time and provide the facilities to handle visiting bitches.

Toddler, Teenager, or Adult?

Generally, you will think of getting a puppy at weaning age—seven to nine weeks—but there are many good reasons for buying an older Beardie. If you have very young children, a twelve-week-old puppy may better contend with their rough handling. If you work away from home during the day so that feeding and housebreaking are difficult, consider a three- to four-month-old puppy that is already trained and able to go longer without attention. If you are buying a show or breeding prospect, the more mature the dog, the surer the choice and, generally speaking, the higher the price. The proven, older broodbitch, the retired show dog that needs a new home, or the mature male ready to show may be just right for your situation. Don't shy away from such opportunities for fear the older dog will not adapt. It may take the older Beardie a little longer to accept you as his master, but he will usually adjust and make an ideal pet.

Pet, Breeding, or Show?

You'll find that most breeders classify their Beardies in one of three basic categories—pet, breeding, or show prospects. One of the breeder's first questions is bound to be, "what quality do you want?"

A Beardie sold as a pet is meant to be just that—a wonderful companion. He will look like a Beardie and will have the typical temperament and personality that may have prompted you to choose a Bearded Collie in the first place. But he will not have all of the fine points of conformation necessary to qualify him for the show ring or breeding kennel. You will find the pet Beardie ideal for herding livestock, for competing in obedience trials, tracking, or other practical work, and you won't need to be as concerned about his sustaining slight injuries or damaging his coat as you would if you used a show dog for this type of activity.

The most important consideration in a pet is temperament. Even at weaning age the young Beardie will exhibit much of his adult personality. By watching a litter at play for awhile you can probably pick out the quietest, the boldest, the most aggressive, and the pup showing the strongest herding instinct. I would not select an extremely frightened or extremely aggressive puppy. (*See* Ch. 15 for a discussion of temperament tests for puppies.)

Breeding and show Beardies are very similar, if not identical, in quality. The young puppy is generally referred to as a "show prospect," since it is difficult to determine with total accuracy just how an eight-week or twelve-week puppy will mature. Exceptional Beardies six-months or over may be classified as "show quality" and will be sold for higher prices than the young "prospects."

At six months the structure is evident, gait and coat are beginning to mature, and type is obvious. Since puppies may be shown at six months of age, the dog may even have begun to prove his mettle in the show ring. A show dog must be an excellent specimen of the breed, possessing all the qualities of temperament, personality, showmanship, and correct conformation that could make him a winner.

"Breeding quality" also denotes show quality or a Beardie only slightly less perfect. The major difference is often the lack of poise or showmanship of the breeding-quality Beardie, especially in females. A dog purchased for breeding should have good temperament, good health, and should exhibit no major faults. A show dog lamed by an injury or one that has lost an ear or a tooth or has been scarred in a fight may also be sold for breeding quality. (*See* Chs. 11 and 15 for more information on breeding and show dog selection.)

WHERE DO YOU FIND YOUR DOG?

Finding the right Beardie may not be easy, and it may take time. If you can locate one or more breeders within driving distance, this is the place to start. You may also find Beardies exhibited at a local dog show (watch the ad column of your local newspaper for date and place). You can probably locate breeders through your local kennel club referral service or by writing the American Kennel Club for the address of the parent club (the Bearded Collie Club of America). The BCCA can then send you a list of breeders.

You may also find advertisements in national dog magazines (*see* "Other Sources").

A good way to develop an eye for a Beardie and meet the breeders is to attend a dog show. Observe the judging carefully, and ask a knowledgeable spectator to help you understand the reasons for the placements. After the breed has been judged, go quickly to the grooming area to discuss buying a puppy with a breeder/exhibitor whose Beardies attracted you. Most exhibitors are busy with preparations prior to ring-time but will be happy to talk with you immediately after the breed classes.

Before you actually make a purchase, try to visit the breeder at home. One clue to a good kennel is consistency of quality and type throughout the kennel, especially if evident through several generations. Another clue is the cleanliness and the kind of socialization and care provided. If the overall type is varied or poor, temperaments are questionable, or kennel conditions unclean, look elsewhere.

What if you can't visit the breeder in person—can you still purchase a good Beardie? Yes, if you are careful. Rely on referrals from knowledgeable handlers or judges or from breeders with an established reputation. Sometimes a professional handler will see and purchase a dog for you if you cannot travel in person. If you choose to write to breeders without a referral, take time to get to know them through letters or calls before you make a purchase.

When buying a dog from other areas of the United States, you can often have him shipped "on approval." Under this circumstance, you pur-

Eng. Ch. Bobby of Bothkennar with part of his first litter.

chase the Beardie with an agreement that he may be returned for a full refund within a specified time period (usually a few days) should you find the dog does not suit your requirements or feel that he was misrepresented. You pay the shipping expenses and assume responsibility for the dog while he is in your possession during the approval period.

Hopefully, you will not find a Bearded Collie in a pet shop—a source we definitely DO NOT recommend. Always buy from a breeder. Most breeders are reputable people who will help you select the right dog for your needs and become your friend and advisor while you are getting started in the breed.

MAKING THE PURCHASE

Every AKC registered dog should be sold with a signed litter or individual registration slip, a pedigree, and a sales contract which includes a guarantee. If the litter registration papers have not come back to the breeder from the AKC, the contract should contain a statement guaranteeing that they will be signed over to the purchaser as soon as they arrive. The seller may hold the registration certificate until certain contractual conditions such as neutering and payment completion are fulfilled.

Guarantees

Ask for and expect a written sales contract/guarantee. A pet will generally be guaranteed to be in good health for a specified period from date of purchase. He may also be guaranteed for good temperament and/or against any debilitating hereditary defects up to the age of two or three years. (This would generally include crippling dysplasia and blindness.)

A breeding-quality Beardie should carry a guarantee that the dog will be capable of reproducing, and either a show or breeding animal should be guaranteed against hereditary defects occurring before three years of age. Since the

Left: three-week-old Beardie puppies.

Lower left: Ch. Glenhy's Marshall Silverleaf, *Glenhy.*

Lower right: Ch. Wyndcliff Stonemark Oliver, *Stonemark,* **at age five months.**

28

monorchidism or cryptorchidism (failure of one or both testicles to descend into the scrotum) is a disqualification in any breed, this should certainly be included in the guarantee on a male.

Contracts for show Beardies may carry any of a number of different terms. Some breeders guarantee that the dog will finish his championship. Other breeders guarantee that the dog will be show quality by their definition at a certain specified age. The more protection you are given by the guarantee, the higher the price you can expect to pay.

Almost every registered Beardie should be sold with some type of contract to protect the buyer and seller. It is important that you understand and agree to these terms. (*See* Ch. 16 for sample contracts.)

Terms of Payment

There are many ways to buy a dog. The best and most usual is outright cash purchase. A few large breeders will accept major charge cards or take time payments, in which case you will be asked to sign a contract and agree that the registration papers be held by the seller until the last payment has been made.

"Breeder's terms" refer to the sale of a male, with stud privileges (use of the dog for breeding) being retained by the seller, or the sale of a bitch with puppies or even litters to be given back to the seller. Sometimes exceptional show animals are sold this way to insure that they and their offspring are properly bred and exhibited. Partial value of the puppies or litters is deducted from the sale price, and the bitch is generally co-owned until the payment in puppies has been fulfilled. If the terms are agreeable to both parties and the two individuals can work together reasonably, such arrangements can be advantageous to both. Terms must be spelled out in writing and clearly understood by both parties.

Permanent co-ownerships offer another method of obtaining a good Beardie. Co-ownerships may be offered by breeders who want to hold on to a Beardie for breeding but who do not have the space or time to keep another dog. Some breeders will sell only co-ownerships to a novice so that they can place the dog but essentially retain control and assure that the dog is shown, promoted, and bred properly. If the beginner is willing to cooperate with the experienced breeder, this may be an excellent way to obtain top-quality stock. Usually, the person pur-

chasing the co-ownership is expected to keep the dog. The two owners may split stud fees or litters, and the sales contract should specify in writing how this is to be done and who is to be responsible for show and advertising expenses.

Occasionally it may be possible to lease a Beardie for a start in breeding without the permanency or expense of buying. Bitches are leased for a five- or six-month period, and the lease must be registered with the AKC. The lessee is generally responsible for the shipping charge, stud fee, and all other expenses when leasing a bitch for a litter, or for promotion costs and showing fees when leasing a stud dog. The lessee is held liable for the dog while the animal is in his care. About the only way to obtain a good Beardie on lease is to become acquainted with breeders and ask to be considered should they be interested in leasing a particular Beardie.

IMPORTING

A number of the Beardies in the United States at this time are either imported or are the offspring of imported dogs. The breed is new to this country, and many breeders initially travelled to England in search of top-quality Beardies from the country of the breed's origin.

However, importing is expensive, risky, and not advisable for the novice breeder. A good puppy can be purchased in England for about $300, but the air fare, duty, crate, and health certificate can nearly double that amount. If you wish to import a dog, the best way is to make a trip to England and pick the dog after a tour of the major kennels. If you cannot do this, you may find an international judge who will select a good puppy for you. You can also depend upon an experienced breeder who has imported previously to find a dog for you.

Brave individuals may want to try writing to breeders in Great Britain and selecting their puppy by correspondence. Select a breeder who is well known or who has been recommended by another importer. A few English breeders want to send some of their best dogs out of the country, while others are concerned about not knowing what kind of home or promotion the dog will receive and are therefore reluctant to export their best.

The seller can usually arrange for transfer of papers and shipping. The airlines require that dogs be shipped in extremely large, heavy,

29

usually wooden crates; hence, the high freight rates. Upon entrance to the United States at either Los Angeles, Chicago, or New York City, the dog will be delayed several hours for a health check. He must then clear customs at your nearest international airport.

Once the dog is here, he cannot be returned, so don't expect him to be shipped on approval. (Dogs going into England are kept in quarantine for six months.) Any guarantee for replacement will be strictly according to the charity of the breeder/seller. Since it is very difficult to purchase an adult, you will probably be importing a young puppy and therefore taking a greater risk in obtaining the quality you want.

The importer must supply you with a three-generation export pedigree and British registration form for your dog. You must then write the American Kennel Club for an imported dog registration form. AKC will instruct you in how to apply for registration in this country.

"Megan," Raggmopp Beardies.

Ch. Greysteel Crackerjack.

Left to right: Ch. Silverleaf Scottish Heather, Ch. Parcana Silverleaf Vandyke, Shepherd's Help From Shiel C.D. Front: Ch. Silverleaf Gifted Artisan.

5 The Comforts of Home

No matter how many new dogs I acquire, the first day at home with them is always enchanting. The new puppy will want to explore every corner, every door, every other animal, and of course every member of the family. His reactions range from hilarious clowning to fright to a well-pulled-off bluff. I can hardly take my eyes, or my hands, off the lovely new creature. I want to play with him, handle him, feel his structure, get acquainted, and at the same time reassure myself that he really is a good dog.

But puppies, like babies, need time for sleep, and they do best if their mealtimes are quiet and undisturbed. You may want to keep your new Beardie closer to the family during the first few weeks while he's getting acquainted, but remember to allow him privacy and rest. His sleeping box, prepared before you brought him home, should be in a warm, draft-free corner away from the mainstream of family activities. A few rawhide chips or rawhide "bones," a rubber ball, and a braid made of old nylon stockings will help entertain him and keep his teeth occupied on something other than dad's new slippers. A rug, old towel, or blanket provides comfortable bedding. If the box is large, you can prepare a bed in one end and spread papers for his toilet at the other end.

EARLY TRAINING

You should begin almost immediately to teach your Beardie what is expected of him. Discourage unruly behavior in the house by keeping him on leash or confined to a small area at first. Discourage chewing of the wrong things, but since all puppies investigate their environment partly by chewing, provide your dog with rawhide or hard rubber toys. Praise him when he chews them. Never give him objects that he can easily tear into small pieces and swallow, except for rawhide.

31

Beardie puppies need to learn that you are "boss." You will be off to a good start with your new relationship if you establish dominance from the beginning, without being harsh. Some physical punishment may be needed until the puppy learns the meaning of the word "No." Use the command firmly in connection with your puppy's name each time he does something that you want him to stop. Usually, tone of voice is sufficient correction. If not, you may discipline the puppy with a sharp jerk on a choke collar, by picking him up by the scuff of the neck and shaking him, or by pushing his head to the ground and holding it there for a minute. Another good corrective measure is a swat with a rolled-up newspaper, but only if it is handy. Corrections must be made within three seconds or not at all. Always accompany the punishment with the command "No."

Praise is also an important part of training. Always praise your Beardie lavishly when he performs as expected and as soon as he stops the behavior you are correcting. If your Beardie is not responding well to your attempts at training, it may be that you are not giving enough praise.

You will probably also want to include the word "Come" in your puppy's early training. Call him to you often while he's with you in the house, rewarding him with praise and a goodie when he comes.

Housebreaking can begin almost immediately, but don't expect a puppy to be perfectly dependable until he's at least three months old. In the beginning it's up to you to anticipate when he has to relieve himself and prevent accidents from happening.

The easiest method of housebreaking is to confine the puppy to a small area—a box, crate, or pen—at night. First thing in the morning, take him immediately to the area where you want him to relieve himself, and wait until he does so. I find it best to avoid the intermediate step of paper breaking and prefer to take the puppy outside from the beginning. Praise him immediately, then return him to the house for a romp. During the day when the puppy is inside, take him out to the same area whenever he is restless, when he wakes from a nap, shortly after a meal, or about every hour. You'll be surprised at how quickly he learns.

For the first few days in the new home, the best procedure is to let the Beardie become acquainted at his own pace. Don't push him to accept new sights, sounds, and experiences. He'll discover them in his own time and be much more confident than if he is rushed. As the puppy begins to feel at home, you can introduce him to all the various aspects of his new life—car rides, hikes, other children, livestock, etc. Some Beardies will be hesitant and will need encouragement from you, while others will bounce right into anything and should be taught to heed your cautions. The first month in a new home, especially for a two- to three-month-old puppy, is a very impressionable period in which the dog-owner bond is being formed. Take advantage of this period to form a relationship of mutual trust and respect with your Beardie.

HOUSING

Beardies need space for exercise and play in order to keep their muscles toned up and their energy level manageable. If you must keep a Bearded Collie confined, allow time in your schedule for walks and romps in the open for at least an hour each day. Provided with this minimum requirement, Beardies adjust remarkably well to nearly any home.

Although most Beardies are house dogs, some owners prepare a space in the yard or garage for their adult Beardies. A draft-proof doghouse or a raised, enclosed box in the corner of garage or porch will do nicely for one or two dogs.

Crates

A Bearded Collie is much too active to be routinely confined to a crate. However, crate training can be a definite asset to any dog. There may come a time when your Beardie must be left at the vet's, stay with a friend, or be shipped to another location. The crate-trained dog will take this in stride.

Select a crate large enough for your Beardie to stand comfortably without ducking and to lie stretched out without being cramped. Wire crates are excellent for kenneling a dog in the house, but wooden or fiberglass crates are preferable for shipping. A shipping crate that is too large may cause the dog to be tossed about and possibly injured.

Crate training is easy. Simply put your Beardie in the crate for a short period at feeding time. Leave him there until he cleans up the food, then release him. This leads to pleasant associations and minimizes bad habits like scratch-

32

ing and whining. Gradually increase the confinement time to several hours or overnight. Give your Beardie a chew toy to alleviate boredom, but don't baby him. If he cries or claws at the crate, correct him immediately by scolding or by slapping the crate with a rolled-up newspaper. Your Beardie's ego is much tougher than he would like you to believe at times, and, in fact, a Beardie that continually gets his way will never be really well adjusted.

How much should you crate a Beardie? Opinions are varied. English breeders dislike crates and believe that much harm is done by using them. While this may be true in isolated incidents, we feel that there is a definite need for the use of crates in the United States. They are a necessity at unbenched dog shows; they provide safety while traveling in a car; and they furnish a clean, easily available in-house kennel where a Beardie can eat and sleep or be confined while you are entertaining, when you are out of the house, or when you just don't want a dog underfoot. Seven or eight hours is maximum for confining any dog to a crate. Obviously, the longer the period of confinement, the more conscientious you must be to provide exercise.

Kennels

If you intend to keep several Bearded Collies for breeding or show, you will undoubtedly want a kennel. There are as many kennel variations as there are breeders. Styles range from made-over poultry or livestock sheds to elaborately constructed custom buildings that architecturally harmonize with the home. Some are unheated, while others boast heating, air conditioning, and even septic systems.

Regardless of style or complexity, certain basics such as dryness, good ventilation, and sanitation must be met. You will also have to consider the zoning regulations imposed by your city, county, or state health department. Always check local regulations before you begin to build.

Either wood or cement block building materials are acceptable. Wood is drier, but concrete is easier to disinfect and clean. With either material, place a layer of heavy plastic sheeting beneath the floor to keep out moisture.

The building should be well ventilated, yet as draft-free as possible. Louvered ventilator windows or fans near the roof at each end of the kennel will provide ventilation; in addition, you may want several screened windows above the dog boxes for air and light. Louvered mobile home windows are excellent if you can obtain them.

The partitions between "stalls" should be sturdy, smooth, and about 6 feet high. I prefer stalls that are 4 feet square, with a larger pen for bitch and puppies. Each stall should have an opening large enough to accommodate a grown Beardie. A swinging door or rubber flap will prevent drafts, and a guillotine door on the inside will keep the opening firmly closed when desirable. Commercial doors are available, or you can build your own by making a sliding wooden door and hanging a rubber automobile flap over the opening.

33

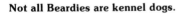

Not all Beardies are kennel dogs.

Runs should be at least 4' x 12' (I prefer 4' x 24') with 6-foot-high chain link fencing. Concrete flooring, definitely the easiest to clean, is costly to install and will wear off the hair on your Beardie's feet and legs. Three-quarter-inch or the smaller "pea" gravel is preferred by many breeders.

In either case, dig the area for the runs to a depth of at least 16 inches. Lay a 4- to 6-inch layer of rock or coarse gravel and sprinkle it heavily with rock salt and *Boraxo®* to help kill odor and worm larvae. Then lay the top surface with about 12 inches of either fine gravel or cement. The top half of the surface gravel will need replacing every couple of years for good sanitation.

My own kennel has 4' x 8' indoor runs, each housing two adult Beardies, and 20' x 40' gravel exercise yards outside. Each Beardie goes outside a minimum of three or four hours a day.

Hard dirt runs or grass areas are difficult to keep clean, and since they encourage infestations of parasites, they are not recommended. You can get by with dirt or grass in a large exercise yard, but be aware that your grooming time will increase substantially if your Beardie is kept on these surfaces.

Sanitation

Cleanliness is essential in a kennel or in any dog facility, and the more dogs you keep, the more important and time consuming this becomes.

Food and water dishes should be washed often. We prefer the hard rubber or stainless steel dishes, since they resist damage and can be disinfected easily. Soapy water with a little *Clorox®* is an old standby for any kennel owner. In addition to cleaning the dishes, use this solution to wash down the building and runs several times a year. Commercial germicidal disinfectants are also available.

Feces should be picked up at least once daily. If flies, mosquitoes, or hookworms are a problem, remove the dogs and spray the premises with malathion, following the instructions carefully. You must keep the dogs out of the area for twelve to twenty-four hours after spraying. Chlorine will help control odors, as will other commercial products, and rock salt will aid in killing roundworm larvae. Sodium borate (commonly sold as *Boraxo®*), applied at the rate of ten pounds per hundred square feet, may be used to control hookworm larvae. Both substances can be harm-

ful to the dog's feet and should be well raked into the gravel or applied to cement and left on an empty run for a day, then washed off with water.

Disease control in the kennel is facilitated by placing a 1-foot deep cement barrier at the base of the fencing between each run. If the runs are gravel, at least 6 inches of the barrier should lie beneath the surface. A 6- or 8-foot solid board fence around the periphery of the kennel is used by many commercial kennels to block airborne germs and noise. If you plan to raise, breed, or ship a number of dogs, a quarantine or isolation run removed from the rest of the kennel is essential. This run may be smaller than the others and should definitely have a cement floor for ease in disinfecting as well as an enclosed top for the safety of visiting Beardies.

KEEPING YOUR BEARDIE SAFE

In addition to the fact that you probably paid a lot of money for your Beardie, he is a living, breathing, cherished part of your family, and you will want to do everything you can to protect him. Yet, many purebred dogs die needlessly each year because their owners did not think about safety. We want to pass on a few tips that will make your dog's life a little safer.

It seems like mere common sense to check your yard, kennel, or other facilities for holes or broken wires, cracks near a gate, insecure latches, and other precarious situations before you bring your dog home. Many new dog owners are not aware that a Beardie (or any dog) in a strange place can become a very adept escape artist. And since Beardies are quite capable jumpers, you will also want to decide if your fences are high enough. Anything less than 6 feet is questionable until the Beardie learns that this is his new home, after which he will probably stay inside fences over which he could easily leap.

While you're checking the premises, look also for chewable items such as accessible electrical cords, exposed fiberglass insulation, or other harmful or poisonous substances. Even adult dogs are likely to chew or swallow foreign objects; it is up to you to keep harmful items out of reach. In general, anything that might harm a child should also be kept from your Beardie. Puppies are apt to tip things over, cut themselves on glass or tin, or step on sharp objects.

The Beardie's inborn herding tendencies can get him into a lot of trouble around livestock. One of my dogs is still (a year later) recovering from a broken leg incurred when a young mare kicked out to protect her newborn foal from the intruding Beardie. Keep your Beardie away from livestock unless he is supervised closely or until he is fully trained to work stock.

Although it seems unnecessary to warn you not to leave your Beardie locked in a closed car in summer, *hundreds* of dogs die annually of heat stroke from this very cause. When outside temperatures approach eighty degrees, the inside of your automobile will register over 100 degrees. If you must leave your dog in a car during the summer, open several windows an inch or two for ventilation, then check on your pet at least hourly.

Poisonous Substances

Many common items are poisonous to dogs if ingested. Among these are chlorine bleach, antifreeze, cleaning fluid, gasoline, fungicides, insecticides, herbicides, rat poisons, tar, suntan lotion, wax, paint and paint removers, hair-setting lotions, hair-coloring lotions, matches, mothballs, shoe polish, children's crayons, some household detergents, disinfectants, aspirin, and other drugs. With the current fad for new and unusual houseplants, it is best to keep all plants away from your Beardie. Many of them are poisonous to dogs, including dieffenbachia, philodendron, poinsettia, and mistletoe. Gardeners should also be concerned that many bulbs, vines such as wisteria and sweet pea, and bushes such as euonymus, rhododendron, laurel, and yew can be harmful to your dogs. Castor beans, especially the seed, are extremely poisonous.

Tattooing

Dognapping has become so common in America that any dog in any community is a potential victim. Absolutely the best safeguard is tattooing. Tattooing is inexpensive, painless, and takes only a few minutes. It can be done by a veterinarian or at one of the many tattoo clinics held in conjunction with shows and matches. Your social security number is tattooed permanently on the inside of your Beardie's right thigh. You should always keep this area clipped so that the tattoo is readily visible. (We do not recommend tattooing on the ear or lip.) Tattooing is the only acceptable, positive legal identification recognized by law enforcement authorities.

Tattooing has been widely promoted since the National Dog Registry, a nationwide organization

formed to aid in the identification of lost, stolen, or stray dogs, came into existence. Your social security number (used in the tattoo), your name, address, and telephone number may be registered with NDR for a one-time fee. Any dogs you own are then tattooed with the number, and a notice is sent to NDR. The listing lasts for a lifetime. If your dog is lost, there is a very good chance that he will be returned to you since state and local police, humane societies, and over 1,500 research labs, medical schools, and other organizations working with dogs have been asked to verify through the National Dog Registry any dog that is delivered to them bearing a tattoo.

You may contact the NDR for information and registration forms at:

National Dog Registry
227 Stebbins Rd.
Carmel, New York 10512

The organization also provides a name tag, which your dog should wear any time he travels. The tag warns, "Tattooed dog registered with NDR." Similar warning signs are available for your car, crates, and kennel.

FINDING A LOST BEARDIE

Should your Beardie wander or become lost, there are a number of things you can do to help locate him. Number one—don't panic! A high percentage of lost dogs are eventually returned to their owners.

If a dog becomes frightened and simply runs away, try to keep him in sight *without* making him feel he is being pursued. As soon as he calms down he will probably respond to your call. If not, try running away from him and he will often follow. If several people are available to help, you can often corner the fleeing dog against a fence or building.

If your Beardie disappears and you can't sight him, act quickly. First call the local humane society, the dog control officer, and the radio station, giving a complete description of the dog and the place where you last saw him. Leave your name and phone number, along with the name and phone number of a friend who can be reached in case you are out. Second, if the dog is newly purchased, contact the old owner should the Beardie try to return to his former home. Run an ad in the local paper, offering a reward for information leading to the dog's return.

Finally, in case the dog is injured, call any veterinarians in the general region, then begin a house-to-house inquiry covering the entire area where the dog was last seen. Ask these residents to call you if the dog is sighted, and to please not chase him themselves. This keeps the dog from becoming more frightened, and he will probably seek water and shelter instead of continuing his flight. Be patient; many dogs are found after one, two, or even more weeks away from home.

THE JET-SET BEARDIE

About as many dogs as people travel these days. If your Beardie is accustomed to going along on family outings, to visiting relatives, and to taking jaunts down to the ice-cream parlor from the time he is a puppy, he will eagerly anticipate an automobile ride. On the other hand, if the only place you ever take him is to the vet's for a vaccination or to a few shows now and then, he'll probably be nervous and may even get carsick. It's far better to start him out slowly at a young age with a few rides to the store or around the block. If he still has a tendency to get carsick, a *Drammamine®* tablet, given about twenty minutes before departure, will help.

If you are going on a long trip with your Beardie, or if he will be flying, make sure that he's wearing a collar with ID tag, rabies tag, and tattoo notice. Don't feed him for twelve hours prior to traveling, nor water two hours before departure. Feed and water him only lightly during the trip. It's always a good idea to take plenty of his regular food and drinking water, because unfamiliar food and/or water easily cause digestive upsets. Additionally, I always like to be prepared by packing a bag containing plenty of newspapers, paper towels, a washcloth, *Drammamine®*, *Kaopectate®*, and a laxative. These prepare me for almost anything!

Shipping by Air

Thousands of dogs are flying about the United States each year with relative ease and safety. New regulations passed in 1977 make air freight shipments of dogs even safer than before. Anyone involved in breeding or showing Beardies extensively will one day ship a dog by air.

Proper preparation helps to insure your Beardie a safe trip. The basics are simple:

1. Make reservations with the appropriate air freight office several days in advance. *Choose a nonstop, direct flight* if possible. If a transfer is necessary, allow plenty of time for it. Ask the freight agent about regulations regarding type of crate and air temperature minimums at point of takeoff and destination. If it's too hot or too cold, your dog may have to wait until a more moderate day.

2. Prepare the crate. *Be sure the size is comfortable but not too large.* Spread a layer of newspaper on the floor, topped by a second layer of shredded paper. Apply a label which notes "Live Dog. Do Not Place Near Dry Ice. Do Not Open Crate Except in Emergency." Prepare a shipping label prominently, giving the name, address, city, and the airport to which the dog is being shipped, as well as your name, address, and phone number. You may note, "Call on arrival . . . ." and indicate the consignee's phone number in case no one is at the airport to receive the dog.

3. *Obtain a health certificate.* Interstate commerce regulations require that all dogs crossing state lines be checked by a veterinarian within ten days or so (depending on the state) and certified to be in good health. A current rabies vaccination is required. To avoid overstressing your Beardie, take him in for the examination a day or two before shipment.

The freight office will request that you have your dog at the airport about two hours before takeoff to allow adequate time for safe and correct loading. *Always place a collar with ID tag on your Beardie before shipment, and put only one dog in each crate.* Exercise the dog just before leaving him at the airport.

At the airport, *check the air bill* carefully to make sure that all information and phone numbers are correct. I like to watch the agent place the air bill on the crate to make certain that the correct air bill goes with my dog. Unless you declare a value and insure your dog, the airline will pay only a minimum figure in case of loss, so be sure to *buy insurance.*

The dog will be placed in the crate and weighed. If you wish, double-check the latch, then leave the rest to the airline. You should remain available, either at the airport or near your phone at home, until takeoff time in case some emergency would prevent shipment. As a final precaution, I always *request that the receiving person phone* to let me know that my dog has arrived safely at his destination.

6 *The Beardie Beautiful*

TOOLS AND EQUIPMENT

Beardies are a "natural" breed, which means that no trimming or sculpturing of the coat is allowed. A clean, healthy, well-brushed dog can grace the show ring or present his best appearance as a pet. A few tips may make your grooming an easy, enjoyable task rather than an ordeal for both owner and dog.

Requirements for grooming tools are minimal. The most important item is a good quality bristle brush. Do not economize on this tool. I recommend a *Mason-Pearson®*-bristle or bristle-and-nylon combination pin brush, or a reasonable facsimile. These come in a variety of sizes and styles. Price may run as high as fifteen or twenty dollars, but the brush is well worth the investment. It will last for years and, aside from keeping the coat in beautiful condition, will cut your grooming time in half. If you cannot justify a *Mason-Pearson®* brush, get either a long, natural-bristle hairbrush or, as a last choice, a metal pin brush. Do not use a slicker brush except to remove a shedding coat because it will tear the undercoat.

You will need a metal comb with medium-spaced teeth, a spray bottle which will adjust to a fine mist, and three general care items—a nail clipper, a tooth scaler, and a long, curved forceps for plucking hair from the ear canal. Add to your list a good brand of dog shampoo (baby shampoo will also work), a bottle of liquid bluing, perhaps some coat conditioner if you live in a dry climate, a bottle of shampoo formulated for use on white hair, and a couple of old towels. If you become an expert you may want to add a few extras of your own, but please remember that a natural look is an essential element of Beardie type. There are plenty of breeds available for the frustrated hairdresser; the Beardie is not one of them.

Throw Out the Scissors

The Beardie is not to be trimmed in any way if he is to be shown. This includes not trimming around the feet or between the pads. If your Beardie has too much hair on the face or still has his wooly puppy coat, you may pluck a few hairs at the inside corner of each eye. Grasp a few hairs between your thumb and first finger, and break the hair off at the skin with a firm twist. The amount removed should be just enough to expose the eyes and show the expression. This is the *only* hair which may be removed, and it should never be trimmed. Plucking is beneficial in avoiding eye irritation as the puppy coat grows. The adult Beardie coat with correct texture and quantity will arch naturally over the eyebrows and expose the eyes.

EVALUATING THE COAT

The correct coat for the Bearded Collie is moderate in length, harsh in texture, easy to maintain, and produces the typical *shaggy* outline. The formula for cultivating a beautiful coat is simply to keep it clean, healthy, and brushed. Assuming the coat has adequate genetic potential, it will develop length and shine in direct proportion to how much effort you exert. A pet Beardie or a show Beardie in good coat needs it to be brushed thoroughly only once a week. Depending on the dog, this will take from fifteen minutes to an hour once you develop a reasonably efficient technique. For a coated breed, this amount of grooming time is quite minimal.

Puppies tend to develop coat in one of two distinct manners. The first type of coat is rather sparse, wiry, and not overly attractive in the puppy stages. This type, however, is usually worth waiting out because the adult coat will come in very harsh, easy to groom, and with the tendency to fall perfectly into place and stay there. Many of the more glamorous puppies actually have soft, wooly coats verging on Old English Sheepdog type. This is alright in a *puppy,* but the coat should change in character until there is less undercoat and a long, harsh, straight outer coat by the time the dog is three years old.

Surprisingly, the profuse puppy coats are more difficult to keep up than the adult coats because they tend to tangle more easily and require more frequent brushing. Likewise, an incorrect adult Beardie coat, tending toward that of either the Old English Sheepdog or the Afghan Hound, will be much more difficult to groom and will need constant attention to look neat. The Old English coat may be curly and carry too much undercoat for a Beardie. The Afghan-type coat is usually dead straight, but silky and limp to the touch. A Beardie with silky coat is often overgroomed (perhaps of necessity) and, when presented in the show ring, looks more like a rangy, overgrown Lhasa Apso (complete with part) than a Bearded Collie. I cannot stress too strongly that this look, although sometimes glamorous, is absolutely incorrect for a Beardie.

TABLE MANNERS

I prefer to groom on a standard grooming table, which I find puts Beardies at a comfortable height for my weak back. Some people use a portable grooming top placed on a crate, a card table with nonslip footing added, or even the floor. I confess that I also occasionally spread an old sheet in front of the television. However, this is only suitable for routine brushing of a well-trained animal.

I start putting my puppies on the grooming table when they are young and get them accustomed to lying down while being brushed. I have only three absolutes when it comes to training. My dogs must come when called, they must stop what they're doing if I yell "No," and they must *never* jump off a grooming table or out of a car until given the command to do so. All puppies and new adult Beardies will try to jump off, but I attempt to prevent it until they reliably understand what is expected. This means not leaving the dog unattended and correcting him if he does jump off. If one "escapes," I grab him, add a sharp verbal "No," and lift him backward onto the table. He then gets a "Stay" or "Wait" command and plenty of praise. This procedure may have to be repeated several times. If so, be sure that your corrections are sharp and definite and consider praise the most important part of the exercise. The dog must be praised for obeying even if you are forcing him to obey; otherwise, he has no incentive to do as you ask. If you know that the dog is thinking about jumping off, correct him before he actually leaps. Be sure to praise him when he stays. In very short order you will have a dog that can be left on a table for several minutes unsupervised. Keep grooming session to thirty minutes or less at first.

38

Besides grooming, table training has other applications. It can provide a simple, impressive means of showing off your dogs. In fact, our first four dogs learned table training before we consciously began teaching it to all of our puppies. On the table they look animated and unrestrained, yet they are confined to keep them from becoming pushy or overbearing to people unfamiliar with the breed. They stand nicely for other breeders to evaluate, and, regardless of the reason for tabling the dog, the situation provides a safety factor. There will be times when you will want to remove your dog's leash or even his collar (especially during grooming). If the dog dives after every distraction at a dog show, he runs a risk of being injured or killed before you can catch him. If grooming space is crowded, I sometimes bring in one less crate than I have dogs and settle down in a chair for the leisure part of the day while my dogs take turns sitting on the table, playing with their admiring public. Our Beardies always make great friends with spectators because they are invitingly friendly (at eye level, yet), and everyone says, "My, isn't he well mannered." I can sit quietly twenty feet away and answer questions when it finally occurs to people to look around for an owner. It definitely takes the work out of grooming, also. You can become exhausted keeping a deathly grip with one hand on an overly exuberant Beardie, while vainly trying to brush him with the other hand.

IMPORTANT: If you demand absolute obedience from your dog in staying on the table,

you must be sure to give him a release command each and every time he is to jump off. You may have to pull him off at first if he has learned to stay properly. I use the command "OK." Other words could be "jump," "hop down," "let's go," or whatever you like. Just be sure that it is consistent and given positively so that the dog understands it as a command and not as part of a conversational sentence.

I also teach my dogs to jump onto the table, but this has certain disadvantages in some circumstances. One bad side effect is that the dog may try to jump onto any grooming table at a show, which can mean keeping a tight lead when walking him down crowded aisles lined with "TABLES" on either side. I learned this trick quickly after one of my champions (yep, one of the same ones I modestly pass off as being so well mannered) landed in the middle of a good-natured (luckily) Old English Sheepdog. I also have one idiot bitch that leaps before she looks. I groom in my basement. If I let her through the door, she'll race down the stairs, around the corner to the family room, and fling herself in the general direction of where the grooming table usually stands. She rarely misses, but occasionally the table isn't set up, or it has been moved a few feet, or someone else has a dog on it. I try to make it a practice to run interference for her or remember to take her down on a leash unless I'm sure everything is shipshape.

If you still prefer the convenience, as I do, of having your dog jump onto the grooming table by

"What are you doing on OUR table?"

"Can she do this, Dad?"

himself, this is how to teach him. It's an easy exercise, because Beardies love jumping in any form. (One comment first—I keep my dogs in a 3½-foot-high yard fence, and they never jump out. From the time they are puppies they are taught the difference between a fence and a table, or obedience jump.) Again, I only allow them to jump on command. With the dog on lead, I use the command "Up" and pat the table. Some dogs will put their front feet up the first time. If so, I praise them lavishly and lift the hindquarters onto the table. If the dog isn't inclined to listen, I talk in a happy, excited voice to him ("Good boy, that's the way," etc.), repeating "Up" as I drag him onto the table by the collar. This can only be done with adult dogs that already know how to stand on the table. Always lift puppies or pregnant bitches both on and off the table. When I want a dog to jump, I lift his front by use of the collar only. After having pulled him up once, I try again, leaving the lead slack and giving the dog a chance to do it himself. He'll probably be hesitant,

so praise is important. If he turns away, jerk him back. After a few times he'll jump on eagerly.

My dogs love their tables and never resent this training once they understand what I want. They will, if given the opportunity, jump onto the tables and play "king of the table" for hours while the other Beardies throw the lucky one envious glances. If I set a table in the yard and go inside for a minute, I'm likely to be greeted by four grinning Beardies lined up on it when I return. Because I do not want the dogs to hop on and off at will, I now fold the tables and stand them on end except when grooming, or else I ban the dogs from the grooming room.

If you have only one or two dogs and a strong back, maybe it's just as easy to lift them. However, I use the "Up" command to get Beardies onto other objects besides tables; for example, the truck I use as a show rig or the platforms used at shows for photographing group wins. It never hurts to think positively. You never know when you'll need it.

Left: an ungroomed Beardie.

40

Bottom row: lay the dog on his side to facilitate grooming.

"Down Boy, Down"

Grooming is decidedly easier if your Beardie will lie on his side and allow you to brush him. Stand him on the table and face his side. Encircle him with your arms approximately at hock level and clasp your hands together. In one motion, lean your body into his and pull his feet toward you. Try to lay him gently into a prone position rather than throwing him like a rodeo calf. He will probably struggle and perhaps become panicky for a few moments. Talk to him soothingly and keep him pinned with your body until he relaxes. Once he feels limp, rest a hand on his neck to steady him and then straighten up. Brush him lightly for a few minutes, then allow him to stand. Again, I prefer a specific release command to allow the dog to stand up. Repeat it a few times and he will soon learn to get up and lie down on command, or at least remain passive as you place him in position. I've had little trouble with even the rowdiest adult males when they were introduced to this procedure. It is the *only* way to thoroughly groom the underside of a Beardie single-handedly. In fact, when the dog is in this position, I can completely groom him in the time it takes to whisk over the top of a Beardie while he is standing. If he tries to get up, hold his head flat on the table and repeat the "Stay" command. He will not be able to get up unless he maneuvers the legs on the bottom side underneath himself, and he is unlikely to manage this unless he raises his head. Grasp the foreleg on the under side in one hand and the corresponding hind leg in your other hand. Pull until the legs are straight toward you and the dog is again flat on his side. You can then begin brushing. You may either stand (this is preferable at first because you may have to steady the dog) or pull up a chair and sit down while grooming.

A secret to keeping the dogs relaxed and willing was passed on from Mrs. Willison of Bothkennar in regard to the breed's foundation bitch "Jeannie":

"... during the whole of her life she refused to be groomed without a running commentary as follows: 'Lie on your back, Jeannie, and let me do your tum, that's a good girl . . . Now sit up and let me do your chest, isn't that nice. Now give me a paw . . . now the other paw . . . Now stand up and let me do your back,' etc. With this method I had her full co-operation. She positioned herself and held up her paws as requested and stayed still even when she had to be combed when shedding her coat."

I do find the dogs ever so much more willing to cooperate if I keep up a steady stream of chatter. I'll occasionally lift the hair from over the eye to enquire of the dog's well-being or allow myself to get close enough for my Beardie to sneak in a lick on my face or hand. Relieving his boredom and making it a game ensures a more pleasant experience for everyone.

THE GROOMING PROCESS

The single technique that must be learned for grooming Beardies is called line-brushing. This is

41

Prevent the dog from standing.

Commonly used grooming tools.

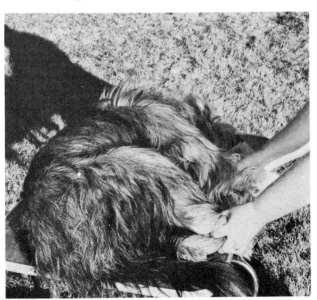

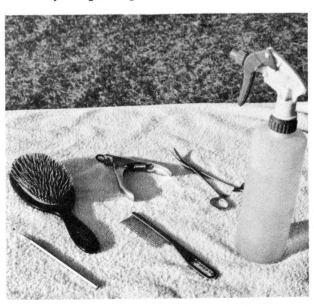

a method of separating the coat into sections and brushing against the lay of the hair until the entire dog has been covered. The hair must be brushed clear to the roots to separate the undercoat and remove dead hair. A dog line-brushed completely once a week should sport a healthy, well-groomed coat. (A damaged coat may need more frequent attention, preferably daily brushing with the addition of some coat oil in the spray during the conditioning period.) With the dog lying on his side, spray the entire coat lightly with water. You will also spray every four or five inches along the line of brushing as you progress along the body. Start on the dog's muzzle and brush a few hairs at a time forward over his nose. Advance toward his neck, brushing a few more hairs with each stroke. It helps to lightly hold the unbrushed hair with your free hand and slide this hand ahead of the brush as you progress.

If you come upon a mat or piece of tangled undercoat while brushing, separate it with your fingers and brush it apart. If necessary, insert the end tooth of your comb and split the tangle, then loosen it with your fingers and comb it out. If you take your time, even the worst mats will come out without cutting or tearing a hole in the coat. Weekly brushing will prevent formation of any but the most insignificant tangles, and if your Beardie has correct coat texture, he will rarely mat.

Half the grooming should take place between the nose and the withers. Areas of very dense hair growth under the ears and on the sides of the neck are often overlooked. Lift the ear up so that the bottom side is exposed. Line-brush under the line of attachment of the ear from muzzle to neck. Don't worry if you can't reach the whole beard. You are to groom only half of the dog from this side and you will need to touch up areas later.

Separate and brush the hair on the inside of the ear and check to see if any hair is growing inside the ear canal. If you find hair, pluck it out carefully following the technique described at the end of this chapter. Next, place the ear back to its normal position and brush the outside fringes. Start at the middle of the skull (remember, you're grooming half of the dog) and line-brush to blend with the completed area. Progress back along the neck. If you have a dog with profuse undercoat, you may want to rebrush this area at right angles to the original brush lines. You will see the difference in the finished look and lack of mats behind the ears. Before going any farther, brush the hair away from your dog's eyes and nose. He will lie much more patiently if he can watch

what's happening. If you have trouble getting through the coat on a puppy, remember that he will become easier to groom as the coat matures.

Next, separate the coat vertically from the middle of the back downward along the edge of the brushed area. Spray one squirt of water along this line and continue brushing. Always move toward the rear of the dog. The coat is still being brushed toward the head, with the brush moving up and down the part and including slightly more hair in each stroke. The body area will be easy to maintain once it has been initially groomed. Repeat the pattern from top to bottom along the dog's side until you reach the loin area.

Now go back and do the front leg. Lift the leg and brush the chest hair and the area around the elbow. Spiral down and around the leg, spraying and line-brushing as you go. The hair on the leg will be brushed straight up toward the body. Separate this hair very thoroughly, paying special attention to the elbow and toes. Brush clear to the tip of the toes, using the comb to separate undercoat wherever necessary. Examine the toenails to determine if they need clipping. (See the end of this chapter for instructions.) Next, continue your line-brushing across the hip and down the hind leg. Be sure to separate all of the hair in the skirts (long hair behind the thigh). When this is completed, turn the dog over and repeat the procedure for the other side. I prefer to have the dog's legs toward me as I groom.

When this is finished, have the dog stand and line-brush down the center of his back. The mature coat should fall into a natural part. You may wish to brush the hair down each side to encourage this, but do not part the back with a comb or other tool. Let the dog shake and lightly whisk all hair back down into its natural lay. Then go to the front of the dog and start line-brushing, working downward on his chest from his throat. Brush the hair upward, but progress down the chest with the brush. When finished, whisk this hair back down also. Then work from the throat to the chin and separate every hair in the beard. You will probably have to comb the beard and face as a finishing touch. The sides of the muzzle are combed down, the top of the skull straight back from the eyes, and the beard forward. The only part left is the tail, which is simply line-brushed around and around from base to tip, with the feather brushed back into its natural plume. You may need someone to hold the dog if he objects to having his tail brushed. When you're

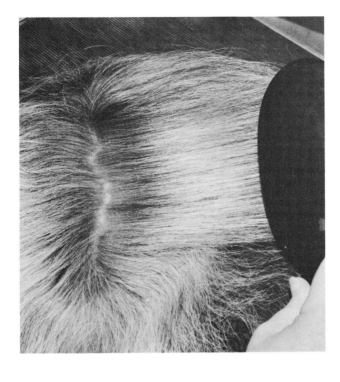

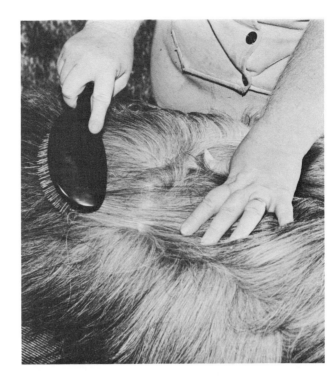

Top left: separate the coat into sections.

Top right: linebrushing.

Middle left: pluck hair growing over the inside corner of the eye.

Middle right: whisk the coat back into place.

Bottom: comb the whiskers down and the beard forward.

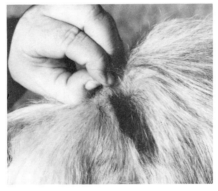

43

finished, he will probably shake. The hair can then be whisked back into position.

Bathing

A Beardie should be bathed only when necessary and at least five days prior to a show so that the texture can return to the coat. The white parts will have to be rebathed the day before the show.

The first and most important step in bathing your Beardie is to give him a *thorough* line-brushing from head to toe, regardless of how dirty he is. If you bathe the dog unbrushed, the under-coat will pack tightly against his body and create a solid mat. Brushing him out afterward will then be more difficult and will tear out considerably more undercoat. I also like to empty the anal glands immediately before a bath so that any residue can be washed off. (Refer to the end of the chapter for details.)

Set out your towels, shampoo, bluing, and a container for mixing. A hand-held spray attachment is extremely helpful and can be purchased to fit almost any shower head. Stand the dog in the tub and wet him thoroughly. I start at the neck and work back, leaving the head for last. I like *Blackout®* or *Darkout®* shampoo for a black or dark slate coat, *Terri-coat®* (which minimizes the softening effect of the bath) for all other colors, and *Snowy-coat®* or *Bright White®* shampoo for the white parts. Baby shampoo is an adequate substitute.

Work some shampoo into the hair around the neck, then lather along the back, down the legs, and finally around the skirts and tail. Let the soap set for two or three minutes, then rinse. Work through the coat with your fingers as you rinse to be sure that the soap is washing out completely. Wet the hair on the skull, ears, and muzzle, being careful to avoid the eyes and ear

The finished product. Best in Show Ch. Shiel's Mogador Silverleaf C.D. ROM, sire of over thirty champions.

44

canal. Rub a small amount of shampoo between your palms and wipe over the skull and ears. The beard and muzzle should then be thoroughly washed with either the white or baby shampoo. After the head is carefully rinsed, relather the feet, tail-tip, and chest with the white shampoo. Rinse and repeat if necessary until these areas are clean.

If the coat is dry, a creme rinse (either a good human brand or a diluted oil-base coat conditioner) may be helpful. Creme rinse should not be applied just before a show because it softens the coat, but it is a useful conditioning aid. As a final touch, rinse the white parts with a bluing solution. Use just enough bluing to color the water sky blue, roughly eight to ten drops to two quarts of water. The hair will dry a sparkling white.

Squeeze excess water from the coat and rub the dog's head with a dry towel. Blot water from the body coat and rub the legs briskly. Allow the dog to shake. When he is partially dry, line-brush his coat thoroughly and repeat when he is completely dry. The line-brushing will go very rapidly if your dog was brushed properly before bathing.

Chalking

Some exhibitors just brush and show their dogs. We prefer to do it this way. Others work a "chalk" powder into slightly damp legs and whiskers for whitening and texture. *FooFoo®*, cornstarch, calcium carbonate, or a mixture of these elements are most frequently used. After it dries, all chalk must be brushed out. No artificial substance should remain in the coat when the dog enters the show ring, and, in fact, is grounds for disqualification.

Routine Care

The following procedures should be performed at regular intervals. It is best to set up a schedule so that they are not neglected. A well-cared-for dog will live a longer, happier life and have fewer health problems over the years.

Ear Care—Any hair growing from the ear canal should be removed. If left, it can form an air blockage and contribute to ear infections. If you do not have a long forceps, pluck as much hair as you can reach with your fingers. This will help but will not remove hair that extends into the canal. This hair is not anchored, and plucking is not painful to the dog. If you have forceps, *carefully* reach as far as possible into the canal and clamp onto the hair. Do not reopen the forceps

but twist around and around until all of the hair pulls loose. Repeat if necessary. If you are still uncertain about this procedure, have a vet or a good groomer show you how easy it actually is.

Occasionally you will want to clean your Beardie's ears. Use rubbing alcohol on a cotton swab. Do not worry about alcohol getting into the canal—it will assist in wax removal and evaporate harmlessly. Clean only the visible surfaces with your swab; never probe into the canal. If a dog scratches his ears continuously, shakes or tilts his head a great deal, or cries out when the ears are touched, he may have ear mites, an infection, or a foreign object imbedded in the ear. Have a veterinarian check the dog if any of these problems are suspected.

Toenails—Should be clipped at least every two weeks unless the dog is very active and wears down the nails on a hard surface. Long toenails cause the foot to spread or splay, making footing difficult. Long nails also force the weight of the body onto the heel of the pad instead of distributing it evenly, resulting in tender, broken-down feet and pasterns.

If your dog's dewclaws (fifth toe located on the inside of each front leg almost at the pastern) have not been removed, be sure to clip them. They do not wear down as the ones on the feet do and can grow in a complete circle and back into the leg in time. Dewclaws are particularly dangerous on Beardies because the breed is active and is prone to tearing the claws off in the underbrush as adults. Also, the coat on the legs

Pluck hair from the ear canal.

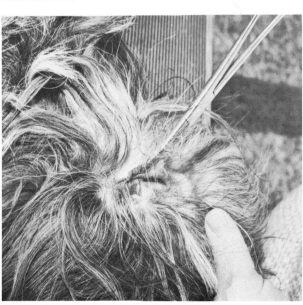

hides the dewclaws from view so that they are easily forgotten and allowed to grow too long.

Hold the foot as illustrated and cut the nail almost to, but not into, the blood line (the pink center of the nail). If you cannot see the quick, remove only the hooked portion of the nail and you will not cut too deeply. After the nail is trimmed, the blood line will recede somewhat as the dog brings the foot in contact with the ground; conversely, in a nail that has not been trimmed for some time, the quick will grow longer so that it reaches closer to the tip of the nail. Since such a nail cannot be cut back as far as it should be with the first trimming, you will have to cut only a tiny bit then repeat the process every few days until the nail has been trimmed back to the proper length. If you should cut too deeply, the nail will bleed but the injury is not serious. A little styptic powder or *Kwik Stop*® will control the bleeding. Your Beardie may remember and be a little touchy about his feet at the next grooming session, though. The properly trimmed nail should just clear the floor when the dog is standing on a hard surface.

There are several kinds of nail clippers, and all of them work well. Most breeders prefer the type illustrated. When your nail clippers become dull so that the nail is pinched or crushed instead of cut, it is time to buy a new pair. Always hold the clipper with the handle *below* the nail, tilting slightly backward. Cutting with the clipper to one side or on top tends to crush the nail rather than make a clean cut.

Foot Care—Because of the requirement for leaving hair between the toes, be sure to check thoroughly for grass seeds and stickers which can become imbedded in the foot. We find that the hair actually protects against the majority of foreign bodies, but those which persevere are harder to detect and may be more easily overlooked than on a trimmed foot. If neglected they can cause a serious infection. "Cheat grass" seed or foxtails are the worst offenders. In areas where these weeds predominate it may be necessary to comb your Beardie's feet daily, or, if he is not being shown, some trimming between the pads may be warranted.

Sore pads are fairly common in any active breed. They can be caused by excessive dryness or cracking, by a bruise, or from too much running on hard or uneven surfaces. Salt used to thaw ice in winter or kill worms in gravel runs may also cause sore feet. There are several commercial preparations such as *Tuf-Foot*® or *Pad-Kote*® which you may apply, or just try a little petroleum jelly or hand lotion to heal cracks. Splinters or other foreign objects in the pad can usually be removed with a tweezer. Swab the area with rubbing alcohol, remove the splinter, then apply first aid cream.

Teeth—Like humans, dogs need the tartar removed from their teeth in order to avoid gum disease. Puppies generally clean their teeth by chewing, but most adult dogs need assistance, especially as they grow older. Dogs that have had their teeth scaled regularly are less likely to lose

Trim toenails to the quick.

Tartar must be scaled from teeth regularly.

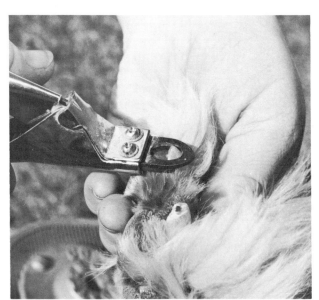

the teeth with age. The rawhide chews, dry kibble, and other products made especially for this purpose are helpful, but if you check your Beardie's teeth at each of your weekly checkups, you will probably find some buildup of discoloring tartar.

Your vet can remove this tartar for a significant fee, which usually includes anesthesia, but if you are economy-minded, buy a tooth scaler and train your puppy to allow you to do the job yourself. If done regularly, cleaning takes only a few minutes. A good quality, sharp scaler, obtainable from your dentist, your vet, or a dog supply catalog, is essential. Begin with the upper incisors. Hold the lips away from the teeth with one hand and use the scaler to scrape from just under the edge of the gum downward with the other hand. Use short, firm strokes, cleaning only a small area of the tooth with each stroke. Be careful not to jab the tongue or lower jaw as you pull downward, but use enough pressure to chip the tartar loose.

After you have cleaned all of the upper teeth, including the molars in the back of the mouth, do the bottom row, scraping from the gum upward on both inside and outside surfaces. Rinse the scaler in an oral antiseptic several times during the process. Complete the job by polishing the teeth with powdered pumice or toothpaste on a soft cloth.

If your Beardie has bad breath even though his teeth are clean, try swabbing the teeth and gums with baking soda or *Happy Breath®*. Strong, persistent breath odor may indicate that your dog has poor digestion or other health problems, and you should call this to the attention of your veterinarian at the Beardie's next checkup.

Anal Glands—These two small glands located below and on either side of the anus secrete a lubricant that enables the dog to expel feces more easily. Occasionally these glands become clogged, accumulating a foul-smelling mass. Irritation of the glands results.

Clogging may be caused by injury to the region, bacterial infection, or by migration of segments of tapeworm into the ducts of the glands. Obesity and lack of muscular tone may be contributing factors in old dogs. Chronically soft feces will also cause retention of the fluid. Closely confined dogs appear to have more difficulty than active dogs.

The most common early sign of anal irritation is when the dog licks or bites at the perineum. As the condition progresses, the dog may drag his anus across the floor or rub it against any rough surface. This action almost always indicates that the anal glands need to be emptied rather than that the dog has worms (as the old wives' tale would have us believe). If the glands become severely clogged, infection will set in and sacs may abscess. The only way to correct the abscess is to have the glands surgically removed.

Removing the accumulated fluid regularly will prevent impaction and will make your Beardie more comfortable. Seize the tail with the left hand and encircle the anus from the bottom with the thumb and forefinger of your right hand. Press the anus firmly between thumb and finger, expelling the vile smelling mass. It may squirt some distance, so either do this outside or in an easily cleaned area, or cover the anus with a tissue or piece of cotton. Repeating this procedure once a month is ample to keep the glands cleaned out, and as stated earlier, I find that the best time to check is before each bath. Be sure to empty both glands.

Eye Care—Prolonged watering or irritation of the eyes is cause for concern, although it will probably occur for a few weeks as the puppy coat grows out and reaches a length where it gets into the eyes. This problem corrects itself as the coat lengthens. For mild irritation, a rinse made from one-fourth teaspoon salt in one-half cup water may be used, or you can buy a bottle of artificial tears for contact lens wearers and use that as an eyewash. Severe irritation, mattering eyes, mild inflammation that does not clear up in a few days, or dilated pupils, haziness over the eye, or a foreign object in the eye signal a quick trip to your veterinarian. Don't put it off. And don't use old medication for a new eye problem. Drops or ointment for use in the eye are very specific to a particular condition and may cause serious injury if used to treat a different condition. Use medications only under the direction of your veterinarian. Avoid giving hepatitis vaccine to a dog with any eye irritation. It can create a severe reaction and possible blindness.

48

Ch. Parcana Jake McTavish in top form!

7 *Shaping Up*

THE HEALTHY BEARDIE

Optimum condition is essential in a show or working Beardie, and it is important for the breeding and pet dog as well. Top condition isn't achieved haphazardly but is the result of a skillfully planned and followed program. Conditioning is an ongoing project. The needs and condition of your Beardie will change from time to time during his life span due to age, environment, stress, and other factors, so you will find it necessary to make adjustments in his diet and routine to compensate for these changes. Each Beardie is a little different. We can offer guidelines, but you will want to experiment a bit with your individual dog.

If you are to maintain your Beardie in glowing health and condition, you must first learn to recognize the signs of good health, as well as the symptoms of illness or poor condition. Whether your dog lives in the house with you or in the kennel, you should be constantly alert to his condition and check him at least twice weekly. At first this will take conscious effort, but as you become familiar with your Beardie, the routine will become second nature.

Good health is dependent upon many factors—heredity, environment, diet, exercise, and grooming, to name a few. A healthy Beardie is bright and active, with a happy, enthusiastic personality. His movements are effortless and smooth with no signs of stiffness or limping, and he does not tire easily. His coat appears glossy and unbroken, and beneath it you will find the skin smooth, pliable, and free from dandruff, scabs, red spots, or parasites.

A Bearded Collie in good condition carries just enough weight so that you can feel the ribs but cannot press a finger between them. Individual show Beardies may look better with just a bit more flesh, but they should never be fat. The muscles should be firm and supple, not soft and flabby. The flesh should fit the body firmly; loose, bouncing rolls of flesh are an indication of poor muscle tone.

You can tell a great deal about your Beardie's health by observing the key areas: eyes, ears, and mouth. A Beardie's eyes may be the window to his soul, and they are also first to clue you that he is not well. In a healthy Beardie the eyes are clear, bright, expressive, and alert. The inside of the eyelids, as well as the third eyelid (the membrane at the inner corner between the upper and lower lids) are pink in color. (The third eyelid may have a dark pigment instead of a pink color.) Redness or swelling in these areas indicates a problem, and so do dull, cloudy eyes. The eyes should not water or contain mucus.

Lift your Beardie's ear leather, and you will find the inside of the ear canal to be pale pink in color. It will be clearly visible if you have kept it free of hair (*see* ch. 6). Bright pink or red ear membranes are abnormal. The ear should have only a small amount of brown wax. Large amounts of brown, orange, or foul-smelling wax are not normal.

The gums are also a vital key to good health; become familiar with the normal color of your Beardie's gums and mouth. Normal gums are either pink or black, and they feel firm and fit tightly around the base of the teeth. Either red, pale pink, yellowish, or white gums are abnormal. A red line along gums which appear to have shrunk away from the teeth may indicate gum disease.

During grooming, run your hands over your Beardie's body. You should find no lumps, swellings, or sores. Become familiar with your dog's respiration patterns both while at rest and after running. Observe his usual sleeping, eating, and urinating patterns. Paying attention to these little details while he is well will enable you to notice quickly any abnormal behavior or appearance. You will catch an illness before it becomes serious and will be able to make minor adjustments in your dog's environment or conditioning program which will keep him in top shape at all times.

50

FEEDING

Your Beardie's diet is the greatest factor in achieving optimum condition and health. Therefore, you will want to choose a high-quality, properly balanced commercial ration. The best commercial dog food manufacturers have conducted feeding trials and laboratory tests and will be happy to provide you with information on the results. Avoid brands which cannot or will not provide this information. Quality food contains minimum levels of carbohydrates, fats, and proteins, as well as minerals and vitamins essential to good canine nutrition. In the United States, an excellent indication of quality is a statement on the label that the diet has been approved by AAFCO (Association of American Feed Control Officials) protocol. An analysis of the ingredients in a particular food is not adequate because an element may be present, but not in a form which the dog can digest and absorb. Also, many nutrients, too numerous to itemize, are required. Toxic substances may be present in low-quality rations. Select a well-known manufacturer whose brand of dog food is recommended by your veterinarian and by other breeders. When you find a ration that maintains your Beardie in good condition, stay with it. Variety is not the "spice of life" when feeding your dog. In fact, changing his diet will often cause him to go off feed or have an upset stomach.

Types of Food

There are five basic types of diets.[1] The first is the homemade diet. It *may* be nutritionally balanced, but because it rarely is, it can cause nutritional deficiencies, excesses, toxicities, and general imbalance.

The second type, generally sold in grocery, pet, or feed stores, was referred to previously as "commercial" dog food. These brands are generally available in a maintenance ration but may also be obtained in a growth ration which has a higher protein and energy content for growing puppies or lactating bitches.

The third type includes foods containing various drugs. These fairly recent products are usually available only through your vet or a specialty house. One type, called *HRH*®, contains drugs to help control heartworms, roundworms, and hookworms. Another brand now being developed will contain a progesterone compound for birth control.

The fourth kind of diet is the Prescription Diet specifically formulated for use in the management of certain medical conditions and available only by prescription from a veterinarian.

The fifth type is the *Science Diet®*, based on a fixed-formula (most commercial manufacturers vary the ingredients depending on availability and cost). *Science Diet®* formulas have been developed for maintenance, lactation, growth, and stress. This ration is highly concentrated as well as highly digestible and needs no additional supplementation of any kind except the possibility of oil for the coat. Since *Science Diet®* has less undigestible bulk, feeding it will result in lower stool volume.

Forms of Food

Three forms of dog food are available: dry, soft-moist, and canned.

Dry Food — Dry foods are cheaper, may be self-fed, and are abrasive enough to help prevent the formation of tartar on the teeth. The disadvantage of this food is that it supplies a great deal of bulk. As a result, a Beardie under stress or with unusually high energy requirements may not eat enough to maintain correct weight. Also, dry food is sometimes deficient in the fatty acids, which aid in maintaining good coat and skin condition. This can be easily offset by adding one tablespoon of vegetable oil to each pound of dry food.

Dry food loses its fatty acids to oxidation and becomes rancid if it is stored for more than six months (less in extreme heat or humidity).

Soft-Moist Food — Many brands of soft-moist (burger-type) foods are being marketed. They are more expensive, cannot be self-fed, and contribute to tartar formation. They *may* contain a higher-quality protein or more energy per pound on a dry-matter basis. They definitely contain higher sugar and preservative percentages.

Canned Food — The advantages and disadvantages of canned food are similar to those of soft-moist. Since each can contains about seventy-seven percent water, more than three-fourths of the cost is for water. A dog must eat a much larger volume of canned food to obtain his daily nutritional requirements, and this makes canned food impractical for Bearded Collies.

To maintain a forty-pound dog, the daily cost for a supermarket-brand dry ration is about fifteen cents; national-brand dry ration, eighteen cents; *Science Diet®* maintenance ration twenty-eight cents; average semimoist ration, forty-one cents; and average canned ration, fifty-six cents.[2]

Methods of Feeding

A dog may be either self-fed or individually fed. The only requirement for self-feeding is to leave food before your Beardie at all times. Self-feeding allows you more freedom to come and go, it is easy, and it requires no mixing, adjusting, or record-keeping. Each dog eats what he wants

Can. Ch. Wishanger Marsh Pimpernel, C.D. with her four-week-old daughter and seven-month-old granddaughter, *Raggmopp*.

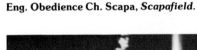

Eng. Obedience Ch. Scapa, *Scapafield*.

when he wants it. Self-feeding helps to discourage the eating of feces. The poor-doer that likes to eat only small amounts at a time will often do best on self-feeding, but some dogs will overeat and get fat. Puppies that are self-fed may overeat, resulting in an overly rapid growth pattern and associated skeletal problems. A self-feeding program must be started slowly to discourage overeating. At first, feed the normal ration, then gradually increase the amount until some food is left at the end of each day. Self-feeding is not recommended for some Beardie puppies until they reach six months of age. You may want to experiment to determine which of your dogs do best on self-feeding programs.

If you feed your Beardies individually, any type of food may be given, and the amount of food and supplementation should be balanced for each dog. Puppies less than six months old and lactating bitches should be fed at least twice daily. In fact, evidence suggests that two feedings per day are better than one for all dogs, although many breeders feed adult dogs only once daily. You can teach your Beardie to clean up his bowl by placing him in an area where he can eat alone and undisturbed. Pick up the bowl in about fifteen minutes, whether he is finished or not. He will soon learn to complete his meal in the allotted time.

Whatever type of food and method of feeding you select, avoid oversupplementing with vitamins and minerals. Improperly fed, supplements can do more harm than good, so they should be used under your veterinarian's direction. Avoid giving table scraps, sweets, or bones to your Beardie. You'll only encourage obesity, begging, or finicky eating. Knuckle bones of beef may be parboiled to kill parasites and can be fed occasionally. Do not give your Beardie pork, steak, chicken, or other small bones. Many dogs have died from a bone-punctured stomach or intestine.

How much should you feed? This is difficult to answer since each Beardie has a slightly different metabolism. Your best gauge is your dog's weight and condition. A dog that is too thin or too fat is probably eating too little or too much, respectively. Generally, an adult Beardie can be expected to consume about four cups of dry food per day.

FOOD SUPPLEMENTS

Many food additives and nutritional supplements are available, but they are generally unnecessary if your adult Beardie is being fed a high-quality ration. It is safer, cheaper, and easier to buy a good-quality, balanced ration than to supplement a low-quality food. Vitamins, minerals, and nutrients must be supplied in balanced ratios to be effective. It is difficult to duplicate scientifically balanced diets by home methods.

Since Beardie puppies between two and six months of age exhibit an unusually fast growth rate, we do feel that they need added calcium and phosphorus, unless *Science Diet Growth*® is being fed. These elements can be safely supplied

52

Jande's famous litter by Ch. Edenborough Happy Go Lucky ex Ch. Beardie Bloody Mary. Six of the nine became champions.

with bone meal, which can be purchased in powdered form from pet supply or health food stores. It is inexpensive and, unlike calcium/phosphorus tablets, is not harmful if overfed. One tablespoon per day may be added to the food during the puppy's first six months of growth.

Beardies living in a dry climate like Colorado, or those fed a dry kibble, may need a coat supplement to furnish additional fatty acids. Many commercial formulas are on the market, or you may simply add corn, vegetable, peanut, or soy oil at the rate of one tablespoon per pound of dry food. Fats from meats other than bacon supply only empty calories instead of the needed fatty acids and should not be used.

CONDITIONING THROUGH EXERCISE

Your conditioning program cannot be complete without planned exercise. The amount of exercise your Beardie gets has as much control over his weight and bloom as does his diet. A fat, soft Beardie needs more exercise, perhaps accompanied by a more restricted diet. A thin or overmuscled dog usually needs less exercise, along with, perhaps, a diet higher in calories. Exercise often improves appetite, and a thin dog that is not eating properly may be induced to eat more by increasing his activity.

Often, neither the kennel dog nor the house pet get the right type of exercise. Both should have at least one hour per day of romping in a large yard or exercise area where they can move freely. The show or working Beardie needs additional exercise, and this is best achieved through road work. Road work means trotting your Beardie for a structured period each day, usually on a leash behind a bicycle or automobile, until he develops his maximum potential gait and endurance. With consistent road work, the Beardie who moves sloppily will tighten up, the good-moving dog will develop a gait that is effortless, smooth, and extended, and the tight dog will begin to move more freely. You can't correct real unsoundness through road work, but you can make the most of what your Beardie is capable of doing.

Adult Beardies should be initiated at about one-half mile per day, moving at a comfortable trotting speed on a loose leash. Do not allow your Beardie to gallop or pace—this develops entirely different muscles. The best surface for road work is dirt or cut grass. If you have only gravel or cement surfaces, you will have to work shorter distances and check continually for signs of sore pads or lameness. The surface should be level or slightly uphill. Never trot a dog downhill—it breaks down pasterns and shoulders.

Never work your Beardie until he is exhausted, stiff, or lame. If this should occur at any point, rest your Beardie a day or two, then shorten the distance worked until it is comfortable for him. By the end of the first week, most Beardies will be ready to proceed to trotting one mile per day. Week by week, gradually lengthen the distance until your dog is easily trotting two to three miles daily.

After your dog has reached his maximum distance, it will take at least a month of consistent, daily road work for him to approach peak performance. After this point, you can maintain optimum performance by working him only once or twice weekly. If you wish your dog to be at his best for show season, start his workouts about three months prior to the first show.

Puppies may be started on road work at about six months of age, but they should be worked much shorter distances and should progress more slowly from one distance to the next. Never tie a Beardie behind a car. Instead, have someone drive while you sit on the tailgate of a station wagon and lead the dog (don't position him where he must breathe the exhaust fumes). Or, still better for you, ride a bicycle. A good trotting speed for an adult Beardie will average seven to eight miles per hour.

CARING FOR THE OLDER BEARDIE

Without your hardly noticing, your Beardie will one day move a little slower and sleep a little longer. His body processes will slow, his resistance will be lower, and his digestion, sight, and hearing will not be as good as they once were. But he will still be an important member of your family and can be depended upon to assist in training the younger dogs and add an air of permanency and dignity to the household. He will be living proof of your healthy line of Beardies and will probably be a super-salesman besides.

The older Beardie requires little in additional care: a warmer, drier place to sleep; encouragement to exercise; and perhaps a special diet lower in protein to help keep his weight down and not overstress his kidneys. Loss of teeth may make food difficult to chew, so switch to a softer food and have his teeth cleaned regularly.

The older dog is often subject to cysts (which sometimes look like pimples on the skin), various infections, deafness, or blindness. In familiar surroundings you may never know that your dog is blind, but he will become frightened and bump into things when taken to a different environment. A blind dog can be taught to respond to sound vibrations, and a deaf dog can respond to hand signals and still live a reasonably happy, comfortable life.

When the day comes that your Beardie can no longer lead a meaningful existence, or when his days are filled with suffering, you should consider ending his misery through euthanasia. No one wants to give up a friend, but often it is the best way. Your veterinarian will inject an overdose of anesthetic, and your Beardie will drift into a peaceful, permanent sleep. The process takes only a few minutes; there is no pain or fright, and no prolonged suffering.

ENDNOTES

[1]*Feeding and Care of the Dog*, Lon D. Lewis, D.V.M., Ph.D., published by Morris Animal Foundation, Denver, Colorado, November, 1977.

[2]From statistics presented by Dr. Lon D. Lewis, D.V.M., Ph.D., at a Dog Health Seminar, Colorado State University, Fort Collins, Colorado, October 30, 1977.

Eng. Ch. Kharisar Karibh Khan (Afghan Hound) and Eng. Ch. Mignonette of Willowmead at Orora, *Orora.*

54

8 In Sickness and In Health

You can protect your pet from many canine diseases by yearly vaccinations and by preventive care. In addition, cleanliness and maintenance of a parasite-free environment will assure that your Beardie stays healthy. You are fortunate to have chosen a breed with relatively few hereditary problems or tendencies to illness. Yet, every dog owner at some point will be called upon to administer first aid or give medication for a minor illness. You will want to familiarize yourself with symptoms of illness, antidotes for poisons, and medical techniques so that you will be prepared.

A Beardie puppy should receive his first immunization at six or seven weeks of age. This shot will introduce into his bloodstream antibodies for the three most deadly canine diseases: distemper, hepatitis, and leptospirosis. A second vaccination should be given about three or four weeks after the first shot, and many vets recommend a third shot one month following the second. (Your vet may advise a slightly different routine, depending upon the type of vaccine used.) This is because the puppy receives antibodies from his mother's milk, and the immunization will not take effect until all of the immunity received from the mother has been lost. This can occur anywhere between six and sixteen weeks of age; therefore, the puppy should be protected from exposure to disease during the first three months, and the last immunization should be given when he is three to four months old. Thereafter, yearly boosters are required.

Rabies vaccinations are required by law and are given when a puppy is six months old. The same state laws also regulate the frequency of booster vaccinations. The American Veterinary Medical Association recommends a booster vaccination for modified live virus rabies one year after the initial shot, then boosters every three years. A certificate of rabies vaccination will be required when you apply for a city or county dog license or a health certificate for interstate shipping. Many localities require yearly boosters.

PARASITES

Parasites are dependent at some point in their life cycle on a host—your dog. They are common in almost any area of the world, and while they generally do not represent a serious problem except in very young puppies, they should be eliminated. They are often the cause of poor overall condition; thinness, dull, dry coats, and lack of vigor.

All parasites complete a life cycle, only part of which affects your dog. This cycle must be considered or you will continue to have the problem even after you have treated the dog.

Internal Parasites

The most common internal parasites are roundworms, tapeworms, hookworms, and whipworms, all of which live in the dog's intestine. You may or may not see the worms or their symptoms. Microscopic diagnosis by a veterinarian is necessary. You will want to have your puppy checked several times the first year and every year thereafter by taking in a small amount of fresh stool for examination.

Roundworms or Ascarids

These white, cylindrical worms are the most common type seen in puppies. Puppies can be born with roundworms, or they can pick up the eggs from contaminated surfaces after birth. Either way, it is safe to assume that almost every puppy will be infected with these worms.

Adult roundworms live in the small intestine where they absorb nutrients from the digestive juices. The worms produce eggs which pass in the stool. The eggs become larvae, are ingested by either the same individual or another dog, and develop into worms to complete the cycle. Some of the larvae will not complete the life cycle but will migrate into the lungs or other tissue to remain in a resting stage. When a bitch becomes pregnant, these resting larvae migrate into the fetus.

Beardies with roundworm infections may appear thin and potbellied. They may have dull coats, diarrhea, or they may vomit or cough. In young puppies a heavy infection may cause death, but in adult dogs the worms don't generally cause a serious illness. Roundworms are easily eliminated with a drug called piperazine. It is safe, can be obtained from your vet or a pet supply store, and can be given to puppies as young as two weeks old. The treatment should be repeated in two weeks, and again in a month to make sure all of the mature worms are killed.

The biggest problem with roundworms is that the eggs can remain alive and infective in the soil for months. Cleanliness is important. Remove the stools daily and control rodents, which serve as an intermediate host to the larvae. Treat the soil with salt or borax (see Ch. 5).

Tapeworms

This parasite attaches to the intestinal wall with suckers. The tapeworm's body is composed of a series of reproductive segments which look somewhat like grains of rice. They may sometimes be seen clinging to the hair or skin around the anus. The adult tapeworm produces eggs which pass in the feces and are eaten by an intermediate host such as rodent, flea, or rabbit. The dog then eats the intermediate host containing the infective stage of the tapeworm, and the worm completes its life cycle by developing in the dog's intestine.

Tapeworms may cause digestive problems, weight loss, or poor condition. Avoid using tapeworm medications available in drug or pet stores because they are generally ineffective and can be dangerous. Your vet can provide a safe, effective dewormer. Again, cleanliness and elimination of intermediate hosts are required to prevent reinfection.

Hookworms

Hookworms are small worms which suck blood directly from the wall of the small intestine. They are one of the more tenacious, and more damaging, parasites. Dogs become infected by ingesting the larvae from the ground or by having their skin or pads penetrated by the infective larvae. Puppies are often infected before birth by migrating larvae.

Symptoms include weakness, diarrhea, anemia, and blood in the stool. The stool is black and looks like tar with a distinctive odor. Heavily infected puppies may die before the worms are detected. Treatment must be administered quickly by a veterinarian, and blood transfusions may be necessary. He may give disophenal as an injection, or diclorvos orally. All hookworm medication can be dangerous and should be used under the direction of your veterinarian. Do not use the over-the-counter medications sold for these worms because they can cause severe side effects.

Whipworms

These parasites live in the large intestine and may cause diarrhea or weight loss. They can be detected only by microscopic examination and require a specific wormer which your veterinarian can prescribe.

Heartworm

Heartworm disease is a very serious problem. The adult heartworms live in the right atrium and ventricle of the heart. The mature worms produce larvae called microfilaria, which circulate in the blood. When a mosquito bites an infected dog, that insect becomes the intermediate host for the microfilaria, which can be passed on when another dog is bitten. Heartworms can be found almost anywhere in the United States but are most common in coastal areas where mosquitoes are prevalent.

Infected dogs tire easily, cough, have difficulty breathing, and are generally in poor condition. Signs of heart failure may occur. However, heartworm may be present for some time before symptoms appear, and it is important to have your dog checked regularly if you live in an area where mosquitoes are present. A blood test is required, and since microfilaria are known to be more active at night, it is best to have the test done late in the day. Treatment is a long and difficult process, and hospitalization is often required.

Protecting your Beardie from mosquitoes is the best way to prevent infection. Researchers are now perfecting a vaccine against heartworm. This medication may soon be available; also, drugs may not be obtained and administered in the dog's food or in pill form to prevent heartworm larvae from developing. Check with your vet about the various protective measures if you live in an area where heartworms are known to be present.

External Parasites

Fleas are by far the most common external parasite found on dogs, cats, and other animals. The small brown insects can be seen jumping about near the dog's skin, where they suck blood. These parasites can significantly weaken the host as well as spread disease. Fleas deposit eggs about the size and color of a grain of salt on their host. The eggs drop off into bedding, into cracks in the soil, or in buildings, into carpets, etc. In about two weeks the eggs hatch into larvae, which then develop into adult fleas.

To control the parasites, you must eliminate them on the dog through the use of medicated shampoo or insecticide powders, then thoroughly clean all bedding and housing or kennel facilities. You may want to fumigate your kennel or spray with lindane, chlordane, or malathion. Burn old bedding.

Lice are small, pale-colored, bloodsucking insects which are far less common than fleas and generally are found only in extremely dirty conditions or around poultry facilities. They can be treated by the same methods used against fleas. Since lice die quickly once removed from their host, it is not necessary to treat the bedding.

Ticks are a problem in some areas of the country. There are many different species, all of which attach themselves to the dog's flesh and engorge themselves with the blood of their host. They cause skin inflammation, may carry disease germs, and cause anemia, weakness, or paralysis. If your dog has only one or two, you can remove them by hand. Apply a little rubbing alcohol to the tick, causing it to loosen, then grasp the insect firmly as close to the dog's skin as possible and slowly pull the tick off. You can then burn it with a match. If ticks are a constant problem, or your dog has picked up a number of them, purchase a good commercial tick and flea dip and spray or fumigate bedding and kennel facilities. You may have to repeat the spraying several times before all ticks are killed.

WHEN YOUR BEARDIE IS NOT FEELING WELL

Once you have learned to observe the signs of good health in your dog and have become familiar with his habit patterns and behavior, it will be easy to determine when he is ill. Any change in behavior or appetite can be a clue. He may be restless, depressed, ill-tempered, or he may whine. His eyes may appear dull and uninterested, or they may water. He may vomit, have diarrhea, shiver, or appear to be uncomfortable. He may show signs of stiffness, lameness, or urinate frequently. A fever is a definite indication of illness.

Since any dog may have an "off day," don't panic at first. Just be observant. Take your Beardie's rectal temperature using any human rectal thermometer inserted about half its length. The normal temperature for most canines is 101.5 degrees, but you should be aware (and also inform your vet) that it is often normal for a Beardie to have a temperature of 102.0 or even 102.5. It will be highest in the afternoon or evening. You should check your dog's temperature several different times while he is healthy to determine what is normal for him.

If your dog appears to behave abnormally for more than one day, or if acute symptoms or a high fever are present, don't wait, take him to your veterinarian for a checkup, or call for advice. It is important for *every* dog owner to locate within close proximity a good veterinarian and establish a good relationship with him or her.

Giving Medication

With a little practice you can give your Beardie a pill easily and quickly. To force your dog's mouth open, grasp his muzzle with your hand over the foreface and let your fingers press his upper lips over the tips of his upper teeth. Tilt the head upward slightly to encourage swallowing. With your other hand, place the pill far back in the center of the base of the tongue. Quickly remove your hand and close the dog's mouth, holding it closed until you feel him swallow. Rubbing the throat will sometimes encourage swallowing. If the pill is particularly large or dry, buttering it will help.

Liquid medication may be given from a spoon, but drawing it into a large syringe, *eye-dropper*, or kitchen baster makes it easier to administer. Pull the corner of the lower lip outward and upward with one hand, forming a

pocket. Keeping your Beardie's head tilted slightly upward, slowly pour the liquid into the lip pocket. Allow the dog to swallow as the liquid is given, but prevent him from lowering or shaking his head.

It is important when giving medications to administer the exact quantity specified. Pills should not be crushed into the food because you can never be sure that they are being swallowed entirely. Liquid medications must be measured accurately. You will find the following conversion table helpful:

16 drops = 1 cc = ¼ teaspoon
 5 cc = 1 teaspoon
15 cc = 1 tablespoon = ½ oz.
30 cc = 2 tablespoons = 1 oz.
 8 oz. = 1 cup
 4 cups = 1 quart = 1 liter

Supplies

Like every good mother, every dog owner should have a medicine chest. Include the following: a rectal thermometer, a good liquid antiseptic soap, cotton swabs, peroxide, gauze pads and a gauze bandage wrap, alcohol, clean towels, a blunt-nosed scissors for clipping around wounds, etc., styptic powder or silver nitrate to control bleeding of small wounds or bites, an old nylon for use as a muzzle, *Kaopectate®*, *Milk of Magnesia®* tablets, a good antiseptic wound spray, a general purpose flea and tick dip or shampoo, *Panalog®* dressing, *Drammamine®*, artificial tears for eyes, activated charcoal, and a

58

Giving liquid medication

Giving a pill.

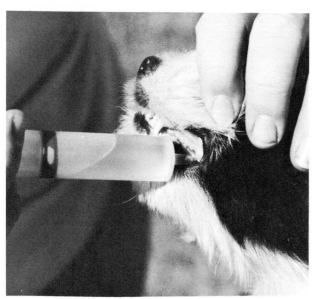

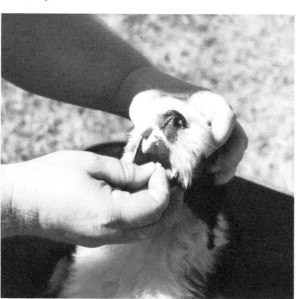

product such as *Bitter Apple*® to prevent chewing.

Some Common Diseases and Problems

Arthritis—Properly called osteoarthritis, this is a disease in which the joints are affected by excess bone growth, resulting in pain and lameness. It can occur in young dogs due to trauma affecting a joint or from congenital joint defects. It more commonly occurs with aging.

Treatment is only symptomatic; there is no way to arrest the development of arthritis. Keep the arthritic Beardie warm and dry, and limit, but do not discontinue, exercise. Do not allow the dog to become overweight. Your vet may prescribe aspirin or *Tylenol*® if the pain is severe, or in more advanced cases may suggest corticosteroids.

Constipation—Constipation commonly occurs from lack of bulk in the diet, but also may be caused by overlong confinement (especially while traveling), internal parasites, tumors, abscessed anal sacs, or old age. One day without a bowel movement is no cause for concern.

A mild change in diet or adding water to the food may help. Two tablespoons of *Milk of Magnesia*® or one of the human laxatives designed to provide bulk may be given, or try a human rectal suppository.

Dermatitis—There are many kinds of dermatitis, or inflammation of the skin—some caused by allergies, some by contact to irritants, and some by infection. The symptoms are similar: red skin accompanied by hair loss in the area, and possibly bumps, scabs, dandruff-like scales, or oozing areas. The skin may feel hot to touch.

Severe dermatitis requires veterinarian attention. You may try treating small areas by bathing the dog frequently and rinsing him with one cap of *Alpha-Keri*® oil per quart of water. Apply *Furaspor*® or some other type of soothing, drying ointment to the area.

Diarrhea—Diarrhea may indicate a more serious disease or infection, or it may be the result of overeating, change in diet, overexcitement, or parasites. The best initial treatment is to withhold food for twelve to twenty-four hours, then limit the dog to a light, bland diet containing broth, cooked eggs, cottage cheese, or rice for several days. *Kaopectate*® can be given every four hours (two teaspoonsful per ten pounds of weight).

Severe diarrhea, diarrhea accompanied by vomiting, or bloody diarrhea signal a trip to your veterinarian. Unchecked diarrhea causes dehydration, which can occur especially rapidly in puppies. Beware of administering some of the commercial products sold by pet supply catalogs. They can be quite strong and possibly dangerous.

Distemper—Distemper is a highly contagious, infectious disease. The germs are airborne, so direct contact with an infected animal is not required. Distemper virus is everywhere; you can even carry the germs into your home on shoes or clothing. For this reason, and because the disease is generally fatal, every dog should be immunized with yearly boosters throughout his life.

Symptoms are erratic. Often, the first signs include fever, listlessness, lack of appetite, stiffness, or vomiting. Later, the dog will probably develop diarrhea, nasal discharge, and coughing. Eventually, the nervous system becomes damaged.

Ear Inflammation—If your Beardie begins shaking his head and scratching at his ears, he may have an ear infection. The inside of the ear may be red or swollen, have large amounts of waxy discharge, or emit a strong odor. First, remove any excess hair from the ear canal by plucking. Try cleaning the ear with a cotton swab dipped in seventy percent isopropyl alcohol. Then place several drops of alcohol into the ear and massage the base of the ear to spread the medication. Severe or continued ear infections should be treated by a veterinarian.

Ear Mites—These parasites are common in some areas of the country. They cause discomfort and scratching, accompanied by profuse amounts of dark reddish brown to grey wax. If you live in an area where ear mites are a problem, your vet can give you drops containing lindane, rotenone, or some other insecticide. Clean the ear with a cotton swab dipped in isopropyl alcohol. You may be able to see the small mites. Drop the insecticide into the ears according to instructions.

Eye Irritations and Inflammations—Eyes are very delicate organs, and even the slightest irritation should not be ignored. Often, dust, pollen, or a foreign object or allergy will cause tearing or mild inflammation. Wash the eye area with a cotton swab dipped in a salt water solution (one teaspoon salt per one cup water), or use artificial tears sold for humans. If the irritation continues, see your vet. Never use anything in the eye that is not specifically designed for ophthalmic use, and never use eye drugs prescribed for one problem to treat another case.

Ophthalmic drugs are very specific; using the wrong one could cause blindness.

Conjunctivitis, or inflammation of the third eyelid, is a fairly common problem. The membrane appears red and swollen. Treatment by antibiotics is necessary.

Enteritis—This is acute, hemorrhagic diarrhea accompanied by cramping of the stomach, gas, and sometimes vomiting. The onset is sudden. Give the dog two tablespoons of *Kaopectate®* to quiet his stomach, and RUSH him to the vet. Causes of enteritis are varied, but sudden death can result unless treatment is begun immediately.

Infectious Canine Hepatitis—Canine hepatitis is not the same as human hepatitis, although it is similar in that the disease primarily affects the liver. It is an acute viral disease characterized by high fever, bloody diarrhea, abdominal pain, and vomiting. Dogs may exhibit an intolerance for light, and occasionally a blue film will form over the cornea of the eye. This condition is known as "blue eye" and can occur from mild forms of the disease, or, rarely, from a reaction to the vaccine. Hepatitis vaccine should never be given to a dog with an eye ulceration because an extreme reaction and possible blindness may result.

There is no cure for the disease. Hospitalization is required, but only the symptoms can be treated. You can protect your Beardie with vaccinations administered yearly in conjunction with distemper vaccine.

Kennel Cough—Tracheobronchitis, called "kennel cough" because it occurs frequently in kennels, shows, or any place where large numbers of dogs come together, is one of the most contagious of canine diseases. It is characterized by a dry, hacking cough or deep harsh coughing often accompanied by gagging. The Beardie's appetite will remain good, and he will have no fever or other symptoms. Like a cold, kennel cough has to run its course, and most dogs recover with or without medication in two to six weeks if kept warm and relatively quiet. Occasionally a stubborn case will hang on for several months. Over-the-counter cough suppressants marketed for humans may be given to mask the symptoms, and your veterinarian can prescribe broad spectrum antibiotics.

A vaccine is now available which can immunize your Beardie against some forms of kennel cough. The immunization can be given separately or combined with DHL vaccine. Be sure to request it if you have a number of dogs or plan to travel or show your Beardie.

Kidney and Bladder Infections—The most common problems affecting the urinary system are interstitial nephritis in the kidneys, or cystitis (bladder infection).

Nephritis is common in older dogs, but it can occur in conjunction with infectious diseases or be caused by the ingestion of poisons. An affected Beardie generally runs a fever, arches his back in pain, drinks increased amounts of water, vomits, and has strong body or breath odors. A urinalysis is required for diagnosis, and hospitalization may be required. Prompt treatment will usually prevent kidney damage in acute cases. Chronic nephritis is controlled by diet and medication.

Cystitis is generally caused by a bacterial infection in the bladder. Symptoms include frequent urination, cloudy or blood-tinged urine, and straining. Females may have a vaginal discharge and may lick themselves excessively. Treatment with antibiotics will be required for several weeks, and the dog should have plenty of water.

If you think your Beardie has a kidney or bladder problem, collect a urine sample within an hour before you leave and take it to your vet. Take your Beardie out on the leash and collect about one-fourth cup of urine in a clean container.

Leptospirosis—Leptospirosis is the third kind of acute infectious disease against which we immunize our Beardies, and the only one contagious to humans. The disease primarily affects the kidneys, causing kidney failure. Germs are spread in the contaminated urine of affected dogs, rodents, or cattle. Rat- or mouse-contaminated foods are a prime source. The bacteria can enter the dog's system orally, through the skin, or during intercourse.

Symptoms include depression, loss of appetite, vomiting, fever, and constipation followed by diarrhea. The dog may be stiff and reluctant to move, often walking in a hunched-up posture with short, choppy steps. Occasionally, the infection is so slight that it is hardly noticed; in others it may cause death. Recovered animals may carry the germs for months afterward.

Vaccination will protect your Beardie from leptospirosis. However, the disease is more prevalent in some parts of the country than in others, and the vaccine, usually administered as part of the DHL package, may not be routinely given. Ask your vet for recommendations, and be sure to inform him if you plan to travel to shows or ship your dog for breeding. The immunity is shorter-lived than other vaccines, and boosters every six months are required in high-risk areas.

Tonsillitis—If you open your Beardie's mouth wide, you can probably see his tonsils, which lie in a pocket on either side of the throat just behind the soft palate. Occasionally, they become infected and appear red and swollen. The dog may refuse to eat or may have difficulty eating, or he may gag, vomit, or have a slight fever. Tonsillitis is often caused by rapid changes in temperature, such as when a house dog is left in the cold too long, or a kennel dog is switched between house and kennel in cold weather. Antibiotics are generally effective in clearing up the infection, but recurrent infections may lead to the removal of the tonsils by surgery.

Tumors—Older dogs, especially, are prone to abnormal tissue growths, or tumors. Tumors may occur internally or on the outside of the body, commonly in the stomach or around the mammary glands of females. Tumors of the oil-producing glands of the skin are called sebaceous cysts. These are usually small, light-colored growths somewhat resembling large pimples. They may appear wartlike. They are usually benign and need no treatment, but can be surgically removed if they become too large.

Heart Disease—There are a number of different heart problems that affect dogs, commonly older dogs. All types generally progress from mild stages to more serious forms and heart failure and can usually be treated and controlled if discovered early. A Beardie suffering from heart disease may tire more easily; you may notice him coughing in the morning and evening, or after exertion. He may gag up mucus. In severe cases you may notice an unusual arrhythmia, or murmur, in the heartbeat, or the dog may have difficulty breathing. Treatment for heart disease often involves regulation of the diet as well as administration of drugs.

Vaginitis—Inflammation of the vagina is not uncommon in bitches. Young bitches may develop a type of vaginitis prior to their first heat. The condition is characterized by a mild irritation and discharge at the vulva accompanied by an unusual attractiveness to male dogs. This form of vaginitis needs no treatment and will disappear with the first heat season.

Older bitches may exhibit a sticky yellowish, greenish, or grey discharge which will cause them to lick the vulva excessively. The mucous membranes may be red or red-spotted. The symptoms may be accompanied by a bladder infection and should be watched carefully. Otherwise, a more serious condition, such as metritis or pyometra which affect the uterus, may develop. Vaginitis can be treated successfully with antibiotics.

Vomiting—Your dog will often vomit when nothing is really wrong other than an upset stomach or the fact that he ate something he shouldn't. He may first vomit food, followed by a frothy clear or yellow fluid. If he vomits only once or twice and has no fever, pain, or other symptoms of illness, don't worry. Just withhold food for about twelve hours, then feed him lightly with soft, bland food for the next day. Don't offer large amounts of water. You can often soothe the dog's stomach by giving *Maalox*® or *Mylanta*® (one teaspoon per twenty pounds of weight).

Vomiting from car sickness usually ends shortly after the movement has stopped. You can sometimes prevent this discomfort by giving *Drammamine*® about one-half hour before leaving.

Severe vomiting, vomiting of blood, or vomiting accompanied by illness or depression should be treated immediately by a veterinarian.

In all cases when your dog appears sick, do not wait. Contact your veterinarian early. Your Beardie cannot talk, and by the time symptoms are observed, the illness may be fairly well progressed.

61

FIRST AID

Applied quickly and correctly, good first aid measures can save your Beardie's life. *They should be used only as a temporary emergency treatment to maintain the life of your dog until professional medical help is obtained.*

Transporting an Injured Beardie

Unless broken bones are obvious, an injured dog may be carried by placing one arm under his body, supporting his chest with your hand, and cradling his body on your forearm. Steady the head with your free hand.

A badly injured dog must be placed gently on a solid board stretcher. Lacking anything solid, you can improvise by placing two sticks through the arms of a jacket or shirt to form a sling. Disturb the dog's position as little as possible.

Applying a Muzzle

A Beardie that is in pain or shock may bite at anyone who tries to handle him. To prevent this, fashion a muzzle in the following manner: tie the mouth shut with a piece of cloth or an old nylon stocking, making two additional wraps around the muzzle with a hard knot under the chin. Bring the two ends of the material behind the ears and tie in a bow.

Checking Pulse

The normal heart rate of a Beardie is 90 to 100 beats per minute. You can feel your Beardie's pulse by locating the femoral artery. Place your index finger inside the hind leg as closely against the body as possible. You can also feel the pulse by placing the fingers over the heart itself.

Artificial Respiration

If you should find your Beardie unconscious and not breathing, but with a heartbeat still audible, you may be able to revive him with artificial respiration.

Place the dog on his right side with head and neck extended so that the windpipe makes a straight line. Pull the tongue forward and out. With the heels of your hands, press the chest moderately hard just behind the shoulder blade, forcing air from the lungs. Relax the pressure, count to five, repeat. The rhythm must be smooth and regular. Continue until the dog is breathing at

his normal rate (about fifteen to twenty times per minute) without assistance. Then treat for shock.

You can also administer artificial respiration by placing your lips over the dog's mouth and nostrils, cupping your hands over them like a cone, and forcing air into his lungs.

Treating for Shock

A dog in shock appears depressed; has a rapid heart and respiration rate; rapid, weak pulse; and pale mucous membranes. He may shiver and feel cold to the touch. Breathing is slow, and the eyes are often glazed.

A dog in shock needs emergency veterinary treatment immediately. Wrap him in a towel or blanket for warmth, and if you are far from professional help, a tablespoon of whiskey may help revive him. Do not give water.

External Heart Massage

If your dog's heart has stopped, combine artificial respiration with external heart massage.

1. With the dog on his back, legs in the air, place the palms of your hands on the sternum, with your fingers on one side of the chest and your thumb on the other side.

2. Alternately compress and release the chest. Compress the chest strongly between thumb and fingers, pushing the ribs together. At the same time, press the sternum downward toward the spine. Release the pressure suddenly.

3. Repeat the compression at the rate of seventy times per minute until the heart starts beating again. A dog can live about three minutes after the heart stops.

First Aid for Specific Conditions

Bee stings—Apply an ice cube to the area and give your Beardie an aspirin tablet. If an allergic reaction sets in, consult your vet. Normally, the swelling will go down in forty-eight hours or less.

Bleeding—Cover the wound with sterile gauze, and apply a pressure bandage by wrapping the injury tightly. Use a tourniquet between an arterial injury and the heart *only* if a pressure bandage will not control the bleeding. Tourniquets must be loosened every ten minutes.

Broken nails—Apply a styptic powder or use powdered alum to stop the bleeding. Smooth the nail with a coarse file after bleeding has stopped.

62 A properly applied muzzle.

Bruises—If the injury is recent and swelling has not yet begun, apply a cold compress. If the injury is swollen, apply a hot compress.

Burns—Run cold water over the area or apply an ice pack for about twenty minutes. Do not apply ointments of any kind. If a burn is serious, take your Beardie to the veterinary hospital immediately.

Cactus or porcupine quills—Remove with tweezers or pliers. Treat with an antiseptic spray.

Cuts and wounds—Wash with a three-percent solution of hydrogen peroxide. You may pour the peroxide directly into the wound, use a cotton swab, or flush the solution into the wound with a syringe or baster. This should be repeated twice daily. Clip the hair around the wound to avoid irritation. Large tears or wounds will require sutures.

Dog bites—Wash with peroxide and treat with a topical antiseptic ointment. Deep puncture wounds or tears will need suturing.

Drowning—Hold the Beardie upside-down by his legs until water is drained from his lungs, then administer artificial respiration if needed. Keep the dog warm and rub his body vigorously. You may be able to revive an unconscious dog with spirits of ammonia held under his nostrils.

Frostbite or chilling—Warm the dog slowly by wrapping him in warm towels. A puppy may be placed inside your coat. Apply tepid water to frozen feet, gradually increasing the temperature to 100 degrees. Do not apply dry heat. Give a tablespoon of whiskey as a stimulant.

Fractures—Move the dog as little as possible. Place him on a board or stretcher and take him to the veterinary hospital as soon as possible. Compound fractures, where the bone has punctured the skin, require immediate attention. Other fractures that are not accompanied by shock can be treated within the day. Do not try to apply splints or bandages.

Heat stroke—An overheated dog will pant, have an increased pulse rate, and will appear anxious with a staring expression. He may vomit, or he may become unconscious. Immerse the dog in cold water, or, if this is impossible, spray him with the garden hose. Massage the skin and legs to encourage circulation, and place ice cubes on his mouth and nose. Do not give stimulants or water. Immediate veterinary attention is needed.

Puncture wounds—Remove small objects carefully and apply a pressure bandage. If the object is large or has punctured the eye or abdomen, let a veterinarian remove it.

Skunk odor—Bathe your Beardie in tomato juice, followed by soap and water. Wash his eyes with a mild salt solution. If you cannot bathe him, you can make him a little more acceptable by rubbing him with a damp sponge sprinkled with baking soda.

Snakebites—Keep the dog immobilized as much as possible, with the wound at the same level as the heart. Use a snakebite kit or make a sharp cut at the wound to induce bleeding. If the bite is on a leg, apply a tourniquet loose enough to slip one finger underneath it, and leave it on

Silverleaf Scottish Heather, *Silverleaf*, at age eighteen months.

A walking cast keeps an injured dog mobile.

63

the dog until you reach a vet. Get your Beardie to the veterinarian as soon as possible.

Swallowing a foreign object—Feed bread or other soft food which will wrap itself around the object. Check with your vet regarding further treatment.

Poisoning

Identifying the poison is of utmost importance. *Call a veterinarian.* If you *cannot* get a vet and you know what the poison material was, administer the antidote and then drive the dog to the clinic. *Do not treat for poisoning unless you are sure what material was ingested.* You can induce vomiting by giving one ounce peroxide in one ounce of water.

If the poison is a contact poison, always wash the contact area with large amounts of water. If the dog goes into convulsions, try to keep him from injuring himself by muzzling him and holding him as still as possible until you get to the vet.

Some common poisons include the following:

Alkalis—Household drain cleaner is the most common of this type. It causes profuse salivation, nausea, and sometimes vomiting. Give a neutralizing acid such as vinegar or lemon juice—two or three tablespoons should be enough.

Analine dyes—Found in shoe polish, crayons, and other household dyes. The lip and oral membranes may turn brown, breathing is labored, and the dog is listless. Induce vomiting with peroxide and give coffee as a stimulant.

Aspirin—Too much aspirin will cause weakness, rapid breathing, stomach pain, and sometimes collapse. Induce vomiting, then give sodium bicarbonate (baking soda) in water.

Bleaches—Cause a general upset stomach. Induce vomiting. Then give the dog an egg white or a little olive oil.

Cleaning fluids—Either inhaling the fumes or ingesting the substance may cause poisoning. For inhalation poisoning, give artificial respiration if needed and move the dog to a well-ventilated area. Wash the eyes with water. If the fluid was swallowed, induce vomiting and give a dose of olive oil. Be careful that the oil does not go down the windpipe and choke the dog.

Cyanide or phosphorus—Found in some rat poisons. They are fast-acting poisons and cause pain, convulsions, diarrhea, and odorous breath. Act fast. Induce vomiting. Get a veterinarian. (Ordinary "strike anywhere" matches also contain phosphorus.)

Ethylene glycol—Radiator antifreeze contains this poison and is readily ingested by dogs. Induce vomiting at once, then give bicarbonate of soda.

Paint—Lead-base paint can cause lead poisoning, either when the liquid paint is swallowed or when excessive amounts of dry flaked paint are chewed from a painted surface. Symptoms include rapid breathing, restlessness, collapse. Induce vomiting and give epsom salts as an antidote.

Pyrophosphates (Malathion, Parathion, Pestox, etc.)—These are absorbed through the skin. Symptoms include pinpoint pupils, salivation, cramps, watery eyes, muscular twitching. Bathe the dog with soap and water and get to a veterinarian quickly.

Strychnine—The kind of poison people use to intentionally poison dogs or small rodents. Violent convulsions with the head and legs extended are a good sign of ingested strychnine. *Do not induce vomiting.* Contact your vet immediately and rush the dog to the hospital. If you know your dog has eaten strychnine but symptoms of poisoning have not yet begun, your vet may advise that you give a sleeping capsule.

Warfarin—A common ingredient in rat poison. It is not supposed to harm dogs, but it sometimes does. The drug acts as an anticoagulant, causing death by internal bleeding. If your dog has eaten warfarin, take him to your vet for a shot which will cause his blood to coagulate. If you wait until symptoms appear it may be too late.

ENDNOTES

[1]Reference sources for this chapter included:

Terri McGinnis, D.V.M., *The Well Dog Book* (New York: Random House/Bookworks, 1974).

Glenn A. Severin, D.V.M., M.S., *Small Animal Medicine Notes* (Fort Collins: Colorado State University, 1969).

Douglas H. McKelvie, D.V.M., Ph.D., *Care and Management of the Racing Greyhound* (Colorado State University, 1974).

9 *Building a Better Beardie*

Merely owning a good dog is not enough for the breeder. He or she becomes obsessed with the desire to produce good dogs as well. Breeding becomes a means of self-expression. As the sculptor manipulates his marble, so does the dog breeder express himself in canine flesh and blood.

Both science and art are involved. The successful breeder has a comprehensive knowledge of the breed and the tools (genetic principles) that he can apply to produce a better Beardie. Artistically, the breeder forms a mental picture of his ideal Beardie according to his interpretation of the Standard and develops a certain "eye" for picking out those individual Beardies that best contribute to this ideal.

There are no shortcuts to becoming a successful breeder. The initial building blocks include a thorough understanding of the breed Standard, the dog's anatomy and structure, the laws of inheritance, and the practical applications of genetics. Knowledge of the history of the breed and of the various types and bloodlines provide necessary guidelines in making breeding choices. Through experience, the breeder begins to develop that "sixth sense" seemingly used by all good breeders in choosing the two individual dogs for producing this ideal.

THE BUILDING BLOCKS

The science of breeding is based on an understanding of genetics embodying the laws of Mendelian inheritance. The principles are complex and fascinating and can be applied to the reproduction of all living organisms from virii to human beings. When enough data on a particular species is collected, theoretical genetics can be practically applied to increase the chances of obtaining the desired results from a planned breeding.

However, learning to understand and use genetic theory is not easy. With each possible inherited characteristic are many considerations, such as: mode of inheritance of the particular trait; number of genes controlling that trait; whether the trait is inherited from one or both parents; whether there are nonvisible, hidden variations; what possible combinations of the trait can be passed on to the offspring, etc. Several sets of genes may control a single trait, and more than one trait may be inherited at one time. When we begin asking questions about a topic as complex, yet relatively unstudied, as the Bearded Collie, the lack of available documentation becomes frustrating. There are no easy answers to the question, "How do I build a better Beardie?" But perhaps as breeders supply the needed data, the pieces will eventually fall into place if the following basics are understood and applied.

Every body is comprised of cells. These are the smallest living units, and although there are many specialized types of cells, nearly all share a similar structure. The outer layer, called the cell membrane, holds the unit together and conducts the inward progress of building materials and disposing of wastes. The membrane contains a jelly-like substance known as cytoplasm. Within the cytoplasm float several specialized units which carry on the chemical processes and life functions of the cell.

In the center of the cell is a smaller body known as the nucleus. Its function is to control the inheritance and the implementation of that inheritance within the cell. The nucleus has a nuclear membrane, nucleoplasm, and the colored threads known as chromosomes. These contain the genes which make an organism unique from all others. The chromosomes, which usually appear as identical pairs, are different in number in every species. Fruit flies are often used for study because their cells contain only four chromosomes, each of which is large and easy to see under a microscope. The complexity of the organism is not determined by how many chromosomes it has. Humans have forty-six chromosomes; dogs have seventy-eight. In the cell, these are long, tangled, and impossible to separate.

On each chromosome are found the "genes," or building blocks, for that organism. A gene is thought to be only a point or "locus" on a chromosome. The actual genetic material is the substance that comprises the chromosomes: the long, spiraled, extremely complex molecules

known as DNA. DNA contains the "blueprint" for all parts of an organism. Chromosomes from cells in your dog's tail contain genes determining his eye color, controlling the aging process, and perhaps triggering a dreaded disease. The chromosomes that are matched pairs are called "alleles." They can be aligned together, with matching points representing genes for the same trait. One allele is inherited from each parent, and only one can be passed on to the offspring. The infinite reshuffling of these genes makes every organism unique.

The messages and timed releases in the DNA are transmitted throughout the body to the proper place by a substance in the cytoplasm known as RNA. RNA serves as a messenger between the nuclear membrane and the rest of the body. The DNA never leaves the nucleus except during cell division (reproduction).

Cell Division

Normal cell division is called mitosis. It occurs during growth of the organism and continues to replace old cells throughout the life of the organism. During this process, the chromosomes duplicate themselves, separate from their newly formed twins, and become two sets of chromosomes, each set identical to the original. The cytoplasm pinches in two, and the cell membrane closes around each new nucleus. Two identical new cells now appear where formerly there was one.

Mitosis, or normal cell division.

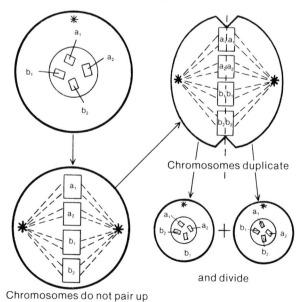

Chromosomes duplicate

Chromosomes do not pair up

and divide

The only exception to mitosis occurs in the "gametes" or reproductive cells. These cells contain only one allele from each set and therefore have only half the normal number of chromosomes. Their sole function is to supply DNA from a parent to an offspring. It is purely chance which of the two alleles transfers to which gametes, and no two gametes will be alike for all traits. These gametes will combine with equally random gametes from the other parent to produce a new entity. This is why no two puppies, even littermates (except identical twins), are exactly alike in either appearance or producing ability.

The division of the sex cells to form gametes is known as meiosis. During this process, the alleles come together in a complicated dance but do *not* duplicate themselves. The corresponding alleles move to opposite sides of the cell, and the cytoplasm divides between them. The result is two new cells, each containing half the genetic material of the original.

Meiosis, division of the reproductive cells.

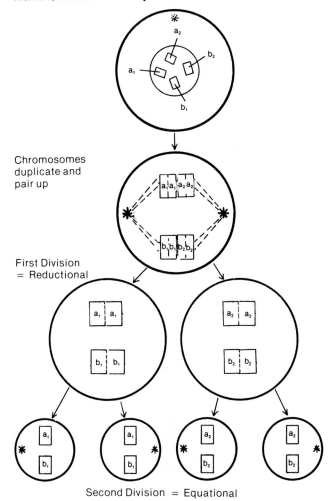

Chromosomes duplicate and pair up

First Division = Reductional

Second Division = Equational

Let's assume that each parent has the following pairs of traits (eye color, tail length, size of spinal column, or what have you). Each gene will be expressed in a slightly different manner, but these alleles all control the same traits.

AaBBcc is the genetic makeup of the father
aaBbCC is the genetic makeup of the mother

Their gametes will contain only one allele for each trait, but the possible combinations are numerous.

The father can produce these combinations:

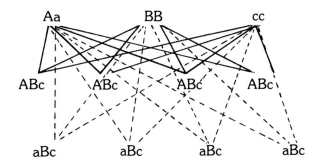

equal chances of ABc, ABc, ABc, ABc, aBc, aBc, aBc, and aBc
    or: ½ ABc and ½ aBc

Combine these with the eight possible choices from the mother which are:
    aBC, aBC, abC, abC, aBC, aBC, abC, and abC
    or: ½ aBC and ½ abC.

To determine the possible combinations of offsprings, form a genetic box:

Parent #1	ABc	aBc
aBC	AaBBCc	aaBBCc
abC	AaBbCc	aaBbCc

(Parent #2)

Equal chance of each result shown within each square

Multiply these by as many traits as you can imagine, and you'll have some idea of why there will always be an element of chance in breeding. Breeders can only improve the odds for a certain result.

Dominant and Recessive Characteristics

In the simplest form of inheritance, a dog carries two genes for a trait (one inherited from each parent). If they are the same, the dog is said to be homozygous for that trait. If they are different, he is heterozygous for the trait.

When the "alleles" (pairs of genes) are homozygous, the "genotype" (genetic makeup) for that trait is obvious in the "phenotype" (the dog's appearance). However, when the heterozygous condition occurs, only *one* gene is apparent in the dog's phenotype. He may be identical to the homozygous dog for that trait (in which case the gene is dominant), but he may carry the opposite trait (if the gene is recessive). When the dog displays the dominant trait, it is impossible to tell just by looking at him whether he is homozygous or heterozygous. However, should he produce a puppy exhibiting the recessive trait, it can be determined that the parent is heterozygous. The dominant gene will completely mask its recessive counterpart, but either one (not both) can be passed on to the offspring. When a recessive trait is expressed, the dog must be homozygous, or "pure," for that trait. A homozygous dominant individual will always produce his own likeness in the next generation, because the dominant allele will mask a recessive which may be inherited from the other parent.

Applicable Facts

1. Each parent contributes half of the genetic makeup of the offspring. *Both* parents must be of good quality before success can be expected.
2. The first two generations contribute most of the genes to a puppy. Dogs more distant in the genetic line have less influence unless they are repeated in the pedigree several times.
3. Littermates may be virtually unrelated genetically and therefore may not produce alike.
4. A recessive trait can be masked completely by its dominant allele. Therefore, the genotype (genetic makeup) must be considered as well as the phenotype (appearance).
5. A dog carrying a hidden recessive is heterozygous for that trait. He can pass on one allele or the other, but not both, to any given puppy.
6. A dog pure for a trait is homozygous for it. He can only pass the trait as he shows it.
7. A dog who exhibits a recessive characteristic must be homozygous for that trait.
8. A dominant trait cannot be present unless at least one parent shows it.
9. Many traits are "polygenic" (controlled by more than one pair of genes) or are influenced by modifiers, so they are not inherited in simple dominant/recessive patterns.
10. Genes located near to each other on a chromosome tend to be inherited together as one unit and are difficult to separate in controlled breeding.
11. Mutations do occur but are very rare. Recessive genes carried by both parents usually account for unexpected results.

GENETICS AND HEALTH

Some health and structural problems can be considered genetic, and a judicious application of basic genetic knowledge to a breeding program can help prevent their occurrence. About one hundred diseases or defects in the dog are known or believed to be hereditary. Some, such as heart, eye, and hip abnormalities, affect the health and usefulness of the dog. Others, such as dewclaws on all four feet, blue eyes, etc., are simply undesirable.

Raising an otherwise promising Beardie only to find that he has a hereditary defect is one of the most devastating experiences that a breeder has to face. It is always a difficult problem, and the temptation is to ignore or disbelieve the diagnosis. The most harmful thing that the owner can do is to mislead others with related stock about the nature of the condition. When a serious genetic defect occurs with a high degree of frequency in a line, its impact can be serious, and, if uncontrolled, it can ruin a breed. Once a defect becomes widespread, it may take generations of carefully selective breeding to eliminate it, if, indeed, it can even be eradicated. Also, many hereditary problems are not easily discernible, especially to the novice; therefore, they go unnoticed and are perpetuated.

Beardies are a relatively unspoiled breed at this point in their history. They are among those breeds that display the least tendency toward hereditary defects. However, there are isolated instances in *every* breed, and several closely related breeds have already seen the devastating effect of breeding afflicted dogs. The only way to avoid problems is to be aware of the possible threats and to be thorough in checking all breeding stock and their offspring.

What is a Hereditary Defect?

A *congenital* defect is present at birth. It may be inherited or be the result of intrauterine factors such as nutritional deficiency, toxicity, or the effect of a drug administered to the bitch during pregnancy. An *inherited* defect is transmitted on the genes. It is possible for a defect to be *both* hereditary and congenital. Unfortunately, not all inherited defects are visible at birth. A dog with progressive retinal atrophy may be normal at weaning and develop clinical blindness by six months of age, while another dog may not develop signs of diminished vision until he is six years of age or older.

Gene combinations that produce defects take many forms. They may be dominant, recessive, or incompletely dominant. They may or may not be sex-linked (i.e., perpetuated by or affecting only one sex because the gene for the defect lies on the sex chromosome). If only one pair of genes is responsible for the defective characteristic, the fault is said to be "autosomal." This is the ideal genetic situation and can be eliminated most easily. However, if more than one pair of genes are involved, as is often the case, the defect will be much harder to breed out. This occurrence is referred to as "multisomal" inheritance.

To further complicate the problem, not enough is known about many defects to enable researchers to accurately determine which type of inheritance pattern is involved. In addition, a breed may be "predisposed" to a problem even though direct inheritance cannot be demonstrated, as in the case of "Collie nose."

A discussion of some of the more common hereditary defects found in Beardies follows. There are, of course, numerous others.

Eye Defects

Eye defects, which have plagued dog breeders for years, may also be present in Bearded Collies. Although veterinarians report that the incidence of eye anomalies in Beardies affects only a small percentage of the total Beardie population, there is adequate cause for being alert.

The Eye Structure—The colored portion of the eye is called the iris. In the center of the iris is the pupil (the dark area), through which light enters the eye.

Basically, the eye is constructed in three layers. The outer layer—the sclera—coats and protects the entire eyeball. A middle layer, called the choroid, lies between the retina and the sclera and is a highly vascular structure. The inner lining of the eye—the retina—is a neural, light-sensitive layer.

Light enters the eye through the pupil, then reaches the retina. Here, the light is converted to nervous impulses which are then transmitted to the brain by the optic nerve. This process produces sight. The area on which the image is projected is called the fundus. The fundus consists of the tapetal, or reflective, part and the nontapetal, or nonreflective, area. The tapetal portion of the fundus has the texture of fine, granulated beading, literally a projection screen. In the center of this area is the optic disc, where the optic nerve and the blood vessels enter the eyeball.

Progressive Retinal Atrophy—Two hereditary retinal atrophies have been identified, and they affect many breeds. One is generalized atrophy, referred to as PRA. The other is central progressive retinal atrophy, or CPRA. Both diseases are progressive and eventually result in blindness. Retinal atrophy may not appear until the dog is two years old or over, making him difficult to eliminate from breeding stock.

PRA is generally attributed to a simple autosomal recessive; thus, both parents may have normal eyes but harbor the damaging recessive genes. PRA advances in stages. Initially, the pupils are semidilated and respond sluggishly to light; there is increased tapetal reflectivity, some loss of granular beading, and the small blood vessels are diminished in size.

Next, the pupils become dilated, and have little response to light. The granular beading nearly disappears, along with the smaller vessels. As the disease progresses, the disc becomes pale and the nontapetal fundus grows lighter in color, developing a mottled appearance. In the final stage, the pupils become fully dilated and have absolutely no response to light. All of the vessels may disappear from the fundus, and the dog becomes totally blind. Both eyes are usually equally affected.

The first warning of PRA that you may observe is night blindness. Initially, the dog will show signs of reduced vision only in darkness or in diminished light situations. Later, he will become day blind as well. Many owners see this as a personality change and wonder why their dog reacts differently in low light situations. They may not realize that the dog is blind until some time after total blindness has occurred.

Central progressive retinal atrophy (CPRA) seems to be less common in most breeds related to the Bearded Collie. Research directed toward how the disease is inherited is being conducted but is inconclusive at this time. The initial signs of CPRA differ from those of PRA. In PRA, night blindness is the first clinical sign, whereas this feature occurs late in CPRA. In CPRA, the owner first observes that the dog has difficulty picking out objects directly in front of him but still has good peripheral vision. Since the central portion of the retina is affected initially, the outer portions continue to function and the dog does not become totally sightless until a later stage of the disease.

At this time, there is only one positive diagnostic method capable of detecting PRA in puppies, and it can only be done by competent specialists. This method is not yet widely available. It is called the electroretinograph, or ERG. The puppy is anesthetized, and a special contact lens is fitted over each eye and connected to an electrical recording device. A strong source of light is then flashed in the pup's eye, and the reaction is recorded. This gives a clear, positive evaluation and saves years of waiting until the disease can be detected by ophthalmic examination. Under regular ophthalmic examination, the disease cannot be recognized until the dog is mature, and it may not appear until he is five years old. By this time he will, if used for breeding, have children and grandchildren also being used for breeding. *All* offspring of an affected dog will be carriers of the defect.

Cataracts—Although little information is available concerning cataracts in Beardies, a related breed—the Old English sheepdog—is plagued with a hereditary form of this problem. The type affecting Sheepdogs is called "juvenile cataracts" and usually appears after six years of age. The condition exists in many breeds and is dominant in some, recessive in others. The mode of inheritance in Sheepdogs is undetermined at this time.

In severe cases, juvenile cataracts progress to blindness. In milder afflictions, they can advance to a certain point, then remain static, causing some sight impairment. Occasionally, a cataract will go into remission and sight will improve.

If the cataract is unilateral (in one eye only), no treatment is recommended. If both eyes are affected (bilateral cataracts), surgical removal of the cataracts is indicated. No early diagnosis is available, and the first positive sign of the condition may be the appearance of a cloudy spot on the eye. Ophthalmic diagnosis is possible at a slightly earlier stage.

Hip Dysplasia

Hip dysplasia is a polygenic, hereditary, developmental condition. It occasionally shows up in puppies as young as eight weeks of age but more commonly cannot be detected until somewhere between the age of four months and two years. The condition is apparently related in some way to the amount of inherited muscle mass around the hip joint as well as to the actual bone formation. It is also influenced by environmental factors such as a too-rapid growth rate, excess weight, and poor diet.

Recent studies indicate that dysplasia may be the result of a deficiency or inability to assimilate ascorbic acid. Puppies fed massive doses of this substance during their growth periods did not develop dysplasia, even though they were from badly afflicted parents. You may wish to discuss these studies with your veterinarian to decide if you want to try a preventative diet for your puppy.

The hip joint is a ball-and-socket joint. The thigh bone of the dog has an offset protrusion at the top in the shape of a ball. Normally, this ball fits into a socket in the pelvis and is held firmly in place by muscles and ligaments. Occasionally, however, the socket is not deep enough or is improperly formed, thus allowing the thigh bone to slip out. Other times, the ball is not properly formed and does not fit well into the socket. Either condition may be diagnosed as hip dysplasia.

A Beardie may go through life with a very mild degree of hip dysplasia that is noticeable only as a sort of hitch in his rear gait, or he may occasionally suffer a great deal of pain. The chances are that most cases go completely undetected unless the dog is X rayed for the condition. If your dog falls easily, sways from side to side when walking, or has noticeable difficulty getting up, suspect dysplasia. There is no cure, although an operation can sometimes relieve the symptoms. Arthritis will accompany an advanced case.

Diagnosis and the OFA—The only positive method of diagnosing hip dysplasia is by X ray.

This must be carefully done, with the dog anesthetized and in an exact position. Even then, mild dysplasia can be difficult to diagnose. For this reason, an organization called the Orthopedic Foundation for Animals (OFA) was established to check and certify dogs of all breeds for freedom from hip dysplasia.

HD is another defect which cannot always be detected in a young dog. If you want your dog certified, wait until he is two years old or more to have him X rayed. A preliminary radiograph should be taken prior to the time the dog is bred if he is to be used before two years of age. When applying for an OFA certification number, your veterinarian will forward the radiographs (X rays), along with an application form and the correct fee (ten dollars) to OFA. There, the radiograph will be identified, given an application number, inspected for quality, and sent to three different veterinary radiologists for diagnosis. A report based on their findings will be sent to the owner and to the veterinarian who took the X rays.

In 1974, OFA adopted the following method of classifying hip dysplasia:

1. Excellent conformation
2. Good conformation
3. Fair conformation
4. Borderline conformation/intermediate (recommend resubmitting new X rays in six months)
5. Mild degree of dysplasia
6. Moderate degree of dysplasia
7. Severe degree of dysplasia

More information about OFA may be obtained by writing the foundation at the University of Missouri, Columbia, Missouri 65201.

Inheritance—Being polygenic in mode of inheritance, hip dysplasia is difficult to breed out of a line or breed of dogs. Many genes are involved, and all must occur in a dog before the condition is expressed. Nondysplastic Beardies may not have any of the genes for dysplasia, or the genes for the condition may be present but not in the right combination for the defect to be expressed. The latter may produce dysplastic puppies if mated with another carrier. In order to consistently produce dysplasia-free Beardies, you must know that the defect was not present in the ancestors of a dog (or the littermates of those ancestors) for at least three to six generations. This, of course, is a tremendous undertaking, and without the cooperation of breeders in obtaining certification and making this information available, it is impossible.

Heart Defects

Twenty-five distinct forms of congenital heart disease have been found in dogs; some rare, others fairly common.[1] Together, they form one of the more common types of hereditary defect.

One form, patent ductus arteriosus (PDA), is fairly common. It is believed to be hereditary and of a polygenic nature. Test matings conducted with mixed breeds show that when a normal dog is mated with a known carrier of PDA, nearly fifty-nine percent of the puppies are affected; when two defective dogs are mated, the ratio increases to sixty-eight percent.[2]

Prior to birth, a blood vessel in the whelp, called the ductus arteriosus, allows blood pumped from the right side of the heart to bypass the non-functioning lungs. At birth, as soon as the puppy starts using his lungs, the ductus normally closes and blood circulates through the lungs for proper oxygenation. The term "patent ductus arteriosus" refers to a condition in which the ductus fails to close after birth, allowing blood to recirculate through the lungs. This overworks and enlarges the heart. If the patent ductus arteriosus is large, the volume of blood shunted to the pulmonary circulation will be correspondingly great and may result in congestion of the lungs and heart failure. This can be evidenced by shortness of breath, rapid, labored breathing, coughing, and, occasionally, collection of fluid in the abdominal cavity. If the ductus is small, the dog may appear normal for years.

PDA is generally accompanied by a heart murmur, which can usually be detected by a veterinarian when a puppy is two to three weeks old. Severe cases develop signs of heart failure before weaning, and it is often possible to feel the throbbing heart vibrating in the chest. Most affected dogs will present signs of cardiac insufficiency before maturity. Chest X rays and an electrocardiogram are beneficial in establishing a positive diagnosis. The condition can be corrected surgically by tying off the ducts, thus eliminating the abnormal pattern of blood flow, and the dog can usually then lead a normal life. If a corrected dog is bred, however, *all* of the puppies will be carriers of the defect.

Monorchidism or Cryptorchidism

When a male Beardie is born, the testes will not be easily felt. As the puppy grows, the testes descend into the scrotum. Sometimes this does not happen, and either one or both testicles remain in the abdominal cavity or do not com-

71

pletely descend. A dog with one testicle descended is called a "monorchid"; one with neither testicle descended is commonly referred to as a "cryptorchid." The condition is hereditary, probably in a simple recessive form. Occasionally, testicle descent can be delayed or prevented by the administration of antibiotics to either the dam or the puppies at critical stages of development.

AKC regulations for conformation showing state that testicles must be normally descended. Therefore, it is unethical for a veterinarian to do surgery to a show dog or give medications that might cause the testicle to come down. When testicles do not descend properly, they are held at a higher body temperature, which has been related to an increased incidence of testicular tumors.[3] Therefore, the best procedure is to have the dog castrated.

In Beardies, both testicles have usually descended by eight weeks of age. Sometimes, the testicles do descend into position, but the puppy may be able to pull them up into the abdomen so tightly that they cannot be palpated. You can be sure that both testicles are descended properly only when they grow large enough to prevent their being pulled out of reach. It is not uncommon for a veterinarian to advise that a Beardie male three months of age without both testicles in position be discarded as a show or breeding prospect. We feel that this is a bit harsh, but a male whose testicles cannot be found at least most of the time by four months of age is a questionable risk. One should be aware of the evidence supporting the claim that dogs with testicles descending late tend to produce monorchid or cryptorchid puppies with greater frequency than normal males.

Although monorchids are usually fertile, they should never be used at stud.

Epilepsy

One of the oldest brain diseases affecting man—epilepsy—also occurs in dogs. There are many kinds of epilepsy and many causes, including tumors, post-traumatic scars, inflammation, and lesions due to infectious agents such as viral infection, mycotic substances, and bacteria. The distemper virus is a very common cause. Only when all other causes have been ruled out should a dog be considered to have "idiopathic" (cause unknown, possibly hereditary) epilepsy. Most cases have specific acquired causes. The idiopathic form has been suspected by some breeders to affect Bearded Collies because it seems to

reappear to a small extent in certain lines. Expert neurologists are clearly skeptical but allow the possibility of this occurrence. No clinical evidence, however, supports such claims. It is also possible that an inherited predisposition makes certain lines more susceptible to outside influences and, therefore, to increased epilepsy.

The inherited form of grand mal epilepsy is characterized by recurring seizures during which the dog may be unconscious. Alternating muscular contractions and relaxation occur, followed by running movements. Profuse salivation, urination, and defecation often occur. Sometimes the dog will howl, become restless, or show marked behavioral changes just before a seizure. After a seizure, the dog usually is physically exhausted for varying periods of time and may be temporarily blind.

Typically, in the inherited form of grand mal epilepsy, seizures begin when the dog is in his second year of life, although they may occur earlier. The convulsions are recurrent, with few, if any, other physical signs. The seizure pattern becomes progressively more severe, with seizures occurring more frequently and with greater intensity. Single seizures are not life-threatening; however, if several occur in a series with little or no time interval (status epilepticus), the dog could die from hyperthermia and electrolytic imbalances. Seizures can usually be controlled somewhat by the use of anticonvulsant drugs.

If a Beardie is known to have epilepsy and all physical causes have been ruled out, the inherited form of the disease should be suspected. Since the cause is difficult to determine, dogs with epilepsy (or ones producing it frequently) should not be kept in a breeding program.

Solar Nasal Dermatitis

Solar nasal dermatitis is referred to as "Collie nose" because it is most commonly seen in Collies and related breeds. It is found in many breeds, usually in ones that have white blazes and a corresponding tendency to have light spots of unpigmented skin on the bridge of the muzzle. Essentially, the condition is an inflammatory reaction of the skin on the nose, and occasionally around the eyes, to sunlight. Studies have been unable to pinpoint the cause. Beardies are slightly predisposed, but inheritance studies have been inconclusive.

The first sign of Collie nose is loss of pigment at the junction of the haired and nonhaired tissue of the nose and sometimes around the eyelids.

72

The hair will drop off; a lesion will develop, then crust, and finally scale. When the scale is rubbed off, the area will bleed. The lesions may spread up the nose to the eyes, into the nares, and possibly onto the upper lip. If the eyes are affected, conjunctivitis may develop. Untreated Collie nose can result in cancer of the nose. Lesions similar to Collie nose can be caused by infections or neoplasia. Therefore, a positive diagnosis should be made before any treatment is started.

Keeping the affected Beardie out of sunlight, and sometimes out of all light, is beneficial but impractical. Topical applications of sunscreen preparations or medicated ointments may help somewhat. Corticosteroids may be prescribed orally. Tattooing the affected area works in many cases but is expensive and usually only temporary. The condition tends to become more severe in summer with increased exposure to sunlight. Beardies with Collie nose should only be bred very judiciously, and careful records must be kept.

Smooth Coats

The very occasional occurrence of smooth-coated specimens in Bearded Collies causes concern to breeders. Some claim that it is the result of impure breeding (probably crosses with Border Collies) during the formative years of the breed. This statement, plus the use of the term "Border Collie throwbacks" instead of "Smooth Beardies" by some breeders, has brought unfortunate and, we feel, unwarranted attention by AKC to this problem in the breed. Smooth specimens occur in many breeds, and breeders simply eliminate and

don't register them knowingly. A dog that produces large numbers of smooths (or any other undesirable characteristic) should be retired from breeding. The only reason we can see for panic is that breeders in the United States chose for several years to hush up the topic and not admit its existence. This, in turn, created panic when novices accidentally produced smooths and did not know what they were. Open communication of any problem is the only way to solve it.

All English breeders with whom we talked were aware of the problem, and apparently, specimens have appeared in very small numbers in most lines. Since most modern dogs trace to the same ancestors, this is not surprising. Inheritance is inconclusive, but the trait may be a simple recessive. In many breeds, smooth coats are dominant, but this cannot be the case in our breed. Multiple gene control or variable expressivity are likely. No line can be completely free of the possibility of producing a smooth, and the only sensible approach is to eliminate smooths and avoid breeding dogs that are known to engender this fault.

Some breeders claim that the temperament (wouldn't *you* become shy if you were a freak kept around just to demonstrate a point?) and structure of "smooth Beardies" are different from normal Beardies. I think that the differences are no more than those which occur from one individual Beardie to the next. The impression made by coat changes the entire look of the dog.

Just be aware that the condition exists and try to avoid perpetuating or increasing its incidence in your breeding program. You will prob-

73

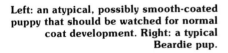

Left: an atypical, possibly smooth-coated puppy that should be watched for normal coat development. Right: a typical Beardie pup.

ably never encounter a smooth individual even after several years of breeding.

Other Defects

Many defects exist in dogs. Distichiasis, a condition in which the eyelashes turn inward, is sometimes seen. Hemophilia—the inability of the blood to clot properly—is a recessive, sex-linked, hereditary defect. A normal male will not be a carrier, but a normal bitch can carry the disease without exhibiting signs of it herself.

There is a small incidence in some working breeds of patellar luxation, a condition in which the stifle joint slips out of position, creating a hopping motion in the gait. This defect is rare if angulation is adequate in the rear. Over- and undershot jaws are hereditary in nature, as are other conditions.

CONTROLLING GENETIC DEFECTS

The sensible approach to genetic defects is to be aware that they exist in our breed and to strive to eliminate from breeding all known or suspected defectives. If a Beardie develops *any* serious structural or physical defect that your veterinarian cannot attribute to injury, illness, or other environmental conditions, suspect the fault to be genetic in nature.

Telling someone not to breed their defective dog is easy. Observing that rule when the defective dog is your own champion or prospective champion is something else. And there's an old saying among dog breeders that the pick of the litter always seems to have the defect. The only real answer, then, is to weigh what this dog can contribute to the breed against the disadvantages of breeding him.

Using the symbol "N" to represent normal, and assuming that it is dominant, and using the symbol "d" to represent a simple recessive defect, we can chart out the expected inheritance patterns. Keep in mind that many defects involve more than one pair of genes, which makes the situation much more involved.

Let's assume that you have a defective dog and you mate it. You probably have no way of knowing if your dog's mate is also a carrier for that defect. But let's assume that the mate is *not* a carrier, making the dog "NN." The results would be:

Parent #2 / Parent #1

	d	d
N	Nd	Nd
N	Nd	Nd

dd plus NN = all puppies Nd, or all carriers

Should you breed the defective Beardie to a known carrier,

Parent #2 / Parent #1

	d	d
d	dd	dd
N	Nd	Nd

dd plus Nd = 50% Nd (carriers), 50% dd (defective)

Now, let's look at what happens when you breed just the carriers—the pups that you produced when you bred your defective Beardie to a Beardie not carrying the defect at all (provided you were able to determine this). You will have

Parent #2 / Parent #1

	N	d
d	Nd	dd
N	NN	Nd

Nd plus Nd =
25% normal puppies (NN)
50% carriers (Nd), and
25% defective puppies (dd)

The only way to prove that a dog is not carrying the genes for a defect is to test-mate him with a known defective dog. Outside of the laboratory, test matings are generally inconclusive and only add to the number of carriers being produced. It takes many litters with different combinations of parents to definitely establish that a dog is a noncarrier. For your protection, and for the protection of the Bearded Collie as a breed, it is far better not to use any Beardie known to have a hereditary defect or known to be a carrier for a genetic defect.

ENDNOTES

[1]Donald F. Patterson, DVM, D.Sc., and R. L. Pyle, VMD., "Genetic Aspects of Congenital Heart Disease in the Dog," in *The New Knowledge About Dogs.* Papers presented at the Twenty-First Gaines Veterinary Symposium, October 20, 1971, Ames, Iowa.

[2]"Congential Heart Disease in the Dog," in *Circulation Research*, XX, August 1968.

[3]Leon F. Whitney, *How to Breed Dogs.* New York: Howell Book House, 1971, pg. 33.

[4]*Ibid.*, pg. 316.

74

10 Color Schemes

Coat color inheritance in Bearded Collies is one of the few areas in which breeders can reliably apply their knowledge of genetics. However, even this concern poses some unanswered questions.

Beardie puppies are born one of four colors: black, blue, brown, or fawn, with or without white and/or tan markings. Most Beardies have some white even if it's just a spot on the chest, white toes, and a few white hairs on the tip of the tail. Genetically, Beardies are one of the two basic colors—black or brown—as determined by only one set of genes. The infinite color variations found in adult Beardies are due to the patterns and modifiers that affect the base color.

Color inheritance in Beardies seems to be the same as in the case of Doberman Pinschers. Black is a simple dominant over brown, but a Beardie may also carry a dilution factor. Lack of dilution is dominant over dilution, so the dog must be pure or homozygous for dilution to show the trait. A diluted black appears as a blue, while a diluted brown looks fawn. Therefore, four genes (two for color and two for dilution) determine a dog's color at birth and the color combinations that he can pass on to his progeny.

The standard symbol designation for genetic characteristics is the first letter of the word representing the *recessive* of a trait (and would appear in lowercase). The corresponding dominant would use the capital of that letter. Therefore, any dog with a symbol "B" would be black. Because it is dominant and can carry a hidden recessive, a black dog could be either BB (pure for black) or Bb (brown-factored). The brown-factored (or heterozygous) black dog can pass on either a black gene or a brown gene (but not both) to his offspring, while the homozygous black can only transfer a black gene. A brown dog would be a homozygous recessive and would be designated as "bb." All of his progeny would inherit a brown gene.

The symbol for dilution will be "d"; that for the dominant non-dilution, "D." A black or brown dog can be either "DD" or "Dd." A blue or fawn dog must be "dd." Remember, we are considering only color at birth so far.

75

The possible combinations are:

Black: (must have one "B" and one "D")
    BBDD—pure for black and nondilution
    BbDD—brown-factored; not dilution-factored
    BbDd—carries both brown and dilution
        factors
Blue: (must have one "B" and be pure for dilution)
    BBdd—pure for black and dilution
    Bbdd—brown-factored and pure dilution
Brown: (must be homozygous brown and have one "D")
    bbDD—brown and pure for nondilution
    bbDd—brown; carries a dilution factor
Fawn: (homozygous recessive in both color and dilution)
    bbdd—brown; pure dilution

The possible results of breeding any two individuals can be determined by constructing genetic squares.

EXAMPLE: A brown-factored black dog with no dilution bred to a fawn bitch. Find the probabilities of producing pups of each possible color from this combination by combining all possible genes that each parent can pass on:

Beagold Black Camero, *Beagold.*

76

Parent #1

		BD	BD	bD	bD
Parent #2	bd	BbDd	BbDd	bbDd	bbDd
	bd	BbDd	BbDd	bbDd	bbDd
	bd	BbDd	BbDd	bbDd	bbDd
	bd	BbDd	BbDd	bbDd	bbDd

RESULTS: BbDD + bbdd = ½ BbDd (blacks carrying factors for brown and dilution) and ½ bbDd (browns carrying dilution factor)

ANOTHER EXAMPLE: Two black parents, each carrying factors for brown and dilution BbDd, may be broken down to these possible gametes:

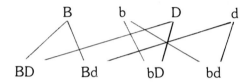

Each combination has an equal chance of occurring.

Parent #1

		BD	Bd	bD	bd
Parent #2	bd	BbDd	Bbdd	bbDd	bbdd
	bD	BbDD	BbDd	bbDD	bbDd
	Bd	BBDd	BBdd	BbDd	Bbdd
	BD	BBDD	BBDd	BbDD	BbDd

RESULTS: BbDd + BbDd = 1/4 BbDd, 1/8 BbDD, 1/8 BBDd, 1/16 BBDD, 1/8 Bbdd, 1/16 BBdd, 1/8 bbDd, 1/16 bbDD, and 1/16 bbdd,
    which translates in appearance to: 1/4 black, 1/8 black, 1/8 black, 1/16 black, 1/8 blue, 1/16 blue, 1/8 brown, 1/16 brown, and 1/16 fawn
    or: 9/16 blacks, 3/16 blues, 3/16 browns, and 1/16 fawns.

It is important to stress at this point that these are statistical percentages and will hold true if puppies from many identical breedings are averaged. Any one litter may have a different proportion of colors, but all will be from the *possible* combinations determined above.

A dog with a brown or diluted parent will always carry recessives for those colors. In some cases, only breeding will determine which genes a dog has inherited and carries as recessive.

WHITE MARKINGS

The white markings characteristically found on Beardies are derivatives of the "Irish" pattern. In its full expression, this pattern superimposes itself on the base color as a white shawl collar, front legs, chest, hind feet, and tail tip. A face blaze may accompany the Irish body pattern.

White found on any part of the Bearded Collie may be broken into three separate inheritable patterns. None have any bearing on the presence or absence of any other white pattern factor present in a given individual. A dog may carry any or all of these factors.

One factor determines the markings on the head and is inherited separately from the white body patterns. On Beardies, anything from a plain face to a wide, white blaze connecting with the collar is acceptable. Predominantly white heads or markings at the skin line which extend onto the ears or past the eyes are considered undesirable. A full blaze, however, can contribute to the most pleasing expressions and must not be discriminated against. Acceptable full blazes seem to be inherited as incomplete dominants. The excessively white and asymmetrically marked heads are relatively uncommon and are probably recessive in nature.

The white appearing anywhere behind the ears can be divided into two factors. The Irish pattern fully or partially expressed is acceptable. It ranges from minimum white points, to a partial collar, to full markings. Any combination is considered desirable as long as it is pleasing to the eye. The full pattern tends to be dominant, but this condition is probably caused by more than one set of genes; therefore, it can be inherited unexpectedly in certain combinations.

There is another unacceptable white body pattern which, when fully expressed, creates a white dog with colored spots. This pattern is also responsible for white body spots or for any white extending past the normal Irish pattern. The genes accountable for this phenomenon are

Left: Can. Ch. Edenborough Blue River, a blue.

Right: Danish Ch. Tambora's Peggy Brown, *Daisy-Belle.* **Browns and fawns sometimes become indistinguishable.**

Bottom left: Ch. Silverleaf Sesame Stick, *Greysteel,* **a brown.**

Bottom right: nose pigment is different for each birth color, even though adult color may be similar. (L. to r.) Bailie, and Eng. Ch. Blue Bonnie of Bothkennar.

referred to as "white factor," and a predominantly white dog is called "white." Whites can have completely colored heads because, as we mentioned before, the white on the head is inherited separately. Full white markings are not an indication that a dog carries white factor. However, white markings up the stifle connecting with the white on the belly usually denote white factor.

White factor is inherited as a recessive. Therefore, two whites bred together would produce all whites, and *all* offspring of a white would be white-factored regardless of their individual markings. Dogs carrying the white factor are not undesirable; however, you will be more limited when selecting a mate for them. Since whites are considered unacceptable by breeders in England and by the majority of knowledgeable Beardie enthusiasts in this country, I feel that a white dog should not be used for breeding. Care should therefore be exercised to avoid breeding together two known white-factored individuals. A dog without white on the stifles may or may not be white-factored. A study of the immediate pedigree and perhaps actually breeding the dog may be the only ways to determine whether or not he carries the white factor. As long as any mismarked puppies, inadvertently produced, are suitably eliminated from any breeding program, it is of no real consequence to try to determine the presence or absence of white factor by test-breeding an acceptably marked dog.

TAN MARKINGS

Occasionally, a puppy will appear with tan markings on the cheeks, eyebrows, legs, and under the tail. These markings can appear on browns or blacks and presumably on the dilutes. The markings generally lighten as the Beardie matures and disappear completely by the time the dog is one year old. Occasionally, they may reappear in a vague suggestion of the original pattern when the dog darkens into his adult color.

Left: unacceptably marked "white" puppies.

Bottom left: tan markings occasionally occur on the face and legs.

Bottom right: white should not surround the eye at the skin.

78

Generally, the tan remains indistinguishable in the adult Beardie, so unless breeders note which puppies are tricolors at birth, it is impossible to guess at a later time. Tan is inherited by one set of alleles. In most breeds the tan markings are dominant. Whether or not this holds true in Beardies can be determined as soon as enough data are collected. If tan is dominant, one parent must have exhibited the trait at birth. Since few records have been kept on this subject, it is difficult to determine which parents were and which were not tricolors. If a tri puppy has two parents, neither of which are tricolors, then the tan markings must be assumed to be recessive.

I have wondered if the tan disappears because it is masked by the greying factor. If so, would the tan remain rich and noticeable on a dog that matures almost completely black? Perhaps this question can be answered in the near future.

GREYING

All factors mentioned so far are present at birth. The most unique and confusing trait in Beardies is the way in which they grey as they mature. This greying factor is a modifier, and it works on all four colors. Nearly all Beardies possess the greying factor to some degree, and no two individuals show identical expression of the trait. Some remain almost the same color as at birth, with a few salt-and-pepper hairs appear-

ing and increasing in number with age. Most individuals grey astonishingly as puppies and at one year of age become a nondescript silver or cream color. At this time, the difference in coat color between a blue and a black or between a brown and a fawn may be indistinguishable. Only the nose color will make the distinction, and sometimes even this variation is subtle enough to cause confusion. This is why it is essential to register a Beardie with his birth color, rather than try to guess how he will look as an adult.

Changes in color first become evident at the roots of the outer coat and become more noticeable as the coat grows. The old color moves toward the tips of the hair and eventually disappears, suggesting that the outer coat continuously grows and breaks off at a certain length.

Coat color usually darkens (sometimes drastically) by the second year, but it always retains some of the frosted, greying effect. Color will change slightly with each new coat; changes past the second year will be very gradual. Rarely does a Beardie come along that does not grey at all. Solid-colored Beardies are uncommon because the greying factor is dominant and widely spread throughout the breed.

Many other breeds possess a greying factor (Kerry Blue Terriers, Shih Tzus, and Yorkshire Terriers, for example). However, in these breeds the coat lightens to a certain color, then remains constant. Beardies are unique in their redarkening of the adult coat color. Old English Sheepdogs and Soft-Coated Wheaten Terriers may come

Greying starts around the eyes. Nose pigment will color later.

New color continually grows from the roots outward.

Can. Ch. Raggmopp Gaelin Image, *Raggmopp*, showing color progression as she grows.

Age twelve weeks.

At age four months.

At age five months.

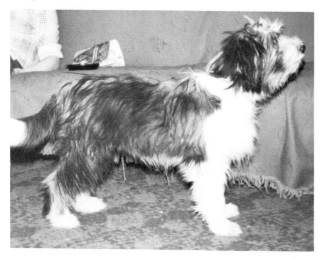

At one year of age.

At two years of age.

At three years of age.

closest to the Beardie in this respect, but even they do not show the variety and changeability of colors seen in the Beardie.

PREDICTING ADULT COLOR

Many people ask how to select a puppy that will mature to a specific shade of color. This is virtually impossible to do, but there are a few hints. The puppy that greys earliest will probably be lightest in color. As the pup lightens, check the color of his ears and tail. The dog will usually darken to match these points.

Because of the variations in greying, it is possible (although rare) for a born-black dog to mature a lighter color than a blue dog. The term "slate" or "grizzle" is used to describe any grey dog that is born black. A black *never* turns into a blue, even if the coat color appears to do so. A blue is born a chinchilla-grey color and must have a dark grey nose and eye rims at maturity. A slate will have black pigmentation.

Greying also varies in browns and fawns, and a brown may occasionally mature lighter in color than a fawn. The adult color for both browns and fawns may be called "sandy." Adult color is more easily predicted in browns than in blacks. The shade will vary with greying, but the color—be it chocolate, red, or honey gold—will be evident at birth. A washed-out or muddy brown will lighten but will remain unattractive. A rich, dark brown or red is desirable.

Blues and fawns appear dull in color at birth but become more attractive within a few weeks. Blacks and browns are usually very rich and shiny at birth, but this intensity never remains even though the coat may have minimal greying.

EYE COLOR

One set of genes determines whether eyes will be blue or brown (brown is dominant), but these colors are subject to four different modifiers which produce infinite variations of shade. Most Beardies have brown eyes, ranging from golden to almost black. Although a grey or brown eye is preferable, blue eyes are permissible with a blue coat color. The blue-white "china eye" can distort expression and is disliked by most breeders. Fawns may have very light-colored eyes, usually hazel, which can still impart proper expression. Browns often have amber eyes, the shade varying with the intensity of coat color. Any eye color that is a soft shade of a color blending with the coat will always contribute to proper expression. Because the coat constantly changes, there will be periods in a Beardie's life when the eyes appear too light or too dark. Most people prefer the appearance of a darker eye, but a light eye cannot be faulted in a light-colored dog. Coat and eye color tend to be inherited together. In fact, a very dark eye in a fawn or a blue dog could look piercing and unnatural.

The eye that changes from baby blue to brown at the earliest age will be the darkest color. Because their adult color will be lighter, brown puppies almost always retain their blue eyes longer than black puppies. A light eye usually indicates that the coat will lighten accordingly. However, some dogs simply have a light eye, and if it accompanies a dark coat color, it is to be faulted. A black dog with yellow eyes looks very harsh in expression.

In many breeds, dark eyes are always preferable. The preference for eye color to follow the coat color is another unique trait in Beardies, and one which necessitates educating the public (including show judges and new breeders).

PIGMENTATION

Pigmentation usually refers to the color of nose and eye rims in a dog. It should also include the lip color and skin color, but these areas are not as obvious at first glance. In some breeds, "pigmentation" is used to describe the color of the pads and even the nails. Beardies are "self-pigmented," meaning that the nose, skin, etc., are the same as the birth color of the coat. A well-pigmented blue nose may appear to be black. However, if the nose is held next to a black nose under a strong light, the difference becomes obvious. Most blues will have an easily detectable Maltese grey color to the nose. In browns, the darker the pigmentation, the better. Fawns will have noses a shade lighter than browns.

At birth, most puppies have entirely or partially pink noses. These should color by a few months of age. Puppies that are fully pigmented at birth or as early as four weeks of age are the safest to select for breeding. As a rule, puppies with white blazes will take longer to reach full pigmentation than plain-faced ones. Also, those with white faces will be more likely to have broken pigment on the bridge of the muzzle. A pink spot above the nose will not be faulted, but it will be more sensitive to sunburn and possibly even to "Collie nose" syndrome. Some pink skin is inevitable when a dog has white markings, but this is of far less importance than the pigmentation of the nose leather itself.

The lips should fill in to a solid color. Spotted lips or pink on the inside of the nostrils indicates poor pigmentation, which in breeding should be compensated for by selecting a strongly pigmented animal as a mate. Nails will usually be pink because Beardies have white feet. Either light or dark nails are acceptable.

In certain adult individuals, pigment seems to "fade," and pink spots appear around the eyes and muzzle. This can be caused by a vitamin deficiency, by allergy, or by heredity. The hereditary form of pigment loss is usually permanent, and care should be exercised if the dog is bred. If your puppy has light-colored eye rims, try exposing him to more sunlight. This condition is often due to a lack of certain vitamins or the inability to assimilate them. Sunlight can correct the problem if this is the cause.

ACCEPTABLE COLOR BREEDINGS

Accepted theory used to suggest that one parent in every breeding should be a black to insure good pigmentation. Many breeders have shied away from breeding dilute (blue or fawn) to dilute, and even from breeding dilute to brown.

Results will vary depending on the genetic makeup of each individual as well as on the dog's obvious color. In all cases, try to avoid breeding together two white-factored or poorly pigmented individuals, and select only acceptably colored stock for breeding. Recommended color combinations include:

1. black to any color
2. brown to black
3. brown to brown (if colors are rich)
4. blue to black
5. fawn to black

If a breeder wants all fawn or blue puppies, two Beardies carrying the dilution factor must be bred. If pigment is good and colors do not tend to degenerate, nothing is wrong with breeding together two dilutes. A well-pigmented dog from one of these combinations is no different genetically from a blue or fawn from any other combination and can be perfectly suitable for breeding. However, it has not been determined if the dilution creating blues and fawns is a constant or if it is accumulative. If the latter is true, breeding blues to blues might increase the chances of pale color, poor pigmentation, light eyes, or a host of possible defects. I have come to the conclusion, based on observation, that the dilution factor is not accumulative and is therefore safe to double, but it is probably wise to avoid doubling up for several generations in a row. Possible combinations which *may* be suitable include:

1. blue to brown
2. fawn to brown
3. blue to blue
4. blue to fawn
5. fawn to fawn

At this point, I recommend that these breedings be left to the more experienced breeders who will be able to recognize if color is degenerating. To be perfectly safe, I advise that one parent usually be a black or a brown, and that at least one (preferably both) be well-pigmented (including inside of the nostrils). Even blacks can exhibit poor pigmentation. (A better theory than requiring one black parent might be to select individuals on the basis of pigmentation rather than on coat color.) At least one English breeder contends that pigmentation is less of a problem in blues and fawns and that these dogs actually improve pigmentation in a breeding program. Is this because breeders are more conscious of pigmentation in a dilute and select only the best ones? And could it be that the willingness to accept *any* black dog for breeding has actually perpetuated or increased the number of blacks with poor pigmentation? Certainly some lines and individuals produce better pigmentation than others. It would seem that this concern becomes a problem only when breeders quit using pigmentation as one of the considerations in selecting breeding stock.

Left: a fawn showing correct light pigmentation and eyes.

Right: incorrect unpigmented nostril. Light eyes — faulted with a black coat.

82

11 Laying the Foundation

With well over one million purebred dogs registered each year with the American Kennel Club, dog breeding is not an avocation to be lightly undertaken. It implies taking responsibility for the puppies you produce and being obligated to breed only because you love the breed and are committed to its preservation and improvement. Moreover, since the Bearded Collie is a relatively new breed rapidly growing in popularity, the Beardie breeder is charged with the awesome tasks of preventing overproduction and its accompanying deterioration of quality, of avoiding fads, and of protecting the breed from loss of the original, unique Beardie characteristics.

If you are willing to accept this charge, there is much to be done. Memorize the Standard. Go over as many Beardies as you can, rating them against the Standard. Your eyes must be able to see and your hands be able to feel the details that create the perfect dog. Visit other breeders. Ask questions, even those "dumb" ones that the novice is afraid to ask. Watch all of the shows in the area. Study the great producers and the various lines and subtypes within your breed. Obtain the pedigrees of Beardies that interest you and research them. Find out what their parents and grandparents looked like and whether they were from top-producing lines. Almost every name on the pedigree should eventually call up an image of that dog.

After a while, you will begin to form a mental picture of how your ideal Bearded Collie should look and act. You must have this ideal clearly in mind before you can progress toward breeding it. Only when you are thoroughly familiar with the breed, when you know what is available, and when you have decided upon your ideal are you ready to begin to create with canine flesh and blood.

FINDING YOUR FOUNDATION STOCK

Selecting the foundation of your kennel should be one of the most important and careful decisions you make. These Beardies cannot be compromises—they must be as close to your ideal and as good in overall quality as you can obtain. Never settle for mediocre stock, thinking that you can upgrade it with successive generations. That path is long and rocky and filled with stumbling blocks. It is also uneconomical and contributes to overproduction of pet stock.

Conformation, pedigree, and producing record weigh almost equally in importance in selecting your foundation Beardies. A lovely animal without a solid lineage of good Beardies behind it will be unlikely to reproduce its own quality. The great winner may or may not be the great producer. Ideally, your foundation Beardies would be exquisite show specimens with a solid, linebred pedigree of top producers behind them. However, you may not be able to purchase such an animal, in which case you should choose either the proven producer of winners or the best youngster you can find with a history of top producers behind him.

A primary consideration in your foundation stock, or for that matter in any Beardie, should be

sound structure. Structural faults in general are much more difficult to improve than such obvious characteristics as coat, pigment, size or shape of eye, or showmanship. Another consideration, if you plan to use your Beardies for work, is herding instinct. If lost from a line, this instinct may be nearly impossible to revive later. Dogs do not inherit the ability to herd, but they do inherit the instinct and certain traits which, with training, enable them to excel in this work.

The Foundation Bitch

The timeworn advice to new breeders has been "start with a bitch," and this is still very valid. A good bitch is a wise investment. If you can improve upon her with each succeeding generation, keeping a daughter each time, you will soon have the beginning of your own line. Keep no pup unless he is better than his parents, at least in some small way, and sell any bitch that, when bred to carefully selected studs, does not produce well in two litters.

Your foundation bitch should have exceptional quality and a solid pedigree. Look for a bitch with a long line of top-producing bitches behind her and you can be reasonably assured that she, too, may produce well. Select a bitch that is not only healthy herself, but that has healthy parents and grandparents. Be sure that her dam was an easy breeder and whelped without problems. These considerations may seem minor, but every experienced dog breeder knows that the bitch that is difficult to breed, that has difficulty whelping, or that is sickly (even though not with a hereditary disease) has a great tendency to produce daughters with the same weaknesses.

Wait for the right bitch. It may take many months to find her, but when you do, it will be worth the time and effort. If you cannot obtain a young bitch, start with an older, proven producer and breed her to the best male available. Hopefully, she will produce a daughter to carry on for you. If you cannot find the perfect bitch, choose one with at least one great virtue. The mediocre bitch with no major faults but also with no major virtues will be less likely to produce the outstanding Beardie than will the bitch excelling in certain qualities but exhibiting a more serious fault. If you must compromise on a bitch with obvious faults, do make sure that the defects can be easily bred out. Also, be certain that you can find a complementary mate. It would be a mistake to begin a

Eng. Ch. Andrake Persephone, *Andrake.* **Top-winning English bitch.**

breeding program with an individual having faults so common that the correct trait cannot be found.

The Stud Dog—Asset or Liability?

Owning a stud dog can be very different from maintaining a small kennel of bitches. If selected and handled properly, a stud may become your most valued asset. In reality, however, most studs become a severe liability to the small kennel—and sometimes it takes the owner several years of mistakes to realize it.

First, a male can be a nuisance. He will undoubtedly become the most dominant dog in your kennel and will not always be a gentleman in proving so. He will harass your bitches, jump on your guests, eat up any profits that you may have anticipated, drown your flowers, become hysterical whenever a bitch comes in season, and demand more grooming and training than the girls. And, by far, the most devastating effect will be to your breeding program. The cost of any decent male will exceed that of the stud fee for the best dogs in the country. Especially if you buy a puppy, the chance of his actually producing well with your bitches is slim. Only a very special few meet the requirements of being both an outstanding individual (and a male who is anything less should be totally eliminated from breeding) and a consistent producer of his best points. Some combine well only with a limited few bitches, and no dog can suit every bitch. Even if you are lucky enough to find a dog that produces well, what about all of his lovely daughters that you keep? They will have to be bred to a different dog when the time comes, yet you will still be feeding, grooming, and picking up after papa. It is *not* cheaper to own your stud. Unless you have a dog that is truly outstanding in some area, we recommend breeding your bitches to established stud dogs.

On the positive side, a male is often your claim to national recognition. He can be your top show dog, an ambassador with the public, and generally your most effective advertisement. He stays in coat more months of the year than a bitch, and he is usually larger and flashier in showmanship. He will have greater potential as a top winner in most cases (although a few notable bitches would call exception to that statement). If you want a show dog, we heartily recommend a male. If he turns out to be a good producer as well, so much the better. Just don't expect all good males to become good stud dogs!

If a promising male is the result of your own breeding, you may wish to keep him to guarantee that he is properly promoted. If you desire a potential stud, you will find it advantageous to purchase a male that possesses virtues needed throughout your bitch line. Just remember that promotion of a stud dog is absolutely necessary if he is to stand to the public. Yet, this promotion can run into thousands of dollars with no assurance of any return.

An adult male that has proven his worth is not likely to be for sale, but he is the best bet if he can be obtained. The price of such a dog may be prohibitive; at best, he will not be cheap. Occasionally, an older dog can be obtained reasonably on the condition that the buyer provide him with a retirement home after he quits siring. This can provide an excellent start for a beginner because the dog will already be trained and will have acquired his reputation. Another possibility is to obtain a young dog (sometimes even a champion) who is surplus to the program of an active kennel. He may be as good and as well bred as their top dogs but too closely related for them to use. Make sure that such a dog is really good and is not just being culled.

Miller's Chocolate Chip, *Miller,* **age four months.**

85

Beardies have the advantage over some breeds of developing consistently; therefore, they can be selected fairly predictably at an early age. Although there is still significantly more risk with a puppy, I would prefer to buy a top puppy than a mediocre adult. It may require growing out two or three puppies to get just the right one, but do not settle for less. A male that is not quite show quality is not suitable to breed. He will only set your program back several generations behind other breeders. Even his best offspring will inherit the ability to pass on his mediocrity.

If you decide to risk acquiring a puppy, select one that is sound, outgoing, and reasonably typey. He should come from a very solid pedigree of quality individuals and preferably be linebred to dogs that are known to produce consistent quality. I would expect a reasonable guarantee of quality and fertility to accompany such a puppy. The more you demand in a guarantee, the more you must expect to pay. Select a deal that sounds fair to both buyer and seller.

DEVELOP A PLAN

Breeders who follow a plan will progress at a steadier rate than those who consider each mating individually. Your goal is to retain the virtues of your foundation stock while improving the faults. The plan, then, becomes a deliberated method for accomplishing this goal.

Suppose you obtain a typey bitch with excellent structure and angulation, good temperament, and natural herding ability. However, she lacks coat and is only mediocre in head qualities. Your plan, then, might be to select males that have superior heads and hopefully somewhat better coats, but that are not significantly lesser in quality concerning structure. You hope to improve the head, obtain moderate improvement in coat, and retain the structure, temperament, and type. In the second generation down from the foundation bitch, you may try for more improvement in head or hope to hold the head qualities that you have gained while going after better coats. In the successive generation, you might want to try setting both of these improved qualities aside while breeding for more elegance and style. Your progress may be slow, but it will be steady. You will generally find that it is better to select one improvement at a time and try to retain the good qualities which you have already obtained, than to go after too many new virtues at once and risk, in the process, losing those strengths that you are beginning to establish.

Selecting for specific qualities is sometimes done irrespective of pedigree, but if many different and unrelated lines are involved, the results may be unpredictable and inconsistent. Therefore, most breeders plan their matings by considering both individual qualities and pedigree. This combination of breeding for a specific subtype, improving faults one at a time, and planning a genetically sound program is the surest road to success as a Bearded Collie breeder.

86

First place brood bitch in 1976 National Specialty — Shepherd's Help From Shiel C.D., second from left, and progeny.

UNDERSTANDING PEDIGREES

Basically, there are three types of genetic programs: inbreeding, linebreeding, or outcrossing. A breeder may use one or all of these forms in his breeding plan, but he must understand each of them and use them appropriately.

Linebreeding

Linebreeding is the safest and most widely recommended long-term program. Linebreeding involves breeding two individuals with common ancestors on both top and bottom of the pedigree. I personally prefer a dog to have at least three-fourths of his ancestors from one bloodline before he is considered linebred and consider anything closer than grandsire to granddaughter to be inbreeding.

In linebreeding, both desirable and undesirable traits are concentrated gradually over several generations. Since all of the faults in the line don't surface at once, they can be dealt with in stages. Uniformity is usually achieved by the second or third generation, and linebreeding can be continued indefinitely provided the line has individuals that offer correction for the particular faults encountered.

The linebred individual is generally most valuable for breeding. This Beardie will be a much more consistent producer than an outcrossed individual. He can be linebred, inbred, or outcrossed to achieve your desired results. You have the choice of linebreeding on an established strain or linebreeding to a certain individual to form a new strain. The linebred Beardie will also usually bring a higher price and be more saleable, especially if he is from a popular line.

Linebreeding encompasses variations from breeding a bitch with her grandsire or grandson to breeding third cousins. Preferably, three or four of the grandparents come from the same general family, with at least one individual appearing several times in a four-generation pedigree.

A linebred pedigree.

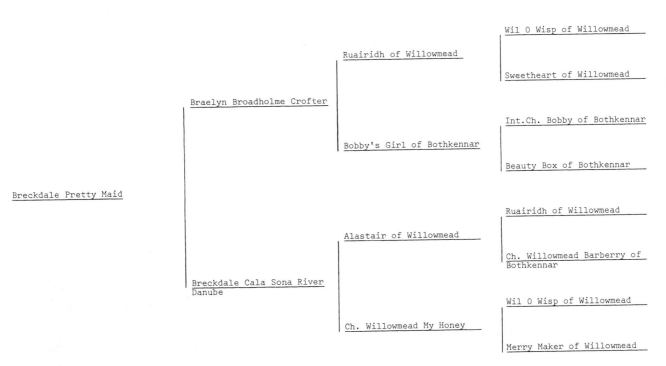

87

Breckdale Pretty Maid

Braelyn Broadholme Crofter

Breckdale Cala Sona River Danube

Ruairidh of Willowmead

Bobby's Girl of Bothkennar

Alastair of Willowmead

Ch. Willowmead My Honey

Wil O Wisp of Willowmead

Sweetheart of Willowmead

Int.Ch. Bobby of Bothkennar

Beauty Box of Bothkennar

Ruairidh of Willowmead

Ch. Willowmead Barberry of Bothkennar

Wil O Wisp of Willowmead

Merry Maker of Willowmead

Inbreeding

Inbreeding involves the mating of two closely related individuals, such as brother to sister, father to daughter, mother to son, or half-brother to half-sister. Inbreeding is the fastest way to establish uniformity in a line because it concentrates the genes of a few individuals and will sometimes set type in one generation.

Inbreeding can only concentrate the qualities already existing in a line; it cannot add new characteristics. It can bring to the surface recessive traits that you did not know existed in the line; these traits will also be concentrated in the genetic makeup of the dog that exhibits them. The poor inbred specimen will be just as prepotent for his qualities as will the good inbred Beardie. Therefore, if you inbreed, you must be prepared to cull your breeding stock ruthlessly.

Inbreeding is successful only if the dogs used are outstanding representatives of the breed and have very few inheritable problems in their background. It is not recommended when there is insufficient knowledge of the dog's pedigree.

After World War II, when the Bearded Collie was being re-established as a recognized breed, inbreeding was used excessively because so few good individuals were available. Therefore, most of our dogs will have either inbred or linebred pedigrees. We should not be afraid of this or be hesitant to use the good inbred dog. A really fine inbred Beardie can have tremendous influence on the breed. However, we should be concerned with establishing more distinct linebred strains as well. Continued inbreeding leaves no place to go for improvement and tends to reduce size and vigor and concentrate undesirable recessives.

Outcrossing

Outcrossing technically means breeding two totally unrelated individuals. This is a nearly impossible feat with Beardies. Probably the best you can find are two individuals with no common ancestor in four generations and hopefully with at least two lines that are not closely related. Breeding two inbred individuals from different lines produces what is known as a first generation out-

An inbred pedigree.

88

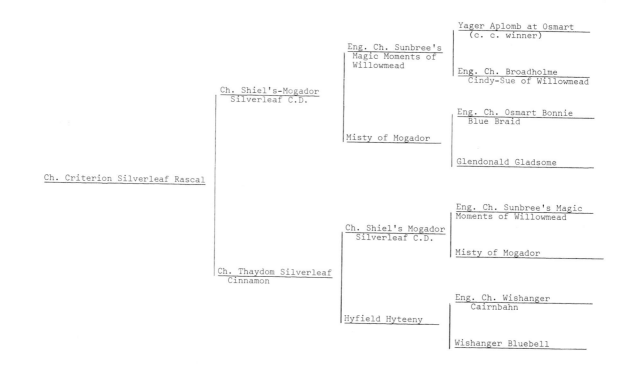

cross. A resultant offspring bred back into either line would produce linebred puppies.

Outcrossing as a general practice is not considered planned breeding unless selection for a specific type is made for several successive generations. Most outcross matings are specifically made to introduce into a line some positive qualities that are weak or nonexistent in the major line. This may be achieved in one outcross breeding or in a series of crosses. The offspring of these outcross matings are usually inbred or linebred into one or the other of the original lines. Outcrossing for several generations becomes a hit-and-miss proposition, and the outcrossed individual is unpredictable as a producer.

PRACTICAL APPLICATIONS

Breeding for the sake of pedigree or type alone is risky; the dogs must complement each other as individuals and combine well on paper. The line must be worthy of concentration or the breeder will magnify his problems.

An outcrossed pedigree.

In selecting individuals for mating, most breeders consider the pedigree of the dog and whether he will fit into their program. Then, by a process known as cross faulting, they will arrive at the individual that best suits a particular bitch. In cross faulting, remember your ideal Beardie. This is your goal. A good match will double the outstanding traits as well as compensate for each fault. Any time that a fault is doubled (both dogs exhibiting the identical fault), the percentage of offspring that will inherit it is high.

When you cross fault, look for the ideal characteristic in the mate to offset the fault. *Never breed a Beardie with a fault at one extreme to a mate with faults at the opposite extreme*—for example, short back to long back—hoping for a compromise. The genetic process does not work that way. In the above example, you would get approximately half of the puppies with long backs and half with short but none with the desired moderate length. Instead, you should breed either the overly short- or overly long-backed dog to one with correct proportions. The same is true of

			Wil O Wisp of Willowmead
		Ruairidh of Willowmead	
			Sweetheart of Willowmead
	Alastair of Willowmead		
			Ridgeway Rob
		Ch. Willowmead Barberry of Bothkennar	
			Bra' Tawny of Bothkennar
Ch. Cala Sona Westernisles Loch Aber			
			Swalehall John Scrope
		Cannamoor Bailie	
			Brasenose Annabelle
	Westernisles Wishanger Beechmast		
			Ch. Wishanger Barley of Bothkennar
		Wishanger Wysteria	
			Wishanger Jessica of Multan

every other characteristic. If your Beardie has a fault, seek a mate that is most correct for the trait.

A good breeder always keeps the overall dog in mind and breeds for balance in all characteristics. If you become overly concerned with one trait (for instance, good angulation), you will tend to develop a line with faults in areas where you have placed less emphasis (heads, for example). You may not want poor heads, but the trend will develop because you ignore the total dog. Keep in mind that you may sometimes have to compromise on your most valued qualities in order to attain quality in other areas. The most talented breeders ever keep the overall ideal Beardie in mind.

Establishing a New Line

The breeder becomes truly creative when he or she contributes to the breed a unique gene pool of individual dogs prepotent for certain exceptional qualities. It is far better to maintain a line that is high in overall quality and that has at least one outstanding characteristic than it is to maintain a kennel of good Beardies having no major faults but also no outstanding virtues. Always consider this when selecting your foundation Beardies and making those important first matings.

With a breed as new in our country as the Bearded Collie, it will be relatively easy in the next few years to establish a recognized line. The danger, of course, lies in the possibility that the new lines will not be as good as the old, established ones.

If you really want to make a mark on the breed, count on spending many years in developing your goal. Select as your foundation the best individuals available and work with existing lines until you are familiar with their genetic makeup. Avoid, if possible, concentrating on only one dog, because no Beardie is perfect. Assess each litter carefully, and when you have made progress, try to determine how it was achieved and how it can be maintained. This is the challenge of establishing a new strain.

Culzean Mogul Madame, *Miller.*

12   *The Family Tree*

One of the most fascinating aspects of dog breeding is the study of pedigrees—learning how others achieved success in their breeding programs. Every Bearded Collie carries genetic material received from several generations of ancestors, and he can pass to his offspring only those factors, good or bad, that he carries. Some of these traits are exhibited in the individual's phenotype (the way he looks), but others are carried as recessives and cannot be observed. We discover these hidden recessives by test breeding and may sometimes determine the probability of their existence through a study of the dog's ancestors.

Since the ultimate goal of every breeding program is to concentrate virtues and diversify faults, the breeder must know where to go to bring in a particular virtue or to avoid doubling on a recessive problem. If the strengths exhibited by a particular dog are not concentrated in his genetic makeup, he will probably produce a hodgepodge of type and quality in his offspring. When a breeder consistently selects with the intent of concentrating certain qualities over several generations, a subtype of Beardie with correct breed type but also with unique strengths of detail (such as correct coat texture, dark pigmentation, correct angulation, etc.) may develop. Thus, a "bloodline" is formed. The breeder who maintains another breeder's ancestral line and type, as well as the breeder who combines many types without achieving uniformity among his dogs, will never achieve an original bloodline. A true bloodline is unique and consistent in reproducing certain virtues particular to that line.

Actually, the Bearded Collie is such a young breed that true bloodlines, such as occur in more established breeds, do not exist. However, various types of Beardies, and kennels that select for the traits which eventually establish a line, certainly can be found. It is essential that the breeder recognize these traits and become familiar with their source so that he may plan breedings more intelligently. Since the breed is too new to the United States for consistent breeding programs to have formed, the authors traveled around England in summer 1977 visiting as many of the Beardie kennels as time would allow. Much of the information for this chapter was gathered during that trip, and, while sketchy, we hope that you will find it helpful. We are deeply indebted to those who so generously supplied photos and information, and we apologize for omitting many others who either did not respond or were not reached.

The following are kennelogs on some of the Beardie kennels that have had a major influence on the breed.

BOTHKENNAR

Mrs. G. O. Willison

As mentioned earlier, the Bearded Collie was actually saved from extinction through the efforts of Mrs. Willison, the first active show breeder of

modern Beardies. Mrs. Willison has since passed on, but she left a heritage of champion Beardies throughout the world.

Mrs. Willison's first bitch, Jeannie, was a brown about twenty-one inches tall, of working parentage. In 1950, a twenty-three-inch slate-colored male, Bailie of Bothkennar, was acquired. After a judge passed the two for registration as purebred Beardies, Bailie and Jeannie were bred. They produced a litter from which Mrs. Willison kept a bitch, Buskie, and three dogs, Bogle, Bruce, and Bravado, and these became the foundation for Bothkennar.

Due to various problems, Mrs. Willison never raised another litter from Jeannie. However, another working bitch, Bess, was obtained. Buskie was bred back to her father, Bailie, to produce Bra' Tawny. When Bess was also bred to Bailie, she produced Briary Nan. At last the breeding program was under way.

Another early Beardie that was passed for registration, Newton Blackie, was mated to Briary Nan. The result was a male, Ridgeway Rob, owned by Clifford Owen. When Rob was mated to Bra' Tawny, they produced Baidh of Bothkennar. Baidh was then bred to Bravado (Bailie ex Jeannie), and they subsequently produced the first Beardie to get a ticket (in 1959) as well as the first Beardie champion, Eng. Ch. Beauty Queen of Bothkennar.

Since Mrs. Willison preferred linebreeding over inbreeding, she used several other Beardies

92

Eng. Ch. Bravo of Bothkennar.

Bawbee of Bothkennar, (left), and
grandsire Bailie of Bothkennar.

Left: Britt of Bothkennar.

Right: Benjie of Bothkennar.

93

Bothkennar Beardies.
Left to right:
Bailie,
Beauty Queen,
Baidh,
Bronze Penny,
Bobby,
Bruce,
and Britt.

of working parentage in her program. Britt of Bothkennar, a very successful sire, was registered from working dog parents. Eng. Ch. Bronze Penny of Bothkennar was a pick-of-the-litter bitch from a litter sired by Bruce out of a red-brown bitch passed for registration as Jennifer of Multan. A daughter of Bailie and Bess was bred to an outcross Scottish dog to produce Eng. Ch. Bobby of Bothkennar.

Anxious to see Bearded Collies accepted throughout the world, Mrs. Willison often sold pick-of-the-litter puppies to beginning breeders. Her stock became the foundation for Willowmead, Wishanger, Osmart, Edenborough, and others. She worked tirelessly to promote the breed and achieve championship status for Beardies in England. When ill health forced her to retire in 1964, she had owned six champions: Beauty Queen, Bronze Penny, Bobby, Bravo, Blue Bonnie, and Bracken Boy.

WILLOWMEAD

Suzanne Moorhouse
The oldest Beardie kennel still in existence, Willowmead, was founded primarily on Bothkennar dogs. Suzanne's family actually owned a Beardie before Mrs. Willison became acquainted with the breed. When the dog died, the Moorhouse family went to Scotland to seek a replacement, and after a long search, they finally located a pair of Beardies working with a shepherd. They inquired about purchasing the dogs, but the shepherd replied that they were more precious than gold. Suzanne and her family consequently came home empty-handed.

Years later, Suzanne purchased Willowmead Barberry of Bothkennar (Ridgeway Rob ex Bra' Tawny) from Mrs. Willison and showed the bitch to her title. Eng. Ch. Barberry was first bred to

Eng. Ch. Willomead Perfect Lady.

Eng. Ch. Broadholme Cindy-Sue of Willowmead, age ten years.

Braelyn Broadholme Crofter, age ten years.

94

More Bothkennars. Left to right: Bannock, Bawbee, Buskie, Bailie, Bond, Bruce, and Briery-Nan.

Britt, an outcross farm-bred Beardie of lovely type and temperament. From this breeding, Miss Moorhouse kept Wil O' Wisp of Willowmead. Barberry was next mated to Eng. Ch. Bobby of Bothkennar to produce Merrymaid of Willowmead. When Merrymaid was bred to her half-brother, Wil O' Wisp, Suzanne got the lovely Eng. Ch. Willowmead My Honey, dam of many champions. Another bitch from the mating of Merrymaid to Wil O' Wisp—Moon Maiden of Willowmead—was subsequently bred to a dog of working lineage to produce Sweetheart of Willowmead, dam of Ruairidh of Willowmead (by Wil O' Wisp). Ruairidh is the sire of Eng. Ch. Broadholme Cindy Sue of Willowmead, Eng. Ch. Broadholme Bonnie Jean, and Braelyn Broadholme Crofter, all well-known producers out of Bobby's Girl of Bothkennar.

At this writing, there are several winning Willowmead Beardies in America, and Miss Moorhouse is carrying on with recently made up Eng. Ch. Willowmead Perfect Lady—an elegant brown—and Willowmead Pure Magic, a slate male.

WISHANGER

Mary Partridge

Another influential early kennel, Wishanger was also established on Bothkennar lines. Barley (Ridgeway Rob ex Bra' Tawny) was purchased

Eng. Ch. Wishanger Cairnbahn.

from Mrs. Willison, and Eng. Ch. Willowmead My Honey (Wil O' Wisp ex Merrymaid) was obtained from Miss Moorhouse. These two Beardies were mated to produce the famous sire Eng. Ch. Wishanger Cairnbahn, a lovely brown known for correct temperament, lovely head, and substance. From the same breeding as Cairnbahn came two other English champions, Wishanger Winter Harvest and Wishanger Cuillin. My Honey, bred to her son Wishanger River Humber, produced Eng. Ch. Wishanger Misty Hollow. Other English champions bred by Miss Partridge include Ch. Wishanger Waterfall, Ch. Wishanger Craggy Tor, and Ch. Wishanger Crab Tree. Apparently, Miss Partridge is no longer an active breeder.

OSMART

Ken and Jenny Osborne

Located high on the moor above Bacup in northern England, Osmart is another of the founding Beardie kennels. The Osbornes were attracted to the breed because of its natural, unkempt look and moderate size and because Beardies had "plenty of brains." Osmart has consistently bred for the "natural" look as well as for soundness, moderate size, and sensible temperament. Jenny is not fond of the overly glamorous, overly groomed Beardies which are often seen in the winner's circle today, and as a breeder and judge she is concerned with keeping the original breed characteristics.

The Osborne's home is a charming old stone farmhouse with a barn (since converted to kennel) attached in an "L" shape. The view from this barren, windswept hilltop stretches for miles across rock-strewn, grassy moors pastured by sheep and cattle. The fact that boarders navigate the steep, rocky road to leave their dogs at Osmart still amazes us.

Osmart was founded in 1962 with three Bothkennar Beardies: Eng. Ch. Bravo of Bothkennar, Eng. Ch. Blue Bonnie of Bothkennar, and Bluebell of Bothkennar. Bonnie was a heavy-boned, solid bitch with a dense coat and a mind of her own that gave her a reputation for being stubborn. When in a bad mood, she would firmly plant her feet and flatly refuse to budge in the show ring. She excelled in the brood box, becoming the dam of five English and one International Champion. Bravo was lighter in bone than Bonnie and very attractively marked, almost black in color. He compensated for her temperament by being the perfect gentleman.

In 1965 Blue Bonnie gave birth to her last litter (by Bravo) and presented the Osbornes with two of their finest representatives: Eng. Ch. Osmart Bonnie Blue Braid and Eng. Ch. Osmart Bonnie Black Pearl. The litter also included Eng. Ch. Osmart Bonnie Blue Ribbon and Swedish and International Champion Osmart Bonnie Black Diamond.

Bonnie Blue Braid became one of the breed's top sires. We were fortunate to see him—a magnificent Beardie with almost human personality, very sound, and with an exquisite head and expression. As a youngster he was aloof and not at all outgoing, which earned him criticism for having an atypical temperament. Nevertheless, Braid showed perfectly and garnered such wins as

a 1973 Best of Breed at Crufts and the Any Variety Progeny class at the 1974 Windsor championship show. Braid has produced many champions worldwide.

Jenny is currently showing a Braid son, Osmart Bracken Brown, whom she says gets admonished by his father whenever he loses a show. At age twelve, Blue Braid is still siring, although he generally can be found relaxing in his favorite chair.

While Braid was born and now lives at Osmart, he really belongs to the Osborne's daughter, Catherine Ryan of Doubletop kennels. Braid was given to Cathy as a puppy, and it was she who had enough faith in the dog to insist that he be campaigned. Cathy also owns the lovely bitch Osmart Silver Secret, and all of the Doubletop Beardies trace back to Bravo and Blue Bonnie.

Left: Eng. Ch. Osmart Bonnie Blue Braid.

Right: Eng. Ch. Blue Bonnie of Bothkennar.

Eng. Ch. Osmart Black Pollyanna.

96

BRAMBLEDALE

Lynne Evans

Also established in 1962, Brambledale has as its foundation Eng. Ch. Heathermead Handsome (by Eng. Ch. Benjie of Bothkennar ex Beehoney of Bothkennar); Brambledale Briquette of Bothkennar (Britt of B. ex Biscuit of B.); and Brambledale Heathermead Moonlight (Bausant of Bothkennar ex Beehoney of B.).

Lynne was attracted by the character of the breed—"that sense and sensibility." She breeds only black or blue Bearded Collies and is noted for producing lovely, clear blue dogs with strong pigmentation.

Representatives of the Brambledale line include: Eng. Ch. Brambledale Balthazar, Brambledale Bathsheba, Brambledale Bluebell, and Int. Ch. Brambledale Billet Doux. Lynne also bred the first United States Champion, Brambledale Blue Bonnet, who also became the first Beardie to go Best in Show, all breeds, in this country.

TAMBORA

Jackie Tidmarsh

Mrs. Tidmarsh established Tambora in 1962 after she had worked with Beardies for several years as a kennel maid for Amberford Kennels. Her foundation bitch, Amberford Bracken (Banter of Bothkennar ex Musical Maid of Willowmead), was obtained from Amberford. Later, while working for Anne Matthews of Hardacre, Jackie obtained Bausant of Bothkennar (Ranger ex Symphony) from Mrs. G. O. Willison. Bausant was a big slate and white dog "full of character" and known by members of the family as a real escape artist. Bausant and Bracken produced Burdock of Tambora, dam of two champions and one dual CC winner.

Probably the most famous Tambora Beardie is Eng. Ch. Edelweiss of Tambora (Ch. Wishanger Cairnbahn ex Burdock), a lovely brown bitch with beautiful dark eyes. Edelweiss was top winning Beardie in England in 1969, and she is the dam of six champions. In her first litter, sired by Ch. Osmart Bonnie Blue Braid, she produced Eng. Ch. Willowmead Juno of Tambora, top winning Beardie in 1971; Canadian Ch. Bronze Javelin of Tambora, top winning Beardie in Canada; and Canadian Ch. Jeanie. Another daughter of Burdock, this time by Blue Braid, is the beautiful black bitch—Hollyhock of Tambora—dam of four English champions.

Although farm raised, Tambora Beardies are true "family" dogs, sharing the Tidmarsh home. Tambora seemed to be in true "Beardie country." Located high above the enchanting old town of Holmfirth in northern England, the farm offers a magnificent view of small country homesites and steep, rugged sheep pastures divided by miles of low stone fences. Holmfirth hosts sheepdog trials in the summer, but we were told that Beardies are rarely seen competing.

Brambledale Bathsheba.

Eng. Ch. Brambledale Balthazar.

Int. Ch. Brambledale Billet Doux.

BEAGOLD

Joyce Collis and Felix Cosme

Mrs. Collis' first Beardie was a fawn, Gayfield Moonlight. Her second, a black and white bitch named Eng. Ch. Beagold Ella, interested Joyce in producing black Beardies. The present Beagold line, concentrating on producing black adult Beardies, stems primarily from the breeding of Ch. Ella to Ch. Wishanger Cairnbahn. Thus, Beagold is also one of the few kennels attempting to concentrate the blood of Cairnbahn.

Located outside the little town of Hitchin, a few hours' drive north of London, Beagold is a country kennel. In true English fashion, the Beardies were turned out to romp for us in the spacious garden.

Beagold dogs will be remembered for their coat color and dark pigmentation. A number of young Beagold Beardies are currently winning in England, and there is now a Beagold champion in New Zealand and one in Poland.

EDENBOROUGH

Shirley Holmes

Edenborough began with the purchase of Ch Bracken Boy of Bothkennar (Bravo ex Blue Bonnie, a brother to Champion Blue Braid) and Blue Maggie from Osmart, a Braid daughter. Bracken Boy was a "family" Beardie and dearly loved by Shirley. Bred to a Cairnbahn daughter, Ch. Wishanger Crab Tree, Bracken Boy sired Rowdina Grey Fellow. Grey Fellow bred to Blue Maggie produced Edenborough's most famous champion, Edenborough Blue Bracken. This large, glamorous, coaty Beardie claims the distinction of being the top winning Beardie in history and the only one to obtain multiple Best in Show wins at championship shows in England. He was the first BIS Beardie in England and is currently top winning Bearded Collie in Ireland. It is a very impressive sight to see Blue Bracken stacked off-lead in the ring, standing like a statue until Shirley releases him.

Left: Can. Ch. Bronze Javelin of Tambora.

Right: Australian Ch. Hopsack of Tambora.

Bottom left:
Eng. Ch. Edelweiss of Tambora.

Bottom right:
Hollyhock of Tambora.

98

Top left: black puppies, a specialty at Beagold.
Top right: Eng. Ch. Edenborough Star Turn at Beagold.

Bottom left: Eng. Ch. Davealex Royale Baron.
Right: Eng. Ch. Beagold Ella.

The lovely bitch, Broadholme Christina, when bred to Blue Bracken, produced four Edenborough champions: Kara Kara, Sweet Lady, Amazing Grace, and Eng. and Can. Ch. Grey Lady.

Located near North Preston, Shirley's Fir Tree Farm is quiet, off the beaten path, yet still easy to find—a kennel owner's dream. The dogs—except for Bracken who was obviously the house pet—are kenneled in a magnificent centuries-old stone barn which has been renovated into a spacious, modern kennel.

Edenborough dogs are noted for their glamor, elegance, and long, straight coats. Since Shirley is interested in seeing Beardies develop a reputation as Best in Show winners, she perhaps places more emphasis on producing glamorous Beardies. She does a little more grooming for the show ring than some breeders prefer. Winning Edenborough Beardies are found in several foreign countries as well as in England, the United States, and Canada. Currently, Shirley is showing offspring of Blue Bracken.

Left to right: Eng. Ch. Edenborough Blue Bracken, Bracken Boy of Bothkennar, and Rowdina Grey Fella.

Eng. Ch. Edenborough Blue Bracken, top-winning English Beardie.

100

ORORA

Bryony Harcourt-Brown

Bryony, like many others, was attracted to Beardies because they are a sound, natural breed with a happy, easily controlled disposition. Bryony hopes never to lose these attributes in her breeding program.

Orora is a relatively young kennel, established in 1970, but is already producing a distinct line of sound, well-balanced Beardies. Bryony's foundation included a brown bitch from Osmart and a black bitch whose dam worked sheep in Scotland. The Orora line is based on Eng. Chs. Wishanger Cairnbahn, Osmart Bonnie Blue Braid, and Edenborough Blue Bracken. Eng. Ch. Mignonette of Willowmead at Orora, a Cairnbahn daughter, was top Beardie in England in 1975 and 1976 and is the only Beardie thus far to be invited to the Contest of Champions. Many other Orora-bred dogs are currently winning in England,

including Eng. Ch. Orora's Sugar Bush and Orora Blue Basil.

DAVEALEX

Derek and Jean Stopforth

Davealex is proof that a small kennel can have plenty of impact on a breed. Upon arriving at Stopforth's, one wonders that they raise dogs at all. The front door of the small apartment opens right onto the sidewalk. But at the back is a small, enclosed patio with a shed, and across the alley is a lovely orchard in which the dogs can romp.

The Stopforths started with a male, Eng. Ch. Davealex Blaze Away at Osmart (Bravo ex Bonnie), as their foundation. He was a beautifully balanced, dark slate dog excelling in head, dark eyes, and expression. He had very correct straight front legs accompanied by good shoulder angulation and was always nicely coated.

Eng. Ch. Mignonette of Willowmead at Orora, a top-winning bitch.

101

Probably the best known Davealex bitch was their foundation bitch, Ch. Cala Sona Westernisles Loch Aber, dam of two English, one Australian, one American, and one Canadian champion, plus many other CC winners. Loch Aber (Alastair of Willowmead ex Westernisle Wishanger Beechmast) was a well-balanced, feminine Beardie with a good head, sweet expression, and good reach of neck. She was an excellent mover with a level topline, but she had a rather sparse coat. Loch Aber was either top or joint top winning Beardie bitch in England from 1967 to 1971, and top or joint top brood bitch from 1971 to 1977.

Davealex Beardies are prepotent for good, steady temperaments, soundness, correct coat texture, and flat, broad skulls. Representative sires that have had impact on the breed in England are Ch. Davealex Royle Baron, Ch. Davealex Royle Brigadier, and Davealex I Own Him. Brigadier is the sire of the all-time top winning bitch in England, Ch. Andrake Persephone.

SUNBREE
Barbara Iremonger

Mrs. Iremonger had the opportunity of working for Mrs. Willison at Bothkennar, and, of course, she fell in love with the breed and eventually started Sunbree. Barbara selects for soundness, character, and intelligence. Among the best-known Sunbree Beardies are Ch. Sunbree Magic Moments of Willowmead, top winner in England in 1973 and sire of Am. Ch. Shiel's Mogador Silverlead C.D., a top winner and producer in the United States. Another son of Magic Moments—Marksman of Sunbree—is becoming an influential sire in England.

Barbara's dogs romp freely about the garden of her lovely home not far out of London in Binfield, Berkshire. Known as the Toll House, this charming country cottage built in the 1700s is furnished with cherished antiques, some of which once belonged to Mrs. Willison. Barbara is currently promoting a young male, Sunbree Sorcerer.

Left: Eng. Ch Orora's Sugar Bush.

Right: Beagold Rena and Buckbean Odyssey. Owner, P. Heller.

Bottom left: Eng. Ch. Davealex Blaze Away at Osmart and Eng. Ch. Cala Sona Westernisles Loch Aber (front).

Bottom right: Eng. Ch. Sunbree's Magic Moments of Willowmead.

102

13 *Planned Parenthood*

The most exciting aspect of dog breeding for many breeders is the planning of future matings. Selection of the right mate for each dog requires creativity, common sense, and a knowledge of genetics, breed characteristics, and the genetic makeup of the individuals involved. But there is more than art to raising consistently healthy, quality litters. Considerable care and effort must be given to establishing an effective conditioning program and preventing the spread of infection, disease, or parasites in the kennel environment. The wise beginning breeder will devote equal attention to each of these factors.

Popular opinion to the contrary, breeding dogs is not a profitable business; more often, it becomes a rather expensive hobby. The first litter may seem a cinch, but with time, the probability of losses and problems increases. The following are average costs that you can expect when breeding a litter of Bearded Collies, providing there are no complications.

Cost of bitch ($1500 purchase price divided by average of six litters produced)	$250
Pre-breeding exam and tests	40
Stud fee (average)	500
Shipping for breeding (average)	400
Feed and vitamins for bitch and litter	200
Puppy vaccinations & worming ($25 ea. x 8 pups)	200
Advertising	100
AVERAGE TOTAL	$1690

Actual costs could be nearly double this amount.

You also need to consider the cost of facilities. While most Beardie bitches are pets whose litters are whelped in the house, a four- or five-week-old litter may be too much for the corner of your kitchen or laundry room. Some type of large puppy crate or an exercise pen is a necessity. The problem compounds if you are contemplating establishing your own bloodline, in which case you may start with more than one bitch and will probably be growing out some of the youngsters. In this case, a kennel may be needed. It must comply with city or county zoning and sanitation requirements, and you may find such plans hampered by increasingly stringent laws and regulations governing kennels.

There are personal and emotional considerations, too. Even the best planned litters may produce a high percentage of pet puppies. Will they find loving homes? Can you accept the fact that defective or unwanted puppies may need to be humanely destroyed? Will you resist the temptation to breed a favorite animal if it carries a hereditary defect or is lacking in quality even though exceptional in disposition? If, having considered all of these factors, you still want to breed your Beardie, there is no time like the present to begin making preparations.

THE BROOD BITCH

About the only difference between keeping a bitch for breeding and keeping one for a pet or for showing is the need to be a little more meticulous about her condition. The prospective brood bitch should be kept in hard, firm, lean condition by feeding her a well-balanced diet supplemented with vitamins and minerals, and by giving her daily exercise. Road work is the surest method of conditioning the muscles, and bitches should also be kenneled in large runs or yards with one or more other dogs so that they are encouraged to run and play. A fat or soft bitch often has trouble whelping.

Brood bitches must be kept free of parasites. Worm checks should be performed at least twice yearly and immediately prior to breeding. Immunizations should be current, and, since they cannot be administered while a bitch is in whelp, they should be given early if you anticipate breeding her during the time that she would normally be scheduled for a booster shot. Every bitch should be checked and certified clear of hip dys-

plasia, hereditary eye problems, or other inherited defects before she is mated.

Opinions differ regarding the age at which a bitch should first be bred. Beardie females generally have their first heat when they are about six months old, and most cycle regularly every six months thereafter. Some individuals, however, are on a four-month cycle, while others come in season only every eight months. English breeders uniformly recommend waiting until a bitch is past two years of age before breeding her. In this country we seem to breed our dogs at an earlier age, but I personally would not recommend mating a Beardie bitch younger than eighteen months of age. Most bitches will continue to produce through their eighth year. It is preferable to skip breeding every other season if the bitch comes in heat on a six-month cycle, but bitches that cycle less frequently may occasionally be bred on successive heats without harm.

The Estrous Cycle

When your bitch comes in heat, a complex series of events takes place within her reproductive organs. The sequence of events leading to heat, ovulation, and possible pregnancy is governed by four hormones—estrogen and progesterone from the ovaries, follicular stimulation hormone (FSH), and luteinizing hormone from the pituitary. Depending upon the influence of these hormones at any particular time, the sexual cycle can be divided into four stages—anestrus, proestrus, estrus, and diestrus.

Anestrus is the period of rest between reproductive cycles and lasts an average of three to six months. Hormonal activity in the bitch's system during this time is low and steady.

During proestrus, the first stage of heat, the ovaries are stimulated by FSH, which causes the follicles containing the eggs to grow. The growing eggs produce estrogen, which causes the vulva to swell, stimulates a red discharge, and increases the bitch's sexual interest. This signals the beginning of the heat cycle. At this time, the bitch will not stand for the male dog, although she will probably flirt.

About the ninth or tenth day of heat, the estrogen level peaks, and the bitch will willingly accept the male. This marks the beginning of estrus. At this time the discharge turns from pink to a clear color, the vulva becomes soft and more swollen, and the bitch will usually "flag" (hold her tail to one side). Shortly after the estrogen peak, the luteinizing hormone also reaches a peak. It is believed that this action triggers ovulation, or the releasing of the eggs. All of the follicles discharge their eggs at approximately the same time, but the eggs are immature and cannot be fertilized for three more days.

The follicles which formerly contained the eggs now become a new gland—the corpus luteum—which produces progesterone. The rise in progesterone and the corresponding lowering of the other hormones stimulate the beginning of the third part of heat, called diestrus. Diestrus occurs about six days after ovulation and marks the end of the heat cycle. The bitch refuses to stand, the discharge becomes brownish and then decreases, and the swelling leaves the vulva. Somewhere between the eighteenth and twenty-first day the bitch will normally be completely out of heat. However, the progesterone level in her system will remain high for about two more months, whether or not she is pregnant. It is impossible to tell at this stage if a bitch is pregnant.

When to Breed

Bitches are unique in that their eggs are released in an immature state. Bitches will accept the dog some five to nine days prior to the time that the eggs can be fertilized. However, the spermatozoa of the dog are remarkably long lived and can remain fertile for up to eight days. Therefore, breeding any time from the day of first acceptance to the day of first refusal to breed generally results in pregnancy. The highest rate of conception usually occurs from matings on the day of ovulation and for up to three days thereafter. Since we know that ovulation generally occurs on the twelfth or thirteenth day of the season, with fertilization taking place three days thereafter, the normal optimum breeding pattern would be on the day of first acceptance (approximately day ten) and again four days later (day fourteen). If only two breedings are made, they should occur three or four days apart. A few bitches are missed because they accept early and are bred on the first day of acceptance, then again two days later.

The estrous cycle of the bitch.

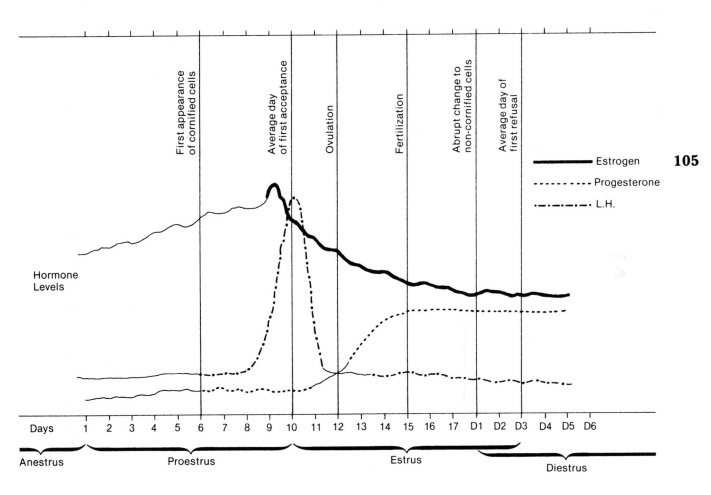

105

If the bitch happens to ovulate later than normal, she may not conceive because the sperm will have died before the eggs matured.

Most Beardie bitches have normal seasons in which the outward signs of heat and acceptance correspond with what is happening inside the reproductive tract. Hence, the success of breeding when nature says "breed." A few bitches, however, will accept on the first or second day of heat or throughout the season. Other bitches may never want to accept at all and will have to be forcibly held for mating. Still others will have silent heats and will show almost no swelling, discharge, or other visible signs of being in season, even though they will ovulate.

The Use of Vaginal Smears

Scientific research has provided a valuable aid for breeders by discovering that vaginal smears may be used to pinpoint the exact time of ovulation. This is especially useful in unusual cases such as we just described or in helping to determine the cause of a bitch "missing."

During her season, three kinds of cells may be found in the vagina of the bitch—red blood cells, white blood cells, and epithelial cells. Numerous red blood cells are present during the early part of the season, but normally there will be only a few white blood cells. (A high white cell count on a slide generally indicates that an infection is present.) It is the epithelial cells in which we are interested. As estrogen levels rise, the vaginal lining (epithelium) thickens. Cells are

sloughed off the surface of this lining and carried away in the discharge. The epithelial cell is larger than the blood cells and resembles a fried egg in appearance. Each cell has a nucleus (yolk of the egg) surrounded by a wide, translucent rim. These cells, which vary in appearance under the influence of estrogen, provide an accurate picture of how the bitch is being influenced by estrogen at this particular time. As her season progresses, the slides will show fewer and fewer blood cells and a gradual progression in the changing shape of the epithelial cells, from the more regular egg shape to an irregular shape resembling a potato chip or a taco. The edges begin to turn up so that the cell looks like a deep "U" and the nucleus is almost, if not completely, invisible. Such cells are referred to as "cornified."

If the bitch is in proestrus when you begin taking smears, you will notice a progression toward the cornified state. The day on which nearly 100 percent of the epithelial cells are cornified marks the beginning of true estrus, whether or not the bitch will stand for breeding. Ovulation occurs approximately six days later. The cells will remain cornified for a total of ten to fourteen days. About the sixth day after ovulation, the cells will change abruptly in appearance as they return to their former, noncornified state. This marks the onset of diestrus. After this point, the eggs cannot be fertilized.

If smears reveal cornified epithelial cells, breed the bitch regardless of the outward signs or the day of her season. If you know the date on

106   Non-cornified epithelial cells and a few blood cells.

Fully cornified epithelial cells.

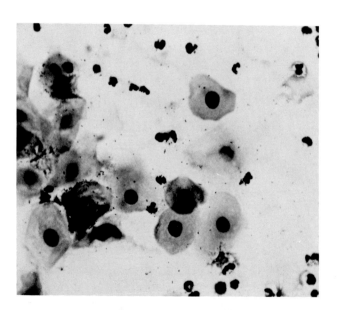

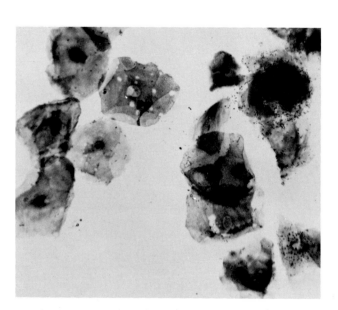

which the cornified state first predominated, you can be sure that ovulation will occur six days later and that the bitch should be bred at that time. If a bitch comes in heat but no cornified cells appear during the season, ovulation has not occurred; therefore, the bitch cannot conceive.

To prepare a smear, insert either a pipette or a cotton swab about one and one-half inches into the vagina to collect the material. Transfer this onto a slide and let it set for several minutes before staining. Fill a small bottle with Wright's stain (or a substitute) and two bottles with distilled water. Follow the instructions that come with the stain you are using. The usual procedure is to dip the slide into the bottle of stain for a specified number of seconds, then into the first water bath for several more seconds. Finally, rinse the slide in the second water bath and prop it on end to dry. When dry, examine it under a microscope that gives good resolution at 100 power.

How Conception Takes Place

A bitch will ovulate about one and one-half times as many eggs as she will actually produce puppies. Providing that live sperm are present in the oviduct, fertilization takes place as soon as the eggs mature. Research has proven that all eggs mature and are fertilized at the same time; therefore, all puppies in a litter are the same age. Size differences in puppies are due to genetic makeup, positioning, and the nutrition that each receives, not to age difference, as is commonly imagined. Puppies lower in the uterine horn tend to be larger and better nourished than those farther up.

It takes only a few seconds for the ejaculated sperm to find their way to the oviduct. If the ova are mature, they will be fertilized immediately. If they are immature, the sperm will surround them and remain motile (alive and able to move) for several days. Once a sperm has fertilized an egg, that egg becomes impervious to other sperm even though it may be surrounded by millions of them. Thus, an *individual puppy* can have only *one* sire. It is possible, however, for a *litter* to have *two* or more sires if all of the matings take place prior to the time that the eggs are mature. In this case, all of the sperm would surround the eggs and wait for them to mature, at which time it becomes pure chance which dog's sperm fertilizes which eggs.

Caring For the Bitch in Heat

A Beardie bitch in season is anything but modest, and often she is an escape artist par excellence, as are most males. Therefore, keep her closely confined, preferably in a crate in the house or in a covered chain link run until she is ready to be bred to the dog of your choice. Be sure to confine her throughout her season until all signs of estrus are gone. The urine odor from a bitch in season will attract males from great distances. You can give your female certain products that will help to neutralize the scent, but it is preferable not to use these if you plan to breed your bitch later in the season. Furthermore, these products aren't always successful. Chlorophyll pills are safe and will decrease odor, but the bitch will still be attractive upon close inspection by the male.

Since sperm remain alive for at least a week, even a mismating early in your bitch's season will probably result in pregnancy. If a mismating occurs, do not breed her to another dog. An estrogen injection given immediately after the mating will prevent conception, but it can also cause serious side effects and is not recommended. Birth control pills that prevent heat, injections that stimulate heat, and hormones given to effect an abortion can all upset the delicate working of the reproductive system, in some instances to the point where a bitch will never again reproduce. Hormones sometimes cause extreme allergic reactions.

SELECTING A MATE

Undoubtedly the most critical part of breeding is selecting the right mate for your bitch. Your search will be long and probably continuous as you watch the young stud dogs appear on the scene each year. Don't wait until your bitch is ready to mate to decide on a stud. Your search should begin almost the day that you bring her home, far in advance of mating.

Most of the basics of selecting a mate apply similarly to selecting an individual (*see* Chs. 4 and 9). The only additional factor that you must keep in mind is "cross faulting," or selecting a mate that does not double on one of your bitch's prominent faults in either genotype or phenotype. He must be strong in the virtues that she lacks and hopefully also strong in some of her virtues so that these may be set. He should not bring in any major new faults, although you may have to compromise and accept a few minor faults along with the needed virtues. To ascertain the faults and virtues that the dog carries but may not exhibit, study his pedigree, his bloodline, and especially his parents and his progeny.

Select a male that is a proven producer of quality and that seems to impart some of his strong points to most of his offspring. Beware of a male that has produced well from one bitch but poorly from several others. He should be structurally sound, healthy, and certified clear of hip dysplasia and eye defects. Avoid like the plague any dog that is producing puppies with genetic defects or health problems. Even though he may be clear, he must be a carrier in order for the puppies to exhibit the defect.

Study the dog's pedigree. A good pedigree will have the superior dogs on the *left* side. All of those "greats" in the fifth generation will have little influence on your puppies. Look very closely at all four grandparents because the puppies often will more nearly resemble the grandparents than the parents. The influence exerted by even these four dogs, or the parents, is not equal, however, and a puppy may closely resemble one grandparent and exhibit none of the traits wanted from the other three.

Unless you can see and go over a stud in person, the selection of a good mate becomes more difficult. Correspond or talk with the owner of a prospective stud at length and ask all of your questions. (Be aware that breeders who spend all of their time writing books are likely to be lousy correspondents!) Ask to see photos from several angles, and try to obtain action photos. A good action shot is worth a thousand words because it will tell you much about the dog's structure and angulation. Ask the opinion of a trusted breeder, judge, or handler of your acquaintance who has seen the dog. Then, since opinions vary and are quite subjective, make up your own mind about the dog.

Contacting the Stud Owner

Since your initial inquiries have been made before the bitch comes into season, your final step is to contact the stud's owner to let him know that your bitch has come into heat and will be arriving for breeding on a specified date. If you are shipping the bitch, have the airline flight numbers and times of departure and arrival handy when you call so that you and the other party can mutually decide on a convenient flight.

If she is leaving your state of residence, your bitch will need a health certificate. In addition, the stud owner may ask for a vaginal culture to determine that the bitch is free of infection, a brucel-

losis test (this blood test usually takes several days, so do it early), and possibly copies of her eye and hip certifications. Now is the time to double-check to make sure that the bitch is free of parasites and that her immunizations are up-to-date. Injections and worm medications may be given while she is in heat but must be administered prior to breeding.

Your bitch should be expected to stay at the stud owner's kennel for several days while she is being bred. In order for her to settle in before the mating, plan for her to arrive a day or two prior to the day of first acceptance, or about the ninth day of heat. The stud fee is always paid in advance. You are paying for the dog's service, not for puppies. Some breeders will guarantee two live puppies or a free return to the male, others guarantee one puppy. The guarantee is a courtesy, not an obligation. In no instance can you expect your fee to be refunded if the bitch fails to conceive. Most stud owners use a contract such as the one displayed later in this chapter to spell out these conditions in writing. Your "letter of introduction" accompanying the bitch should contain her name, registration number, age, number of previous litters, if any, and the date that her current season began. She should be returned to you with a contract or letter stating the number of breedings and the dates.

THE STUD DOG

As a stud owner, your first responsibility is to be totally honest about your dog. You must have him tested and certified free of any common hereditary defects. In Beardies, I recommend both a hip X ray by a qualified radiologist to test for dysplasia (studs over two years of age should have an OFA number) and an eye examination by a qualified ophthalmologist for PRA and cataracts. If there is any question, the dog should not stand at public stud; using him may also hurt your own program. The dog should have no known serious health problems in his immediate background.

No one owns a perfect dog. It is your responsibility to know your dog's faults as well as his virtues and to be sure that the latter outweigh the former. An honest evaluation of the dog and his suitability for a particular bitch must be given to the bitch's owner. After a few litters, you should recognize which traits your dog produces in a majority of his offspring and which faults he will not correct. This is almost as important as the traits he possesses. You must be firm in refusing to breed any bitch that is substandard in quality and in referring those unsuitable for your dog to a more compatible male. It takes effort to do this tactfully, but most people respect an honest effort to preserve quality in the breed.

The owner of a popular stud generally refers puppy buyers to breeders who have mated their bitches to the dog. Are you willing and able to provide this service? This by no means implies that you are responsible for selling the puppies— at times there is no market for anyone. Yet, there is a greater chance of selling puppies sired by a well-known champion rather than by an unknown dog. However, if an unfinished lesser-known dog appears to be a better choice for a bitch, you shouldn't hesitate to recommend him.

The stud owner must have adequate facilities to care for visiting bitches, he must be able to handle the breeding efficiently with no danger to any of the parties involved, and he must have reasonable transportation connections with the rest of the country. He should have a good veterinarian close at hand and good public relations with his neighbors so that they won't object to the extra barking dogs coming and going. He must also be willing to put the time and money into showing and advertising his dog fairly extensively. This is not only for personal publicity but is an obligation to the people who have used the dog.

Most adolescent males will begin mounting other dogs. This is normal and should be corrected only if carried to excess. While most Beardies are eager breeders, it is important that your young stud not get the idea that he will be punished for mounting a bitch. Try to separate him or distract him rather than correct him for mounting. Do not let him be dominated constantly by an older male during adolescence. The youngster is insecure enough during these months and needs to feel that he is "top dog" at home.

From the time you acquire your puppy, you must establish yourself as the dominant personality. If you are firm, yet consistent, in requiring that he must do *what* you tell him *when* you tell him, he will become a delightful, well-mannered Beardie. If you let him "get the upper hand," he can become unmanageable when mature. Males will challenge you more than most bitches. However, if you do not let him get away with the first few things, he will accept you as his boss and try very hard to please you in the future.

Conditioning the Stud Dog

Conditioning of a male can begin when he is very young. During the growth months, he should receive the best nutrition possible for full expression of his genetic potential. He should be fed a balanced diet with adequate protein and calcium for optimum growth. A fat puppy is not necessarily a healthy puppy. The best condition is hard and muscular with just enough weight to cover the ribs. The male puppy should be encouraged to get plenty of exercise and should receive all of his vaccinations and checkups on schedule. Take note of the age at which both testicles descend. It is preferable that they be normally descended by eight to twelve weeks of age.

A stud dog should be kept healthy and in hard condition. If he is used heavily, a slight increase in protein in his diet may be warranted. Stick with a good, balanced ration as a basic diet. Your male should also be periodically checked for evidence of brucellosis or infections. You will probably want to require his bitches to be examined as well. You must be particularly careful to eliminate parasites in a stud dog because he can contaminate the bitches with whom he comes into contact. Treat any problems immediately and do not allow the dog to breed any bitch while he has a communicable problem.

A common problem found in breeding-age males is sheath infection. Check the penis for signs of discharge or inflammation. If this exists, work some topical antibiotic into the sheath and repeat twice daily until the condition corrects. If your dog is subject to recurring infections, have him examined by a veterinarian for possible cause. Clipping some of the hair around the penis and keeping the area clean may help.

109

Handling the Mating

Never leave your dog alone with a bitch in season or allow him to breed her unassisted. The possibility of injury to the male is great, and you will not know if the bitch has actually been bred and, if so, when. Plan to conduct a mating in a quiet place with good footing. The procedure can take from ten minutes to an hour, so use a place that is comfortable for this length of time. Rough concrete, carpet, or rubber matting provide good footing. Keep both dogs under control at all times and wait a few hours if they are uncooperative. Some bitches need restraining, others are eager to stand for the male. An experienced male will usually know when to breed a bitch. Believe him, even if the timing seems odd. You may miss a bitch with an unusual cycle if you breed her strictly according to the charts.

Check the bitch for any obstructions that will require veterinary attention. If she has an excessive amount of hair around the vulva, comb it aside or trim a small area immediately surrounding the vulva. Check her discharge. It should be light pink or clear, and she should flag her tail to one side if you touch her hindquarters. If you are unsure about correct breeding time, have a vaginal smear taken. The first breeding usually takes place between the tenth and twelfth days of estrus, with a second breeding occurring two to four days later. If smears have not been taken and the bitch still stands willingly, a third breeding can take place. One breeding is all that is necessary if the timing is right. Do not routinely breed your male at less than thirty-six-hour intervals. Repeated daily use will deplete his sperm count, as sperm needs approximately thirty-six hours to mature.

Whenever possible, two people should assist with the mating. This minimizes the potential of injury to either dogs or people. One person will hold the bitch's head. Put a choke collar on her and attach a six-foot leather lead. Wrap the leash firmly, but not tightly, around her muzzle and behind her neck. If you prefer, you may use a muzzle made of an old nylon stocking (see Ch. 8). Few bitches actually need to be muzzled, but even the gentlest bitch may bite if she becomes frightened. Have the bitch's handler place one hand on each side of the bitch's neck just behind her ears and firmly grasp the wraps of the muzzle, talking reassuringly to the bitch and holding her steady throughout the mating. This person may sit in a chair and hold the bitch's head on his or her knees if preferred.

The second person assists the stud. Kneel or sit beside the bitch and place a hand under her flank to steady her. If she tries to lie down, you may have to support her weight on your knee. Hold her tail to one side as the dog mounts. If he penetrates and forms a "tie," help him turn so that the two dogs stand tail-to-tail until the tie breaks (usually ten to fifteen minutes). If the dog has trouble penetrating, place one hand under the bitch's vulva and guide her against the dog as he thrusts. Try to guide him into the proper position without dampening his enthusiasm.

Once the dog has tied and turned, hold him steady with the collar so that he doesn't pull. Restrain the bitch from throwing herself to the ground or jumping. In this vulnerable position, the male can be badly injured, which is why no one should allow a dog to breed unassisted. It is usually the male that is damaged, often ruining a valuable animal for future breedings.

After the dogs break apart, confine them separately in a quiet area for half an hour.

Financial Arrangements

The stud owner is not required to guarantee live puppies, but most breeders do. I guarantee two live puppies to a certain age, or else the bitch may be returned for a free service at her next

110   Ch. Ha'Penny Moon Shadow, a group winning dog.

Ch. Gaymardon Bouncing Bogart.

heat. Many breeders guarantee one live puppy either at birth or to a specified age. These arrangements are individual and may be altered to suit both parties. The only requirement is that both parties clearly understand the terms and that the agreement be recorded in writing. A young, unproven dog may have a lower fee or delayed payment for stud fee. The owner of a very old dog may allow him to be used for a partial fee, with the remainder due when the bitch is determined to be in whelp. The following contract suggests one possibility. Both parties should keep a copy of the written agreement.

BREEDING DIFFICULTIES

It would be impossible to cover in this book all the reasons why a bitch fails to conceive or carry a litter to term, or why a stud quits siring. Every breeder at some time or other will be confronted with a problem of this kind. About half of the problems are freakish, one-time occurrences. Others include:

Abortion

Until the emergence of canine brucellosis, abortion was considered to be rare in bitches. The

---

STUD SERVICE CONTRACT

The _____ stud dog, _____ ; _____
        breed   name   color

registration # _____ owned by _____

was bred on _____ to the bitch_____
                  date   name and reg. #

owned by _____ of _____ ;
              name   address

_____   _____
        phone   bitch's color

Policy for approving bitches:
Bitches must be approved by the stud's owner before being accepted for breeding. Bitch owners must be willing and able to provide proper care for the litter and agree that no puppies from the resultant litter will be sold to pet shops or other wholesale outlets.

Bitches must be in good health and condition at the time of breeding and must be free of hereditary defects, parasites, or infections. They must be of good conformation and temperament and must be physically suitable for breeding to the selected male. A recent negative culture and brucellosis test are required.

A culture or veterinary examination may be required at the owner's expense if any problem is suspected.

Stud owner's responsibility:
We promise the best possible care and handling of the bitch, but cannot accept responsibility for accidents which happen while she is in our care. Our stud dogs are guaranteed to be in the same good health required of the bitch. A culture or veterinary examination is required.

Guarantee:
_____ guarantees at least two living
(name of kennel)
puppies to the age of three weeks. If less than that number result, the owners of the bitch are entitled to a free return service to any male owned by
_____ subject to the availability of the dog requested.
(name of kennel)

Stud Fee:
Stud fee is payable at the time of service and is not refundable.
Fee $ _____ Paid in full?   Yes   No

Special Provisions:

Signed: _____
                  owner of bitch

Signed: _____
                  owner of stud

Address: _____

_____

Phone: _____

111

death of one fetus will not cause a bitch to abort. Rather, she will resorb or partially resorb the fetus. If a problem occurs very early in pregnancy, the bitch will probably resorb the entire litter. Fetuses that die in the last week of pregnancy will most likely be delivered along with the rest of the puppies. Abortion, therefore, is only recognized during the fifth to eighth week.

Beginning about 1962, an infectious disease characterized by abortion and by infertility in males and females occurred in epidemic form in all regions of the United States. By 1968, the disease had been diagnosed in over eight hundred bitches in thirty-eight states.

The most striking characteristic of brucellosis, *B. canis*, is that abortion usually occurs between the forty-fifth and fifty-fifth days of gestation, without any forewarning and without fever or illness in the bitch. Most aborted litters are stillborn or die shortly after birth.

Bitches commonly exhibit a vaginal discharge for several weeks, and most fail to conceive thereafter. A few, however, may deliver normal litters a year or so later.

In males, this infection may be accompanied by scrotal dermatitis and painful swelling of the scrotal sac, which is often followed by testicular atrophy and sterility.

At present, no known cure or immunization exists, although research is currently underway. The disease is detected by testing for elevated serum antibody titers with a standardized tube agglutination test. Dogs should be checked two times, thirty days apart. Suspect brucellosis when a bitch aborts late in pregnancy or fails to conceive twice in a row. Suspect *any* male that has associated with a bitch that has aborted or failed to conceive. The bacteria remain active for at least a year, and the infection is spread through the urine as well as by genital contact. When one dog in a kennel is infected, the brucella generally spread rapidly throughout the entire kennel. At this point, the infection can only be controlled by isolating all new dogs and eradicating all infected dogs.

Failure to Conceive

Inability of a bitch to become pregnant when bred at the correct time by a fertile male can result from infection in the uterus, a hormonal imbalance, or disease. A bitch that has had distemper, leptospirosis, or other serious infectious disease may never come in heat. Other bitches come in heat quite often, yet never conceive.

Generally, this situation is caused by ovarian cysts or by overproduction of one of the hormones, which prevent ovulation. A tumor or infection in the reproductive tract will often prevent conception.

Some veterinarians induce heat by giving pregnant-mare serum to bitches. This is a dangerous practice, because horse serum contains large amounts of protein that can cause extreme allergic reactions in dogs. If you wish to artificially stimulate your hormone-deficient bitch to come in season, request that the vet use pure FSH (follicular stimulating hormone), not pregnant-mare serum. FSH in its pure form should not cause allergic reaction.

False Pregnancy

Occasionally bitches, bred or not, will have all of the symptoms of pregnancy—the uterus will enlarge under the influence of progesterone, and the mammary glands will fill with milk. At about the time that they would be due to whelp, these bitches may go through the process of nesting and, in rare cases, even labor. It is difficult at first to determine whether such a bitch is really pregnant, the only difference being that the whelps cannot be felt. False pregnancy ends at about the time that a normal pregnancy would terminate. It does not harm the bitch, and little is really known about what causes the condition. Some bitches with a history of false pregnancy never conceive. Others conceive normally when bred.

Obstructions in the Bitch

A bitch may have a stricture or a hymen which prevents penetration by the male during breeding. These must be broken or dilated, or in severe cases corrected by surgery. To examine the bitch, wear a thin rubber glove and lubricate a finger with surgical jelly or a small amount of *Vaseline®*. Insert the finger about three inches into the vagina of the bitch. Any obstruction should be obvious within that distance. If the vagina is too small to penetrate, the bitch may be too early in her season, but more likely she will need to be dialated or bred artificially. I recomment not breeding a bitch that cannot be bred naturally because this condition tends to be hereditary. You may find a bitch who is difficult to breed because the vulva is lower than the vaginal canal, and the male is unable to penetrate. Try lifting the vulva between two fingers so that the male has an unobstructed passage.

Resorption of Whelps

If a bitch conceives and something goes wrong—hormonal imbalance, injury, toxicity from medication or poison—before the sixth week of pregnancy, she will simply resorb the dead puppies or those that her body cannot sustain. Resorption sometimes occurs so early in the pregnancy that one may never know if the bitch was actually pregnant. In some cases this problem can be corrected by giving repositol progestrone after breeding and repeating the treatment at two-week intervals through about the sixth week. The injections will have to be given with each breeding since the deficiency does not correct itself.

Sperm Counts

A sperm count is a microscopic examination of a dog's semen. It will determine if sperm is present, if it is in sufficient quantity for the dog to be a reliable sire, if it is motile, and if the sperm's morphology (form) is normal. A semen sample must be collected from the male immediately prior to examination. The container must be heated to body temperature and held inside an insulated sleeve to keep the sperm motile. It is easier to stimulate the male if a bitch in season (any breed) is present to excite him. Morphology of the sperm is more easily determined if the slide is stained.

Sterility of the Stud Dog

There are two primary reasons for a stud to quit siring besides brucellosis or infection. One is the inability to produce live sperm. This problem is usually caused by a hormone change within the body (sometimes a hereditary concern) which, if complete, will eventually lead to testicle atrophy. A biopsy of the testicle can tell if the dog is producing semen, but unless done properly the scars from this operation can guarantee permanent sterility. A series of hormone injections *may* temporarily restore fertility, but excessive use of hormones will cause the body to quit producing them altogether, and result in testicle atrophy. A change in diet and exercise may be beneficial.

The other cause of male sterility is a blockage preventing sperm from being ejaculated. In this case a biopsy will reveal that the dog is producing viable sperm, but a check of the semen finds only carrying fluid present. In this case, hormone injections are detrimental. A blockage may be helped surgically depending upon its location. Seek help from a specialist in breeding problems if you decide to attempt this procedure.

Occasionally a dog becomes sterile for seemingly no reason, then suddenly begins siring again. This may be due to overuse, condition, diet (hormones in some commercial feeds and from poultry used in animal feed can be harmful), or a temporary hormone reversal. A dog who has not been bred for some time should be bred at least twice to his next bitch, because the first ejaculate may contain aged or dead sperm.

Recommended procedure in determining sterility in a stud is to take a sperm count and a brucellosis test. If these are normal, a bitch's missing is not the male's fault. If sperm is nonexistent, even after a change in environment, a testicle biopsy should be conducted and treatment scheduled accordingly. Prognosis is usually poor for correcting male sterility.

Thyroid Imbalance

An over or under active thyroid can cause failure to conceive. If enough thyroid is not produced, the bitch will not ovulate. She will usually tend to be overweight and lazy and have a greasy-looking coat.

Thyroid malfunction can easily be detected through blood tests and corrected by the administration of the hormone, but it is one conception problem that few veterinarians consider. If your bitch will not conceive and you suspect thyroid deficiency, request a blood test for thyroid level. This problem is usually hereditary, but may be aggravated by living at high altitudes. Consider carefully before perpetuating the tendency.

Uterine Infections

113

While the uterus of a nonpregnant bitch is remarkably resistant to infection, the pregnant or pseudopregnant uterus is quite susceptible to infection from a variety of bacteria. Therefore, the period between breeding and whelping, and immediately after birth of a litter, are key times to check your bitch for vaginal discharge, odor, or other signs of infection.

There are a host of potential low-grade uterine infections. Most are characterized by some type of discharge and may be treated with antibiotics. Several more serious types also exist.

Acute Metritis—This infection occurs from bacteria introduced during whelping or, less commonly, during breeding. The chances of metritis are increased in cases of abortion, retained whelp or placenta, or lacerations of the uterine wall. Bacteria isolated from infected bitches include staph, strep, and E. coli.

The bitch appears depressed and has a foul-smelling, dark reddish discharge. She is feverish and does not want to eat. Neither will she care for her litter if she has one. Treatment with antibiotics is required immediately, and spaying is sometimes necessary.

Pyometra — This is by far the most serious uterine infection. The cervix closes under the influence of progesterone after the end of estrus, and the infected uterus fills with pus that cannot drain. The bitch may be mildly depressed and will have an odorous, pus-filled discharge. She will want to drink unusually large amounts of water and may run a temperature. If not treated immediately, she will become very ill. The infection does not respond well to any drug, and the only hope of saving the bitch is immediate removal of the uterus.

CULTURING AND TREATING INFECTION

Any time that a colored or foul-smelling discharge is noticed, that a bitch aborts or fails to conceive, or that uterine infection is suspected, a uterine culture should be taken. If infection is present, the veterinarian can learn from the culture what organism is causing the problem. Common infections include staph, strep, and E. coli. A culture to determine sensitivity to specific drugs should follow any positive growth. A culture from a bitch is more accurate if taken while she is in season. Semen from a male can also be cultured.

Healthy newborns are sleek, well filled-out, and strong nursers.

114

14 The New Generation

During the first few weeks after a bitch has been bred, no dependable signs of pregnancy appear. Occasionally, you will observe a slight change in the bitch's behavior, or her nipples may appear pinker and the vulva softer than normal. There may be a clear discharge from the vulva. None of these signs are reliable clues, however, so feed and condition any bred bitch as if she is pregnant until proven otherwise.

If the eggs were fertilized, they will move from the oviduct down to the uterus, where they will implant themselves into the uterine wall about twelve days after the onset of diestrus. As the whelps grow in size, the horns of the uterus, normally about seven inches long, will also increase in length, often to several feet by the end of gestation. By the twenty-fourth to thirty-fifth days of pregnancy, the whelps will have grown to about the size of a ping-pong ball and can often be palpated with your fingertips. The two horns of the uterus generally lay below the intestines. Sometimes they rest along the abdominal floor, while other times they lay well up in the abdomen just behind the rib cage. Take the bitch's abdomen between your thumb and forefinger and gently, but firmly, palpate from the rear toward the rib cage. The fetus at this stage will feel like a small lump. It is impossible to tell how many puppies a bitch will have because some of the fetuses will be carried high and out of your reach. After the thirty-fifth day, the fetuses will be surrounded with fluid and will be impossible to feel.

The pregnant bitch must be kept in good muscular condition so that she will have plenty of strength to expel the whelps. During the early weeks of pregnancy, her regular routine or training need not be discontinued. The house dog should have several hours of free exercise in the fresh air each day, or at least half an hour daily of roadwork on leash. During the last two or three weeks of pregnancy, the bitch that is heavy in whelp will not be inclined to run or work. She should be prevented from jumping, herding, or

Whelping chart. "Date bred" / "Date due to whelp" for each breeding month.

Bred Jan	Due Mar	Bred Feb	Due Apr	Bred Mar	Due May	Bred Apr	Due Jun	Bred May	Due Jul	Bred Jun	Due Aug	Bred Jul	Due Sep	Bred Aug	Due Oct	Bred Sep	Due Nov	Bred Oct	Due Dec	Bred Nov	Due Jan	Bred Dec	Due Feb
1	5	1	5	1	3	1	3	1	3	1	3	1	2	1	3	1	3	1	3	1	3	1	2
2	6	2	6	2	4	2	4	2	4	2	4	2	3	2	4	2	4	2	4	2	4	2	3
3	7	3	7	3	5	3	5	3	5	3	5	3	4	3	5	3	5	3	5	3	5	3	4
4	8	4	8	4	6	4	6	4	6	4	6	4	5	4	6	4	6	4	6	4	6	4	5
5	9	5	9	5	7	5	7	5	7	5	7	5	6	5	7	5	7	5	7	5	7	5	6
6	10	6	10	6	8	6	8	6	8	6	8	6	7	6	8	6	8	6	8	6	8	6	7
7	11	7	11	7	9	7	9	7	9	7	9	7	8	7	9	7	9	7	9	7	9	7	8
8	12	8	12	8	10	8	10	8	10	8	10	8	9	8	10	8	10	8	10	8	10	8	9
9	13	9	13	9	11	9	11	9	11	9	11	9	10	9	11	9	11	9	11	9	11	9	10
10	14	10	14	10	12	10	12	10	12	10	12	10	11	10	12	10	12	10	12	10	12	10	11
11	15	11	15	11	13	11	13	11	13	11	13	11	12	11	13	11	13	11	13	11	13	11	12
12	16	12	16	12	14	12	14	12	14	12	14	12	13	12	14	12	14	12	14	12	14	12	13
13	17	13	17	13	15	13	15	13	15	13	15	13	14	13	15	13	15	13	15	13	15	13	14
14	18	14	18	14	16	14	16	14	16	14	16	14	15	14	16	14	16	14	16	14	16	14	15
15	19	15	19	15	17	15	17	15	17	15	17	15	16	15	17	15	17	15	17	15	17	15	16
16	20	16	20	16	18	16	18	16	18	16	18	16	17	16	18	16	18	16	18	16	18	16	17
17	21	17	21	17	19	17	19	17	19	17	19	17	18	17	19	17	19	17	19	17	19	17	18
18	22	18	22	18	20	18	20	18	20	18	20	18	19	18	20	18	20	18	20	18	20	18	19
19	23	19	23	19	21	19	21	19	21	19	21	19	20	19	21	19	21	19	21	19	21	19	20
20	24	20	24	20	22	20	22	20	22	20	22	20	21	20	22	20	22	20	22	20	22	20	21
21	25	21	25	21	23	21	23	21	23	21	23	21	22	21	23	21	23	21	23	21	23	21	22
22	26	22	26	22	24	22	24	22	24	22	24	22	23	22	24	22	24	22	24	22	24	22	23
23	27	23	27	23	25	23	25	23	25	23	25	23	24	23	25	23	25	23	25	23	25	23	24
24	28	24	28	24	26	24	26	24	26	24	26	24	25	24	26	24	26	24	26	24	26	24	25
25	29	25	29	25	27	25	27	25	27	25	27	25	26	25	27	25	27	25	27	25	27	25	26
26	30	26	30	26	28	26	28	26	28	26	28	26	27	26	28	26	28	26	28	26	28	26	27
27	31	27	May 1	27	29	27	29	27	29	27	29	27	28	27	29	27	29	27	29	27	29	27	28
28	Apr. 1	28	2	28	30	28	30	28	30	28	30	28	29	28	30	28	30	28	30	28	30	28	Mar. 1
29	2			29	31	29	July 1	29	31	29	31	29	30	29	31	29	Dec. 1	29	31	29	31	29	2
30	3			30	June 1	30	2	30	Aug. 1	30	Sep. 1	30	Oct. 1	30	Nov. 1	30	2	30	Jan. 1	30	Feb. 1	30	3
31	4			31	2			31	2			31	2	31	2			31	2			31	4

116

Whelping chart, courtesy of Gaines.

doing other strenuous work and should be encouraged to exercise freely in the yard or taken for long walks on leash. A bitch that is closely confined is prone to whelping difficulties.

About the fourth week of pregnancy, the bitch's appetite may increase. If she is self-fed, just make sure that she is not becoming obese. If you feed her individually, change to two meals per day and increase her food intake as she requires, making sure that she does not overeat and put on unnecessary fat. Providing you feed a professional ration such as *Science Diet®*, simply switch the bitch over to the "lactation" formula during the fourth or fifth week of pregnancy and continue this diet until her litter is weaned. Additional supplements are not needed. However, if you continue to feed a standard maintenance-type food, additional protein, calcium, and phosphorus will be needed during the final weeks before whelping. Small amounts of raw liver, lean beef, or cottage cheese are excellent sources of protein, and bone meal supplies the best and safest calcium/phosphorus supplement. Calcium and phosphorus must be balanced at a ratio of 1.2 to 1. An unbalanced mixture can be harmful.

As whelping approaches, the bitch will appear quite obviously pregnant by her enlarged abdomen. About a week prior to whelping, the puppies "drop," leaving the bitch with a sunken-in appearance in the loin areas. Her nipples will enlarge and turn pink in color, and the mammary glands generally will fill with milk. The bitch should now be kept in the house where you can keep a close watch on her condition. She will need to go outside frequently because her bladder will be crowded by the growing puppies.

About ten days before the litter is expected, move the bitch to her whelping box. This will give her time to get used to sleeping in a new area, and you will be prepared if the litter happens to come early. I use a large wooden whelping box which has 24-inch sides. It also has a hinged board on the front which can be lowered to make one side 12 inches high. You can easily build your own from one-half- or three-quarter-inch plywood. You may want to add a rail around the inside of the box about 4 inches from the floor to prevent the bitch from crushing her puppies against the sides of the box. If the box will be placed on a cold or drafty floor, raise if off floor level with two-by-four boards. An average size whelping box that could accommodate bitch and puppies for the first three weeks after birth would be about 48 x 48 inches. Substitutes for an actual whelping box include the bottom of a fiberglass crate or a wire crate which can be opened from the top. Place a board or piece of cardboard around the base of a wire crate to prevent drafts. A cardboard box may not be suitable because some bitches will tear it to shreds in short order. Whatever you use, it should be cleaned, disinfected, and lined with newspapers prior to whelping.

You will need to assemble a few supplies near the whelping area. My list includes a large stack of newspapers, several large towels, sterilized scissors and hemostat, dental floss, and several plastic garbage bags. I also have on hand

117

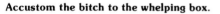
Accustom the bitch to the whelping box.

a piece of indoor-outdoor carpeting to use in the whelping box after whelping, a can of bitch's milk replacer, and feeding tube, and some liquid glucose. If you are experienced at whelping, your vet may also supply you with some oxytocin to keep on hand for uterine inertia. He will instruct you in its use, and these directions must be followed explicitly.

SIGNS OF APPROACHING LABOR

All Beardie bitches are individuals, and it is difficult to predict just how they will behave prior to whelping. Some announce the event by nesting for several days in advance; others nonchalantly go into labor and whelp their puppies without so much as a murmur. The surest clue that whelping is imminent is a drop in the bitch's temperature. Start taking her rectal temperature morning and evening about ten days prior to her due date. At first it will hover in the neighborhood of 101.5 to 102 degrees. A few days before she whelps, it will drop slowly to around 100 degrees, and just before the onset of labor, her temperature will drop abruptly, usually to 97 or 98 degrees Fahrenheit. If no signs of labor occur within twenty-four hours of this drop, the bitch should be examined by a veterinarian.

The bitch will usually have a clear, profuse discharge from the vagina at this time. The young bitch having her first litter will probably show only slight enlargement of the mammary gland, but the

118

Restlessness marks the start of prelabor.

older, proven broodbitch may be heavy with milk. The bitch may refuse to eat during the day or so preceding whelping, but again, each bitch is an individual and may not follow an expected pattern. She will probably seem restless and uncomfortable, and the young bitch, not knowing what to expect, may be a bit nervous.

Your final preparations should be made now. Bathe the bitch, or at least wash her hindquarters and stomach with an antiseptic soap. Keep the discharge cleaned up as much as possible to prevent the hair from matting. Finally, clip the inner layers of feathering from the bitch's hindquarters, and especially clip the hair around the vulva. This will keep the area clean and prevent a puppy from becoming entangled in the long hair. Also comb the hair away from the breasts. Most of it will be loose and will come out as you comb. Clip the feathering at the sides of the belly and any hair that still remains around the breasts.

Prelabor

This is the early stage of labor during which much is happening inside the bitch's body to prepare the puppies for birth, but outward signs may be difficult to detect. This stage lasts from two to thirty-six hours.

During this time, various hormones effect a series of events. The whelp, which has been attached to the uterine wall by the placenta (through which the whelp receives its nourishment and oxygen supply), prepares to detach. The cervix and birth canal dilate to allow for the passage of the puppies. The contractions at this time are weak and cannot generally be seen or felt. The bitch, however, becomes increasingly uncomfortable. She may scratch feverishly at the newspapers in her box, pant, or possibly vomit. Between these fits of activity, she will probably lie quietly asleep in her box. As time passes, the bitch may begin to lick vigorously at her rear parts or sit and watch her sides with much curiosity.

You should not interfere at this stage, but do keep an eye on the bitch. Note how long the prelabor stage is lasting, and be concerned if it continues much longer than twenty-four hours. If the bitch wants to go out, let her relieve herself but make sure that she does not drop a puppy in the yard. If you think that whelping is progressing abnormally, or if it has been more than twenty-four hours since the bitch's temperature dropped or she began prelabor, take your bitch for an examination. If a puppy is stuck or an obstruction exists, the bitch may not go into labor at all.

Excessive nervousness, pain, bleeding from the vulva, or a foul-smelling discharge at this time all warn of problems that should be dealt with by your veterinarian. A bitch should also be checked if she goes past the sixty-third day with no signs of going into labor.

I trust my own common sense at a time like this. Some vets will advise you to wait if you just call and consult them on the telephone. If you are concerned, insist on an examination. Most Beardies are easy whelpers, and if problems arise, they usually are serious enough to require veterinary assistance.

WHELPING

During labor, the contractions increase in intensity and can sometimes be seen as the abdominal wall hardens and then relaxes. The bitch may be seen straining as though she is having a bowel movement. By now the whelps have begun to detach from the uterus and move into position in the birth canal. Puppies at the base of the uterine horns will be whelped first. The whelp, the cord, and the placenta are all contained in the outer sack. This sack is filled with amniotic fluid, which acts as a cushion for the whelp. A second sack covers the whelp itself. Whelp and placenta are connected by the umbilical cord, which contains two umbilical arteries and one vein. As the puppy, enclosed in this double-layered sack, moves down the birth canal, the water bag is forced out in front, where it helps to soften and dilate the passage. It finally bursts during a contraction, and the fluid lubricates the vagina, making the way easier for the whelp.

Watch for the breaking of the water bag. If you notice the fluid or see wet papers in the whelping box, you can be sure that the first puppy is on the way. If the water bag ruptures and no puppy appears within an hour, or if the bitch goes into hard labor and suddenly stops having contractions, there may be complications. Sometimes a puppy can get jammed at the junction of the uterus and the birth canal; if so, you will need veterinarian assistance. Do not give oxytocin before the first puppy has arrived because the contractions stimulated by the shot could cause the uterus to rupture.

The Puppy Arrives

Puppies are born either head first, which is preferable, or hind feet first, which is known as "breech." In the head-first position, the sack filled with dark fluid is seen first. A young bitch may become frightened and try to bite at the sack as it appears. If this happens, prevent her from tearing at the sack or the puppy by grasping the hair at each side of her neck just behind the ears, holding the head rigid. Lift her completely off the floor so that she cannot struggle against you. Don't bend recklessly over her head—you could be bitten accidentally. The next contraction should cause the puppy to come free and drop to the floor of the whelping box. You can then release the bitch and let her get back to the work at hand.

The puppy will generally still be enclosed in the translucent sack; he will be attached to the placenta by the umbilical cord. Occasionally, the placenta will not come out with the puppy and the bitch will sever the cord, leaving the placenta inside her body. It should be expelled with the next puppy. You should be observant of this and ask a veterinarian to check any bitch that you suspect has retained a placenta, since this condition can cause infection of the uterus.

The pressure encountered during birth will stimulate the puppy to start breathing, and if he is not removed from the sack within a minute or two, he may suffocate. Most bitches will instinctively begin cleaning the sack off of the puppy. If she does not get the puppy out, you will have to take over for her. Grasp the sack between the folds of a clean washcloth and pull forward, away from the puppy's head. The sack will break easily. Use the cloth to wipe away fluid from the nostrils and mouth, then give the puppy back to his dam.

The bitch will likely turn her attentions to eating the placenta, and in the process will sever the attached umbilical cord. The placenta contains hormones that stimulate the uterus to contract after whelping. These hormones also stimulate the production of milk. Bearded Collies are remarkably efficient when whelping and are likely to resent your interference. Observe, but stay out of the way unless a bitch is having trouble or is not taking care of the newborn. A maiden bitch sometimes will not realize that the expelled mass of fluid and tissue contains a puppy. In this case, remove the puppy from the whelping box so that you can work on him without upsetting the bitch or getting bitten, and proceed to cut and tie the

119

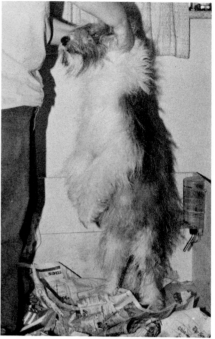

Top: hard labor begins. Lift the bitch if she tries to snap the whelp.

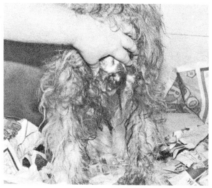

Left and bottom: a puppy arrives.

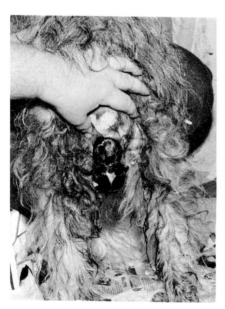

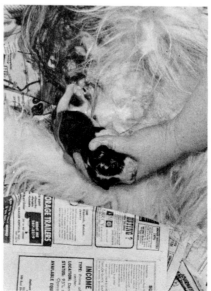

Top: most bitches whelp unassisted.

Middle left: the puppy is attached to the placenta at birth.

Middle right: if the bitch delays, clamp and cut the umbilical cord.

Bottom left: leave the cord clamped for a few minutes to stop bleeding.

Bottom right: remove puppies until the bitch has finished whelping.

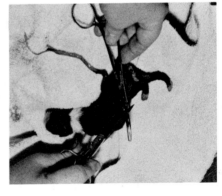

121

cord. Take the cord between your thumb and forefinger and milk the blood in the cord toward the puppy. Then, holding the cord firmly near the puppy so that no pressure is on the navel, use the thumb and forefinger of the other hand to pull and tear the cord about one inch from the puppy's body. (If you prefer, you can clamp the cord with a hemostat and sever it with a sterilized, dull scissors. This causes more bleeding than does tearing, so leave the hemostat clamped on the cord for several more minutes.) A cord that continues to ooze blood, whether cut or severed by the bitch's teeth, should be tied off with a loop of dental floss about one-half inch from the puppy's stomach. Knot twice, then cut off any excess string so that the bitch cannot pull on it.

Some puppies need to have the fluid cleared from their lungs and trachea. If you hear a puppy "rattling" when he breathes or see one having difficulty breathing, you will need to shake out the fluid. Hold the puppy between the flat palms of your hands, being careful to support his head. Raise your arms straight out in front of you, then bring them sharply downward, stopping abruptly with the puppy's head held straight down. Repeat several times if necessary. Take a good hold and, as long as his head is firmly supported, don't be afraid of shaking the puppy too hard.

Additions to the Family

A Beardie can be expected to have from four to twelve puppies, with seven being the average litter. Most bitches whelp at fifteen- to thirty-minute intervals, but it is not unusual for an hour to elapse between puppies. Near the middle of whelping there is usually a longer rest period of up to two hours.

The first puppy may be able to nurse for a few minutes. Generally, this serves to stimulate contractions. Since a Beardie will usually fuss if you take away all of her babies, I leave the first puppy in the box until the second one is born, and so on. Since the bitch will often nest between puppies, and since each puppy is usually preceded by considerable fluid, it is not advisable to leave all of the puppies with the bitch. They could get chilled or injured. Instead, place them in a small cardboard box just outside the whelping box and cover the box with a towel for warmth. Small or weak puppies should be placed on a towel-covered heating pad that has been turned to its lowest setting.

During the midwhelping break, or at any time when the bitch is resting, the puppies may be placed with her to nurse. Newborn puppies should be dry and warm before nursing. They can go as long as an hour without food.

Keep the box clean and add fresh papers as the others become torn and wet. If a bitch has an extremely large litter, try to keep her from eating all of the placentas, as they will most likely cause diarrhea. However, you may never get the chance to take them away, and if so, don't worry about it.

Whelping Complications

More than two hours between puppies, more than one hour since the onset of hard contractions, or complete cessation of labor when more puppies are obviously inside the bitch signal a call to your veterinarian.

Sometimes a large puppy, or one that is in the breech presentation, will have difficulty coming through the pelvic opening. A little assistance will generally free the puppy. Have someone hold the bitch so that she cannot snap, and take hold of the puppy with a clean washcloth. Pull him gently and firmly down toward the bitch's stomach. Never pull straight out. If he still doesn't come loose, pull him gently to one side, then to the other.

You may pull a puppy either by the feet or by the head, depending on which is protruding. However, try not to pull on only one foot. A gloved finger may be able to find and free the other foot. Never pull a puppy that is presented upside down. Instead, try to turn him over, or seek veterinary assistance.

If you have not succeeded in freeing a puppy, or if the puppy is too far inside the bitch for you to grasp, take your bitch immediately to a veterinarian. You will probably have to muzzle her and load her in a traveling crate. The other puppies may be safely left in their heated box.

Uterine Inertia—The most common problem that bitches encounter when whelping large litters is uterine inertia. The bitches simply wear out and stop having contractions in the midst of delivery. Sometimes a short rest and a couple teaspoons of brandy in a bowl of milk will revive the bitch, and she will resume having contractions. An injection of oxytocin (pituitary hormone), one cc. intramuscularly, will often revive the contractions. The bitch should start contractions within fifteen minutes after receiving the injection. If a puppy has not arrived within forty-five minutes, it is best to seek veterinary assistance.

122

Impossible delivery—If a bitch, for whatever reason, cannot whelp a puppy or a litter naturally, your vet will perform a caesarian section. He can usually remove all of the puppies while they are still alive if you have taken reasonable care and have not waited too long. While the bitch will be groggy for twelve to eighteen hours afterward due to the anesthesia, the puppies will be able to nurse as usual. You may need to remove them from the bitch to prevent her from falling on them at first. You should also rub the puppies' stomachs after they eat to stimulate defecation. Within a day, the bitch will be caring for them normally.

POSTWHELPING CARE OF THE BITCH

The bitch will probably be thirsty after whelping and will appreciate a drink of water or warm milk. She will not want to eat for several hours, and after all of the puppies are cleaned and dry, she will probably fall asleep.

For the first two or three days, the bitch should be fed lightly and often, gradually building up to her regular ration by the third or fourth day. Broth, cottage cheese, and a little raw liver are good in the interim. Mix her food into a soft gruel and feed only small portions at a time, even though her appetite may become voracious. Plenty of water should be available to her at all times.

The bitch's temperature will rise to 101.5 or 102 after whelping. If everything is normal, it will not exceed 102.5. A high temperature or a greenish or pus-filled discharge probably indicate an infection that will require immediate treatment. Some discharge and bleeding are to be expected, but excessive blood loss is cause for concern. Immediately after whelping, as well as while a bitch is in heat, are prime periods for the occurrence of uterine infections, so your Beardie should be carefully watched.

Some bitches seem to give all of their nourishment to their puppies and are therefore prone to "nursing fits" or eclampsia, caused by having all of the calcium drained from their system. The bitch will appear to stare wildly, wobble, or she may go into convulsions, walk stiff-legged, or limp. An injection of calcium, if given immediately, will correct this condition. If left untreated, a bitch could die.

Most bitches whelp and raise their Beardie puppies without complications, so you can relax and enjoy the experience of watching a litter thrive and grow.

Sandoonagh Keli of Cauldbrae and litter, *Glennamoor.*

124

A typical Rich-Lin puppy.

15 All Beardies Great and Small

Watching your newborn Beardie puppies can be awe inspiring. They are so strong and sleek, with a color intensity that makes them resemble little seals. The blacks and browns look like they have been polished to a fine sheen; the blues and fawns are flatter in color but have an iridescent look dusted on the tip of each hair.

If you have not already done so, clip the long hair from directly around each of the bitch's nipples. If left, the pups have a more difficult time nursing. The long hairs can wrap around the nipple, shutting off the milk supply. If undetected for a few days, the nipple can actually be severed from the body. I have nearly had this happen to two different bitches, so it is a very real possibility. A couple of minutes spent clipping these hairs (preferably prior to whelping) will avoid any problems.

The puppies will search out their first meal as if directed by radar. A healthy pup will fight his way through the other pups until he finds a nipple and latches on. The tongue will wrap around the nipple, and after the first few frantic tugs, the puppy will lay almost still, with his tail held stiffly straight behind him. He will cause little commotion unless a littermate tries to nose him out. If a puppy cries while nursing or frantically crawls from one nipple to the next, the bitch may not have enough milk. A shot of oxytocin during the first twenty-four hours following whelping may help to bring down the milk, but stimulation from the pups' nursing may be all that is needed.

It is extremely important that all pups nurse well during their first twenty-four hours of life. The milk produced immediately after whelping is called colostrum and contains the antibodies that give the puppies immunity against various diseases during their first few weeks. This immunity is more complete if the bitch has had recent vaccinations. Be sure that the litter has enough functional nipples. The number of nipples can vary from dog to dog, and some Beardies have very large litters. If there are too many pups, you may have to supplement the feeding for some or split them into two groups and alternate the bitch's time between them.

The second immediate concern is that the bitch licks the puppies. Most Beardies are good about this, but the puppies' urination and defecation are controlled strictly by outside stimulation. The first bowel movement, called meconium, is very dark brown in color and should occur during the first hour after whelping. Constipation at this age can result in death. As long as the bitch licks the puppies and checks them periodically, everything should be fine.

If any of the umbilical cords begin bleeding, remove the puppy to a separate box and apply a hemostat to close off the cord. Bleeding should stop, and the clamp may be removed after a few minutes. You can tie the cord with a piece of dental floss if bleeding persists. If cords are cut to roughly 1-inch lengths, the danger is less than if the bitch chews them very close to the body. If the cord is left too long, the bitch may keep pulling at it, which stimulates bleeding and can also cause an umbilical hernia. A small amount of lost blood is not significant; a large volume can substantially weaken the puppy.

Most Beardie mothers are possessive and efficient with their puppies. These traits are admirable and should be encouraged. Beardies so far have very few breeding difficulties. If a bitch is not a good mother, especially after her first litter, she should not be considered a prime brood bitch, and you should be aware that these traits will probably be passed to some of her daughters. Beardies will remain a strong breed only as long as breeders do not perpetuate weaknesses.

EXAMINING THE PUPPIES

Each puppy should be checked for abnormalities and overall condition. Start with the head. Are markings satisfactory? They need not be symmetrical, but a puppy with a predominantly white head looks more like an Old English Sheepdog than a Beardie. Be aware that blazes will narrow to about half their width by maturity. Open the mouth and check for a cleft palate, a condition in which an opening in the roof of the mouth allows air and milk directly into the nasal passage. A puppy with this deformity will have trouble sucking, and often milk will bubble from the nostrils. The cleft can vary from a wide gap to a narrow hole near the back of the palate, which is difficult to see. There is no cure, and any defective puppies should be "put down" immediately.

Look at the way in which the jaws meet. If the puppy had teeth, would they meet in a scissors or level bite? If a puppy is undershot or badly overshot at birth (¼ inch or more), he may later have difficulty eating. Therefore, you may want to consider disposing of this puppy now. Bites that are abnormal at birth are much less likely to correct than ones that become problematic during development.

Check nose, lip, and gum pigment (most will be pink at birth). Are the gums very white, or do you notice any other deviation? Anemic puppies or ones that show a bluish cast may have a heart defect or a severe parasitic infection (especially hookworm). Watch these puppies very closely for

Three day old puppies.

The same puppies at one week of age.

a day or two to see if the color corrects. If so, the color was probably due to oxygen deficiency during birth and no treatment is necessary. If the condition persists, consult your vet. Parasites can usually be treated, but defective puppies should be diagnosed and euthanized immediately.

Next, look at the body for mismarks, club feet, kinked or bobbed tails, or any obvious deformity. Club feet are usually due to a cramped position in the uterus and may correct themselves by the time the puppy is old enough to walk. Most other problems will not correct.

If some puppies really need to be destroyed, do so immediately by having your vet administer an overdose of anesthetic. This is painless and quick. Very few Beardie pups are defective, but problems will increase if breeders perpetuate the "weakies." It is selfish and foolish to try and raise puppies that are not healthy, normal, typical Beardies. You do not need them yourself, and they cannot be sold to someone else. It is much easier to dispose of a puppy immediately before you form an attachment to it. Neither you nor the bitch will miss it after a few hours, and your conscience will be clearer if you are firm about your responsibility from the start.

EARLY ENVIRONMENT

The puppies should now be placed on a surface that provides proper footing. Most Beardie mothers will not tolerate newspapers (which are unsuitable anyway) or loose towels for bedding and will root them into the corners of their box, leaving the puppies on a hard, bare surface. I find the best liner for a puppy box to be a piece of indoor-outdoor carpeting cut to fit the exact size. This is washable (it's best to have two pieces to alternate while one is being cleaned), difficult for the bitch to remove, and provides excellent footing for the puppies. If this is unavailable, try Astroturf® or an anchored sheet or large towel.

Proper footing allows the puppies to have traction while nursing. Beardies are notorious for whelping a week early and for having puppies that grow at a tremendously fast rate. While early pups usually look as strong and healthy as full-term pups, their ribs are softer and more easily crushed by the body weight. If the pup is forced to remain on a slick, hard surface, the rib cage will become flat on the bottom, restricting lung capacity and forcing legs to flail helplessly to the sides. In most cases, this condition corrects itself

when the puppy is placed on proper footing. In extreme cases, a pup may become a "swimmer," a condition in which the puppy's front legs are unable to reach under his body and he is supported solely by the chest. Lung capacity is decreased, and heart failure may occur. A swimmer can sometimes be helped by suspending the body inside a cardboard tube. Tape the puppy's body to the top of the tube so that the chest can eventually drop to a normal position, and control his weight by limiting feedings. Fat puppies are more susceptible to swimmers syndrome.

Be sure to keep the puppies' toenails clipped short. They are very sharp and can scratch the bitch terribly while the puppies nurse. If she gets too sore, the bitch may not feed the puppies as long or as often as she should. I once clipped the nails of the females in a litter but got interrupted before finishing the males. I forgot to go back, and not until I realized that the boys were falling behind in growth did I catch the significance. They hurt the bitch, and she kept pushing them away, while the bitch puppies with their shorter nails were cared for well. I recommend clipping nails every third or fourth day.

The puppies must be kept draft-free. They can catch pneumonia easily in a drafty place, even though the temperature is warm enough. I like a box with 12-inch to 24-inch sides. If a wire crate is used, tie cardboard at least 6 to 8 inches high along the bottom of each side.

I do not use supplemental heat with Beardie pups unless the litter must be separated from the dam (if puppies are orphaned or if a large litter is split into two boxes). I find that a house temperature of about seventy degrees is adequate for healthy pups. If you have a sick or weak puppy, a heating pad or heat lamp may be used to bring the temperature in the box to eighty-five or ninety degrees. Do not overheat the puppies so that they dehydrate. For this reason, a heating pad that covers only part of the box is safest. Puppies kept on carpet need less additional heat than those kept on paper.

WEAK PUPPIES

Some puppies get off to a bad start. Either they are smaller and get pushed away from the food, or they are thin and weak and just can't seem to snap out of it quickly. If a weak puppy is getting pushed away from the dam, hold the larger puppies back so that the small ones can nurse unobstructed every few hours.

Occasionally, a weak puppy will not have the strength to hold onto a teat but can still nurse if held to the dam. Hold this puppy to the bitch and keep him awake and nursing at least fifteen minutes every two hours until he becomes stronger. Making a cupped bed out of a bath towel and propping the puppy against the bitch may suffice if the other pups are removed. Never deprive the healthy pups for a sick one that will probably die anyway. The weak puppy that doesn't show drastic improvement during the first two days is a very poor risk.

Extraordinary means should not be employed to keep puppies alive. Puppies that are this weak rarely make suitable adults, even in a pet capacity. Heat, food, and fluids are all that should be offered, and these only for a limited time.

Tube Feeding the Weak Puppy

A puppy can be fed with an eyedropper or premature baby bottle, but neither method is very efficient. If you must hand-feed an entire litter or a sick puppy, learn to tube feed. At first it is a bit unnerving, but done properly, it is better for the puppy and far easier and quicker for you.

You will need a ten cc. plastic or glass syringe and a "number five" rubber catheter. You can obtain these from a vet supply house or from your local hospital. These tubes are used on premature human babies.

Hold the puppy with his head stretched forward. Put the tip of the tube at the puppy's last (rear) rib and, following the curve of the neck, measure to the end of his nose. Mark this point on the tube with a piece of adhesive tape or a bit of nail polish. Boil the tube and syringe to sterilize them.

To feed, attach the tube to the syringe and draw up about one cc. more milk than the puppy will need. Place the pup on his tummy on a flat surface. Open the mouth and insert the tube. Since it probably is still dripping with milk, most puppies will start to swallow the tube on their own. It is important to keep the puppy's head down and forward while inserting the tube so that the tube will slide easily down the esophagus. If the tube hits an obstruction, do not force it. Instead, withdraw it slowly and start over. The tube should slide easily to the mark that you made earlier. If it doesn't, it may be in the lungs.

You may check this in two ways if you are not sure. Draw the milk back into the syringe, remove the syringe from the tube, and listen. If the tube is in the lungs rather than in the stomach, the pup's breathing should be quite audible when the tube end is held to your ear. You may also place the end of the tube in a glass of water. If bubbles appear, the tube is in the lungs. With a little experience, you will be able to insert the tube into the stomach easily every time. Care is always necessary, however, for should you inject the liquid into the lungs by accident, the puppy will catch pneumonia and probably die.

128

Measure the catheter before feeding.   **Insert the tube gently.**   **Inject the formula slowly.**

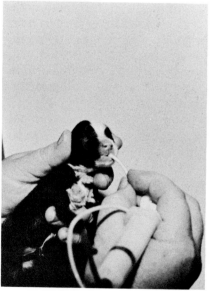

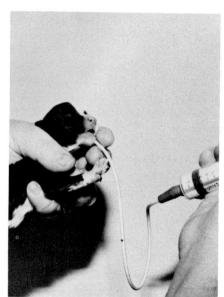

Luckily, it is very rare that the tube does not enter the stomach as desired, and if it inserts to the mark, you are safe.

When you are sure that the tube is all the way into the stomach, press the plunger of the syringe very slowly until about half of the desired feeding has been given. Check the stomach. It will begin to fill out. If it looks full and stretched, the puppy has had enough. If not, rest a second, then continue forcing the liquid into the stomach until the full amount has been given. Wait a few seconds, then withdraw the tube quickly.

With practice, you will be able to feed an entire litter in just a few minutes. The puppy exerts no energy in getting his food, and strong puppies will soon be able to go six hours between meals. Start orphaned puppies eating from a dish by three weeks of age and wean them as soon as possible.

Feeding Particulars

The easiest and best formula to feed is a bitch's milk supplement, such as *Esbilac®*. This solution is readily available in either dry or liquid form from any pet supply store or through veterinarians. If you use the dry form, mix only enough for one feeding at a time. Follow directions on the can for mixing and storing. The liquid form is much more satisfactory for young puppies. If you absolutely cannot obtain a bitch's milk replacer, mix one egg yolk with one-half cup of whole homogenized milk. Heat all formula to about 100 degrees and test it on your wrist to make sure that it feels neither hot nor cold.

Newborn puppies and very small, weak, or sick puppies should be fed every two hours. Larger, stronger puppies can manage with feedings every four hours, and by the time they are one week old, every six hours. It is important to establish a schedule and stay with it. Irregular feedings cause colic. If the puppies cry between feedings, they are probably hungry, and either you are not feeding enough or you need to feed more often. No matter how hungry a puppy is, he should be fed slowly. A puppy that guzzles milk will almost surely get colic.

Each puppy needs an individual amount of food, and it depends on the weight and health of the pup. Sick puppies should not be overfed; in fact, it is always better to underfeed than to overfeed. As a general rule, a twelve-ounce Beardie puppy should get about one and one-half ounces of formula per day. Divide this by the number of feedings per day to arrive at the amount per feeding. Vary this to suit the puppy. Six feedings, one every four hours, would mean that this puppy would receive one-fourth ounce at each feeding. If the puppy is small or ill, feed at two-hour invervals and do not allow over two cc's each time at first. The amount and the interval between feedings can be gradually increased over the next few days.

While a puppy on supplemental formula will not gain as fast as a pup raised on bitch's milk, he should gain at least an ounce every couple of days. If he is getting enough formula, the puppy will sleep contentedly between feedings and his stomach will look full and round. The puppy that is being overfed will look bloated, and his stools will become curdled and yellowish. Cut the strength of the formula in half at the first sign of diarrhea, and cut back on the amount. If diarrhea continues, you may want to switch to liquid glucose in water for a few feedings. It might also be wise to have your vet check a stool sample for coccidia.

Do not forget to rub the tummy of a puppy to stimulate defecation and urination if the puppy is not being placed with his dam between feedings. (See following section for method.)

Danger Signs in Young Puppies

If you pick up a puppy and he feels limp, cold, clammy, or lifeless, you must act quickly to find and treat the condition. Common causes can be starvation, constipation (causing toxemia), overheating, or chilling.

Chilling—First check the temperature of the box and adjust accordingly. A chilled puppy should be warmed gradually by rubbing him briskly to stimulate circulation then carrying him around under your shirt or coat. He can also be placed under a heat lamp or on a heating pad, but be careful not to cause shock by raising the temperature too quickly. Heating pads should be set on low heat. Do not feed a chilled puppy until he has been thoroughly warmed as he will be unable to properly digest the formula.

Constipation—If the pup's tummy is full, and if the pup appears normal in color and healthy to outward appearances but does not rouse and nurse, then he may be toxic from constipation. Stimulate him by rubbing the tummy with damp cotton balls. If this does not bring relief, and if the puppy strains or whimpers and cries, give one cc. of warm water as an enema. You must inject the solution slowly to keep from causing too much pressure. If this does not give relief, get the puppy to a veterinarian right away because the bowel or rectum may be blocked, twisted, or ruptured, and further stimulation could cause complications.

Overheating—An overheated puppy will cry and scream and may pant or hyperventilate. Remove him from the heat immediately and keep him quiet until his body has returned to a normal temperature. He will usually be red, limp, and exhausted, and he may be dehydrated.

Sore eyes—Occasionally, a puppy's eye becomes puffy and pus accumulates under the lids. This must be removed by gently pressing around the eye socket to force the matter out of the lids. Clean the eye area with a cotton ball dipped in warm water. If the eyes are not yet open, the eyelid may have to be slit. Use a sterile scalpel and just score the surface, or else have your vet administer treatment.

Diarrhea—This is common in puppies and may be caused by defective milk from the bitch, colic, overeating, incorrect formula mixtures, parasites, or any of a number of infections. Curdled, extremely foul-smelling or bright yellow feces are serious indications signaling a call to your veterinarian.

Ordinary diarrhea may be treated first with four drops of *Kaopectate*® every four hours. If the puppy is being hand-fed, dilute the *Esbilac*® formula to half strength, or feed only weak glucose water (*Karo*® syrup dissolved in water) for twelve hours. If the diarrhea has not been curtailed in twelve to sixteen hours, it is time to call your veterinarian. The puppy may require antibiotics, which should be employed only if a specific outside cause for the infection is known.

Check for dehydration (which is recognized by loose skin) and treat if necessary. Pinch the skin together. If it stays together when you release it instead of returning to the way it was, then the puppy is dehydrated. Again, this condition is very serious in a tiny puppy. If the pup is only mildly dehydrated and is nursing well, just watch him and make sure that the condition corrects within a couple of days. If he is in bad shape, inject a five-percent dextrose and water solution (preferably with electrolytes) under the skin in several places. Repeat two or three times a day until the dehydration is no longer evident. It will take a lot of fluid to correct the condition, so don't be afraid to inject several cc's. Severe dehydration can kill a puppy within twenty-four hours.

PUPPY DISEASES

Colic and Enteritis—A puppy that cries when touched and that doubles up is probably colicky. This is common in puppies, as in babies, and generally is not cause for alarm. Usually, colic is caused by gas in the stomach and intestines, which is precipitated by the puppy swallowing air, either while bottle feeding, tube feeding, or nursing. Colic can also be caused by overeating or by bad milk. Give the puppy eight drops of *Kaopectate*® and rub the tummy with cotton to stimulate release of the gas. If the puppy develops diarrhea, treat it accordingly. If the entire litter becomes colicky, the cause is probably in the bitch's milk or is due to parasites. Alkaline milk is quite common and necessitates hand-feeding the

130

Hold a puppy in this manner to assess his structure.

litter. You can check this by using *Testape®*, available at any drugstore.

Enteritis is a more serious stomach and intestinal inflammation. The puppy will scream and show obvious signs of intense abdominal pain, which occurs rather suddenly. Get the puppy to a veterinarian fast.

Pneumonia — This is caused by a puppy becoming chilled, getting milk or other fluid into the lungs, or by a virus. Mechanical pneumonia, caused from fluid going down the windpipe, is probably most common. You will at first notice labored breathing followed by a rattling noise in the chest. The puppy will cry at first, then become limp and pale, later turning blue. Your vet can put the puppy on antibiotics, but the death rate is very high. Usually, the best treatment is to simply keep the puppy warm and tube feed until he regains his strength.

Other Diseases — Septicemia is a term used to describe a puppy that has a system full of various forms of bacteria. The feet, nose, and pads of the feet will turn a fiery red color, and the pup will "mew" like a kitten. Prognosis is poor, and a bitch that regularly produces septicemic puppies should be cultured while in season for the presence of *E. coli* or other bacteria. If the bitch requires antibiotics every time she is bred, she is a questionable brood animal.

Herpes virus is also usually contracted from the bitch. The puppy will develop profuse yellowish-green diarrhea. A fat, healthy, week-old puppy will just stop eating and begin to scream endlessly, followed eventually by dehydration, labored breathing, painful whining, and death.

Autopsy will reveal liver damage, and the virus can generally be isolated.

Although the cure for these symptoms is unknown, some breeders believe that adding vitamin K or feeding raw liver blood several times a day can benefit both bitch and puppies. Prognosis is usually poor, and again, it may be best to simply weed out the sick puppies and continue with the healthy ones.

EVALUATION OF YOUNG PUPPIES

It is difficult to keep your hands off of the newborn pups. Some bitches become frantic if you pick up their babies, others proudly display them for your approval. Either way, you should not fuss with the puppies to the point that it deprives them of sleep or food. They need all of their strength at this age for survival and growth. Still, besides checking for defects and health, you will want to note your first impressions and evaluations of the puppies.

I recommend evaluating puppies for structure at birth, at about three days (to verify the initial look), four weeks, eight weeks, six months, one year, two years, and at full maturity. This progression will help you recognize the growth patterns and normal development for puppies of your line. All lines develop slightly differently, and with experience you will learn to recognize characteristics peculiar to your line. Most puppies develop uniformly and are consistent in comparison to their littermates throughout development. **131**

The same dog, Ch. Parcana Silverleaf Vandyke, *Parcana*, showing similar traits as an adult.

It is beneficial to watch all puppies from a litter to see how they mature.

The head is the most obvious part to evaluate in a tiny puppy. The head should be broad, rectangular, and relatively flat in skull and on the sides and have a broad, blunt muzzle. The muzzle should merge smoothly into the skull on the sides with no dip below the eyes. The skull and top of the muzzle should be parallel (viewed from the side) and separated by a distinct "stop" or break between the eyes. The underjaw should be full and rounded at the chin by birth, with the same scissors bite preferred in an adult. If the head looks rounded, pinched in muzzle, or Roman-nosed, recheck at three days to see if it has filled out, as some heads are rather compressed at birth. Sharp ridges from the eye back along the sides of the skull generally indicate that the skull will broaden and probably flatten with age.

Next, check overall proportions. The head should fit the body. If the head is too large, the puppy will probably grow into it. If too small, it will probably remain too narrow or "snipey" for the dog. The neck should be moderately long and arched and should be held proudly when the puppy nurses. The body should be long in rib cage, with ribs slanted toward the tail, and the loin should be strong, well muscled, and not overly long. Angulation can be evaluated by holding the puppy as illustrated and measuring angles between shoulder and upper arm and between pelvis and stifle. The ridge to measure along the shoulder blade is obvious since the layer of fat has not yet formed under the skin of the puppy. Angulation both front and rear should be as close to a right angle as possible. The upper arm and shoulder blade should be the same length (be sure that you are measuring actual length of each of these bones). The stifle should be quite long and hocks noticeably low set. Tail set and croup cannot be evaluated until sixteen weeks of age, when the pelvis drops to the adult position.

Depth of chest can be checked, however, with the best chests reaching the point of the elbow. Many are shallow at birth but improve by eight weeks of age. Rear legs should hang straight and parallel (viewed from the rear) when the puppy is relaxed. Fronts will probably be a bit crooked at birth, but straight front legs are a real bonus. Bone should be moderately heavy and can be best evaluated by examining the diameter of the legs in proportion to the body. Coats will be flat and preferably harsh, the more profuse

ones being thicker on the back of the neck and on the back of the front legs.

At three days of age, the puppies should present a more perfect picture of this description. By this time, the layer of body fat will be filling out the outline and the heads will be looking stronger.

DEWCLAWS

At three days of age, right after the evaluation is made, the dewclaws should be removed. A dewclaw is the fifth toe located like a useless "thumb" on the inside of the front legs. Although not required to be removed by the breed Standard, dewclaws invite injury to the dog later in life if they are left intact. They catch easily in underbrush and can be painfully ripped off, and the nail will grow into the leg if neglected. Beardies almost never have hind dewclaws, but these *must* be removed if present.

Dewclaws can be snipped off at the skin line with large sewing shears, or they can be removed with a small, sharp hemostat. I prefer the hemostat because it does a cleaner job of removing bone and causes less bleeding.

Have someone hold the puppy on his back in a spread-eagle position. With the hemostat as close to the leg as possible, close it over the dewclaw and crush the toe. Remove the clamp and reapply in the same manner at ninety degrees.

Remove dewclaws when pups are three days old.

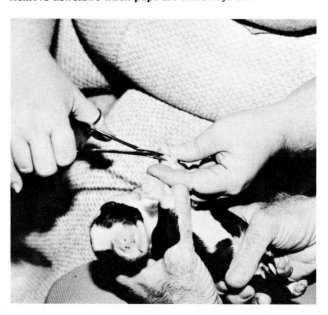

132

This prevents most bleeding and removes a minimum of skin. With the hemostat clamped shut, twist it sideways as if you were rolling it along the leg. Apply enough pressure to lift off the dewclaw. I prefer to go back and grasp any remaining bone fragment with the tip of the hemostat and pull it loose. It is almost impossible to go too deep, and anything that can be grasped is safe to remove. This prevents lumps in the legs or the possibility of the nail growing back. Sometimes the dewclaw breaks off cleanly with the first operation.

Apply silver nitrate to the wound to seal it and stop bleeding. You will find that puppies complain because they're being restrained, but once placed back in their box, they show little evidence of pain. Neurologists assure us that pain does not consciously register in a puppy until five days of age, and by then the area is nearly healed. No further treatment of the area is required.

THE TODDLER

At any time after three weeks of age, the pups should be moved to a larger pen, but they should still have a draft-free bed, especially at night. A pen or large crate is suitable. I like to use either a 4- x 4-foot or a 4- x 8-foot portable exercise pen, depending on the number of puppies and whether the pen will be set up inside or outdoors. If possible, keep your puppies near a traffic area in your home where they will be exposed to all kinds of attention and new sounds and sights. Be sure that the puppies can see out of their enclosure. Those confined to a solid-walled box never develop as desirably in a mental and emotional capacity. I also like to start putting puppies on the table to be brushed at this age, and early leash-breaking can be started as long as it is kept fun.

Expose your puppies to all possible noise and confusion—vacuum cleaners, television, children,

Right: a three-week-old puppy showing a weak head. Note snipey muzzle with dip under eyes and sliding stop.

Bottom: a good, blocky head on a three-week-old puppy.

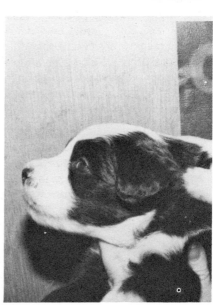

133

washing machines, etc.—but don't deliberately frighten the puppies. Normally, Beardie puppies accept all of these things in stride and adapt easily to any situation. For a puppy that shows tendencies of shyness at this age, a little extra patience and attention can do wonders. Do not snatch him up every time he comes to you or he will begin ducking away. Puppies want to play on their own level and feel insecure if they never have their feet on the ground. This is hard to do, but make a conscious effort to keep your hands off of the pups some of the time.

The Four-Week-Old Puppy

At four weeks, the puppies should be up on their feet and the bodies can therefore be better evaluated. Front legs should be straight by now, and stance should be square all around. The body may appear shorter because the puppy has grown rapidly in height and is not yet balanced. The muzzle should be square, but the head may be a bit longer and leaner overall because it is now lengthening. Watch for the puppy that falls into a trot most of the time when moving. He will probably become your best mover. As eye color changes from baby blue to the adult color, the first eyes to change will be the darkest color. Also, the first pup to open his eyes will have the largest eyes, the last one will have the smallest.

Temperament Testing

Several sophisticated tests can evaluate basic temperament traits in young puppies, but here are a few very simple tests which can easily be done at home and which, if conducted when the puppy is exactly five weeks old, will be fairly accurate. Since most Beardies have good temperaments, testing is not necessary, but it can help match specific puppies to the right homes and help avoid problems caused by the litter "peck order."

Take the pups individually to a place where they have never been, preferably a closed room, and have a stranger to the puppies do the testing. The person should not speak to the puppy throughout the tests.

Set the pup down, leave him, and observe the reaction he gives. Does he sit huddled up? Does he check out his surroundings? Is he suspicious, curious, or observant? This test tells a lot about self-assurance and how the pup will react to a new environment.

Set the puppy at one end of the room and walk to the other. Kneel down and clap your hands. Does the puppy come? Does he ignore you or run the other way? Responsiveness is the key this time.

Hold the puppy on his back on the floor for a minute, still not speaking to him. The dominant puppy will struggle and fight the entire time. The submissive pup will lie quietly and let you pin him. The pup that is sensible and has a nice combination of both traits, making him easier to live with, will fight until he realizes that he's overpowered. He will then become quiet, accepting you as his boss.

134 Quality four-week-old puppies at Orora.

A six-week-old litter at Thaydom. Note good stops and forefaces.

Next, cradle the puppy in your hands with his legs dangling just a couple of inches off the floor. Hold him this way for thirty seconds and see if he struggles. Most pups will lie quietly for a few seconds and then struggle. A very aggressive puppy will throw a tantrum and perhaps try to bite, and a very timid one will remain passive. A puppy that trembles when placed on a table is also likely to be timid.

If one puppy is aggressive to all tests, and another is submissive you may wish to separate pups into two groups or put the leader in with older dogs that will "knock him down a peg." These tests are more accurate than just playing with puppies because pups react differently when on familiar ground with their own people.

Weaning

Puppies should be weaned at five weeks of age if they are normal and healthy. Mine begin eating dry *Science Diet Growth*® or *Lactation*® along with the dam at about three weeks of age and are weaned directly onto the dry food at five weeks. This avoids the digestive upset that accompanies soaked puppy foods and keeps the puppies healthy and sleek without overeating.

The reason why I wean puppies this early is because Beardies are unusually precocious and have such a rapid growth rate. If pups remain on the bitch past the age of five weeks, the dam's condition weakens to the point where it takes several months for her to regain her weight and coat. If the pups are removed at five weeks, the bitch will bounce back in very short order. I take the bitch away for a few days, then let her return to play with the pups and help with their socialization. Check a fecal sample at this age and worm the puppies if necessary. The first DHL shot should be administered at seven weeks of age.

The Beardie goes through emotional development with distinct stages not unlike his physical growth. Weaning time is stressful for the puppies, and the eighth week is a critical period in developing response to people.

A puppy should be friendly and quick to respond to your attention. However, at about three months of age all puppies display what is known as "avoidance behavior." This is nature's way of allowing the puppy to learn to discriminate between friend and foe. He will probably act as though he wants to play but will remain just out of reach or run away if you approach. Ignore him, and he will soon be in your lap. Within a few weeks he will be back to being the friendly, aggressive puppy he once was. Except for these few weeks, he should be self-assured and eager to please.

EVALUATING THE OLDER PUPPY

At eight weeks, the puppy should resemble a miniature adult in structure, head, and proportions. Croup and tail set may still be a bit high, and the coat will be rather wooly and of a more or less uniform length over the body. Beard and feathering will not yet be pronounced. The puppy should have broadened again in skull, and the flatter the skull, the better. Ear set can now be evaluated, and the very small, fly-away ears can

135

Seven-week-old puppy with excellent front and body proportions. Pepperland Rolling Stone, Silverleaf.

be detected if they exist. The bite may be starting to go slightly overshot, or it may still be a scissors bite. Movement can begin to be assessed accurately, and stance and angulation should again be a mirror image of the adult. By this time, eyes should have become their adult color, and nose pigment should be nearly, if not completely, filled in. Most males have both testicles descended by eight weeks, and this is most preferable. Males that do not have both testicles descended should be held back until this condition improves if they are to be sold as show or breeding prospects. The rest of the puppies may go to new homes if they are healthy and vaccinated.

During the next few months, the puppy will go through a tremendous growth period and at times will appear to go off in quality and balance. Most notable is the tendency in nearly half of the puppies to go overshot, sometimes very badly, in bite. This may improve by six or seven months of age but more likely will take until about eleven months to correct completely. Although discon-

certing, most bites improve if they were correct at birth. At about three months of age, the puppy loses his baby teeth. The baby canines must be pulled if they do not loosen as the adult canines appear. Otherwise the bite may develop improperly.

Puppies tend to grow hind end first, making them high in the rear. They then catch up in the front in a seesaw pattern. After a rapid growth spurt, bone will appear more fine and angulation more straight until the balance returns. Pasterns may become a bit weak at three months, but the feet should point forward.

At six months, the puppy will probably be solid, sound moving, and starting to develop a heavy puppy coat. His head should be broad and squared off, his tail carriage more like that of an adult, and his front legs straight. Males without both testicles descended at this age are probably hopeless. Bitches may appear small at this age. Males should be nearly twenty inches at the withers by now unless they have experienced a

Middle left: an excellent head for an eight-week-old pup. Davealex His n' Hers, Davealex.

Middle right: Silverleaf Send In The Clown, *Silverleaf,* at age four months.

Bottom left: Ch. Silverleaf Gifted Artisan, *Artisan,* at age six months

Bottom right: Am. Can. Ch. Shaggylane's Beamin Pride and Joy in puppy coat.

136

set back or are from a slow-growing line. Bites may be correct or overshot.

Between six and eighteen months of age, a Beardie will enter adolescence. This period of confusion and uncertainty usually occurs from seven to eleven months of age. His instincts are becoming stronger, puberty has arrived, yet the dog is still a baby in many ways. The conflict is evident in his behavior, and he may become submissive or wary of strangers. It is best not to stress a dog during this age, and training should be delayed until he outgrows his unsureness. By one year of age, most Beardies have regained their former composure in any situation with no special help from their owners. Some dogs remain in adolescence throughout their second year. Beardies experience no major changes after two years of age and once again become charming extroverts. Formal obedience training is best started after the dog has become an adult emotionally. He can perform the exercises at a younger age but will not be as steady or as happy about doing so. Males have more trouble with adolescence as a rule, and breeding a dog often speeds up his transition to an adult.

At one year, the puppy coat may be starting to shed, substance will have miraculously vanished, and the dog, although of full height, will look more immature and less impressive than he did a few months before. Bite should be correct by now, and longer, harsher hair should be evident over the withers. During the next few months, the dog will look very "intermediate" in development and may shed coat from the front half of the body, leaving the impression that he looks like two dogs sewn together in the middle. Don't despair. Every Beardie goes through this stage and you cannot hurry it.

By two years of age, many dogs will have filled out, and the coat length should be improving. Color, which probably went very light at one year (except in the ones that remained nearly black), will be noticeably darker, and the puppy coat texture should be less evident. Hair will not be growing over the eyes so badly, and beard and feathering should be lengthening. Beardies should be over any adolescent quirks by now, and the dog will be looking more and more like a glamorous adult Beardie. Body may be a bit thin, but bone should be ample.

Beardies mature between three and four years of age, depending on their line, their condition, whether they've been bred, etc. Although your two-year-old probably looked great at home, the mature dog will look ever so much more impressive. The long, harsh, mature coat has changed his overall appearance, and his body is now very solid and well muscled. Coat color may still change slightly from year to year, always growing in from the roots and breaking off at the tips in a constant rainbow of shades. The mature Beardie will hold this quality and look into old age, making the long wait well worth the time and tears shed along the way.

Hair on a puppy's face is often too wooly.   **Ch. Nel-Von's MacDuff O'Silverleaf, Nel-Von, demonstrating lack of coat during the adolescent stage.**   **137**

A puppy grows up. Betse at three months of age.

Betse at eight months of age.

Betse at one year. Note adolescent coat pattern.

Ch. Parcana Silverleaf Betse Ros C.D., *Silverleaf,* maturing nicely at age two years.

16 Bye, Bye Beardie

Selling your Beardie puppies will generally be a rewarding experience as the new owners discover the unique, loving personalities of their new pets. Selling puppies can also be frustrating and sometimes time-consuming. It is not always easy. Some breeders cannot keep up with the demand, while others find themselves with a dozen half-grown Beardies for which there is no market.

The key to Beardie sales is two-fold: 1) having a reputation for top-quality dogs, since there is little market for mediocre pets and 2) advertising properly and educating potential buyers.

HELP THE PUBLIC DISCOVER BEARDIES

The very best publicity is simply to let your Beardies be seen. Take your dogs everywhere—to dog shows, matches, obedience and conformation classes, to the shopping center, to outdoor sports events where dogs are allowed, to the park, or wherever the public will be exposed to your Beardies. Then be prepared to spend a little time answering questions: "What kind of dog is that? A Bearded what? Are you sure it isn't an Old English with a tail? I had a mutt just like that as a kid."

Beardies will sell themselves if given the opportunity. Most successful breeders have found that their best market comes from people who have met and become enchanted with a Beardie and who will reserve a puppy from the next litter even before the bitch is bred. Here, too, lies a key to selling all of your puppies: breed only the number of pups for which you feel sure there is a market. Some of your puppies should always be spoken for, or at least the demand should be evident, before you breed, and you should never breed unless you want a puppy yourself.

Since the breed is new and you are likely to be flooded with questions, it is helpful to have printed information that you can give or mail to persons wanting to know more about the breed. The Bearded Collie Club of America publishes a leaflet explaining the history and chracteristics of Beardies, but you may also want to prepare your own flyer that describes your particular line of dogs. This will save you a great deal of time in writing letters and explaining the breed. You can follow up in more detail once you know that the person is seriously interested in buying a Beardie. Never lower your prices to make a sale. People who are genuinely interested in and will care for the dog will not barter. If they cannot afford the price, they may not be able to care for and promote the dog properly. You can accept payments if you like, but keep prices competitive with those of other breeders. Otherwise, everyone, as well as the breed, suffers.

ADVERTISING

Advertising on a national level is a necessity if you are establishing a kennel and hope to make a name for yourself in the show world. Advertising of this type does not mean advertising a litter of puppies—it means image-building and keeping your name before the public over a period of time. Reputations are not made in a day, and the new breeder should not expect instant acceptance. It takes time—often several years.

Your first ads may simply introduce your kennel name and your foundation Beardies. If you accumulate show wins of any consequence, keep your public informed with follow-up ads. Also, you may "blow your horn" about exciting additions to your kennel or about your Beardies' producing a winner, finishing a championship, or winning an obedience or herding trial. Simply advertising puppies will not generate much interest until you have proof of the quality, intelligence, or ability of the parents and the reliability and experience of your breeding program.

The time that it takes to become nationally recognized in the breed is directly correlated to the amount of advertising done on a national level, the number of times your Beardies win, and, of course, the fact that your dogs are really top-notch. You will want to experiment with various magazines to see which ones give you the best results. Several all-breed magazines have

large readership, and some magazines are devoted exclusively to working breeds or Beardies. Your first ads might include a series of three or four running in consecutive issues, followed by smaller ads every second or third issue over a year's time. We cannot stress enough that you should not expect instant results from the first one or two ads. It takes time, patience, and skillful promotion to build a reputation as a breeder. Once you have achieved this, sales will not be lacking.

Preparing the Ad

Anyone seriously interested in writing good advertisements should read a book on the subject. Your local library probably has several. We will try to cover some of the basics.

1. Be concise. Keep your copy short and to the point.
2. Don't try to cover too much in one ad. Limit your ad to one subject: a win, an introduction, a stud, or a litter.
3. Develop an identity through a logo, slogan, unique typeface, etc.
4. A headline is sixty percent of your ad's effectiveness. Put a lot of effort into a good headline.
5. A photo, if it is a good, honest one, is worth 1,000 words. Use photos whenever possible. If you aren't a good photographer, hire a professional. It will pay off. A poor photo is worse than none at all.
6. Keep ad layouts simple. You can have a layout designed for around ten to twenty-five dollars. Again, professional help may be worthwhile. If the magazine staff does your layout, tell them what you want to emphasize, how large to make the photo, etc.
7. Since most magazines use offset reproduction, you can have your logo from letterhead or cards reproduced for no extra cost. Just furnish a clean black-and-white copy.
8. Use repetition. Repeat your logo. Repeat the qualities that you emphasize in breeding. You may even repeat ads occasionally. Keep your name before your public.
9. Besides the large national magazines, you may want to try farm publications for your working Beardies or the local newspaper for your pets. Experiment with various media.

Stud Promotion

Promotion of a stud dog can take many forms. Some of the most standard methods include general advertising in breed publications, distributing stud cards or kennel brochures, handing out printed business cards, and showing your dog. Be sure to always present a stud dog well groomed and in attractive, healthy condition. You may wish to consider hiring a professional handler to gain exposure for the dog in the show ring over a wider geographical area. Much of your dog's impressiveness can come from your own enthusiasm for him, but keep your presentation honest and within proper limits.

When advertising your dog, again remember that repetition is important. People need to know that you'll be around for more than a month, and your ad has to be current when they start looking for a stud. Repeat the same two or three points that you wish to stress in each ad and use a *good* photo. Vary the photo every few ads, but never run a poor shot of the dog. If you do, it is the only one that people will remember.

As with general ads, do not clutter your copy with too many words or ideas. Choose a simple theme and leave plenty of white space. Feature the dog's name prominently and stress a few of his special assets. New wins or titles can be listed, along with your name, address, and telephone number plus stud fee, if you wish. Tell just enough to make the people contact you for more information. Pride in your dog will show without gushy superlatives.

Keep in Touch With Other Breeders

Most breeders find that a good many of their puppy sales come from referrals from customers or from other breeders. You can do your fellow breeder a favor by keeping in touch and referring buyers to them when you don't have a Beardie for sale. They will do the same for you. Pet buyers often buy spontaneously and may not wait for your next litter. Find them a good puppy while they are looking, or they may end up with another breed or with a Beardie from an undesirable source.

The best and easiest sales of all come when acquaintances or friends of a previous customer come to visit. Each satisfied customer who has purchased a healthy, correctly dispositioned, honestly represented Beardie from you has the potential of bringing you many more sales. Each dissatisfied buyer who feels that his dog was misrepresented, overpriced, or impossible to live with because of a bad disposition can do you irreparable harm. Always keep this in mind when selling your puppies.

PREPARING YOUR PUPPIES FOR SALE

Proper preparation can make or break sales and may be a large factor in the satisfaction of the buyer. Beardie puppies are ready to go to new homes at the age of eight weeks. Before they leave, they should have had their first DHL shot, should be eating solid food well, and should have been weaned for at least two, and preferably three, weeks. The immunity will not be as effective if the puppy has not been weaned for this length of time before receiving his vaccination.

To help the new owner get off to a good start, most breeders like to send them home with a packet of helpful aids. This packet should, of course, include the puppy's registration form, pedigree, and sales contract stating terms of the purchase and guarantee. But you will also want to include worming and vaccination records and instructions for the puppy's care and training. (We highly recommend that you include a copy of this book or other source of breed information. You can increase the price of your puppy enough to cover the cost and do the buyer a big favor.) Perhaps you can also include a small bag of food that the puppy is used to eating and some rawhide chew chips to keep him occupied the first night in his new home.

The puppies should be bathed, groomed, and have their nails trimmed. Each may have a small collar and should have had a lesson or two in leash training. Check each puppy to make sure that he is healthy and eating properly. If any problem exists, wait until it is solved before you let the puppy go.

MAKING THE SALE

Your first contact with a buyer is usually by telephone. You should not try to sell a dog immediately; instead, sell the buyer on coming to look. Sales are generally not made until the buyer walks through your door.

Always get the potential buyer's name and phone number so that you can follow up if necessary. Ask for specific information about the buyer's wants and needs and determine whether you have a dog that might be suitable. If not, refer him elsewhere.

If you have a Beardie that might be suitable, move immediately into a conversation about when the buyer can come and look. Tell him just enough to entice him, but explain that seeing the puppy is the only way to make an intelligent choice. Offer to show your adult dogs and tell the buyer more about the breed. Let him know that you have plenty to offer besides a puppy.

If the inquiry comes by mail, you will need to approach the situation a little differently. If you have several puppies available, your first letter should give a little information about each one to test the buyer's interest. You may send a pedigree and photos of the puppies, the parents, or both. Later letters, narrowing down the sale to one possible individual, should be as detailed, explicit, and honest as you can make them. Point out the pup's virtues, and quickly, but thoroughly, go over the faults. Do be honest about the Beardie. Shipping is both costly and risky, and your reputation depends upon your reliability.

Presenting the Dog

You have made an appointment for the potential buyer to visit, and the puppy is ready. Now, much depends on the quality of your stock and on your ability as a salesperson.

I like to bring buyers into my office where trophies, ribbons, and photos are displayed. Let them relax a bit as you get acquainted and find out in more detail what they want. No dogs are allowed to be present at this point except for one friendly, attractive, well-mannered adult.

142

I like to think that every good breeder screens his buyers. There are some people to whom I simply would not sell a dog. Certain people are not suited to a Beardie's temperament, while others do not have suitable quarters in which to keep a large, active dog. I try to determine these factors in that initial face-to-face conversation. Sometimes your common sense and intuition have to be your guide, but you can learn much by asking questions about the person's experience with dogs, his facilities, his awareness of the expense of keeping a dog, and his attitude toward neutering a pet. If you are dealing by long distance, your insight may not be as clear, but be sure to talk long enough to establish as many answers as possible. Be absolutely certain that the person has a fenced yard, and refuse to sell a puppy to anyone who does not. That dog would likely end up lost or dead in a few weeks, and your conscience would always be troubled by it.

When the discussion ends, I bring in one puppy at a time. I generally do not take buyers into the kennel unless they are breeders or have some particular reason that makes it necessary. It is a good health precaution to limit the visitors, especially to your puppy room, because these people have probably been shopping at other kennels and may be spreading disease or colds. Also, pet buyers can be quite turned off by seeing too many dogs at once, particularly in a kennel situation.

If the buyer wants to see the mother or father, if available, I bring the dogs in one at a time. Several adult Beardies competing for attention can overpower a visitor. It is sometimes helpful to show the buyer an adult Beardie of the same color and type that the puppy is expected to be as an adult. Give the buyer all the time that he needs in looking over the pup, playing with it, and getting acquainted. Sales cannot be rushed. Beardies will sell themselves to the right people, so there's no need for high pressure. Sometimes it will be evident that a particular puppy and

A litter at Nigella

person are just not suited for one another. If this happens, remove that puppy quickly and bring in another if you have one. If you feel that the people are not suited for your dogs, tactfully explain that a personality conflict would make neither the buyer nor the puppy happy. Recommend a different breed or kennel that you feel would be suitable for their consideration.

Closing the Sale

Once you see the buyer starting to make up his mind, reassure him that he has made a good choice. Point out all the positive aspects of this Beardie, but also briefly mention his faults. Ask for a commitment from the buyer. "Shall I brush him up for you?" "Do you want to take him now or pick him up later?"

SALES CONTRACT FOR BREEDING OR SHOW DOGS

_____ Kennels agrees to sell the following_____
                                                                                    breed

                                                                       phone _____
to _____
                                name

of _____
                address

for the sum of $ _____ .

Registration Number _____   Sex _____

Name _____   Color_____

Sire _____   Date whelped _____

Dam _____

This animal is guaranteed as follows:

☐ To be free of show disqualifying and serious faults except those due to injury or neglect after sale.

☐ To be fertile, and to be free of all hereditary defects affecting its suitability for breeding.

☐ To be healthy and of sound temperament for the first forty-eight hours after date of sale. It is recommended that the buyer have the animal examined by a reputable veterinarian during this time period.

☐ Terms of replacement shall be as follows: A full refund will be given for any dog returned in good condition during the first two days. Credit for the amount of purchase less $ _____ (pet price) will be given for any dog that matures at less than the represented quality at twelve months of age, provided the original dog has not produced a litter and is immediately neutered. (Replacement may be given provided the dog is returned to the seller in good condition, under certain circumstances.) A free replacement will be given for any dog which, for hereditary reasons, is unsuitable as a pet as determined by the seller up to three years from date of sale.

The buyer agrees:

☐ To use the kennel name _____in the registered name of the dog if it has not been individually registered at the time of sale.

☐ In the event that the dog is later sold, the seller will have first chance to repurchase it.

☐ No puppies produced by this dog or bitch will be sold to pet shops or other wholesale outlets at any time.

Papers:

☐ Are supplied with this contract or will be forwarded upon receipt from AKC.

☐ Will be signed over to the buyer upon fulfillment of the following terms:

Special Provisions of Sale:

Date _____

Signed: _____
                                Buyer

Signed: _____
                                Seller

Address _____   Phone _____

Witnessed by: _____

143

Never reserve or hold a puppy without a nonrefundable deposit, usually about one-fourth the purchase price. You may find yourself missing other sales while the first buyer fails to pay for and pick up the dog.

Make out the papers, explaining the registration form and how to fill it out. Cover the contract in detail, making sure that every aspect is clearly understood (see samples). Adjust the contract to suit each individual sale. Terms for time payments, if used, should be spelled out in writing, and the contract should be signed by buyer, seller, and a witness. Whenever the contract calls for time payments, puppies back, or neutering of a pet when it is old enough, the registration papers are customarily held by the seller until all terms of the contract have been fulfilled. The buyer gets the original contract; the seller keeps a copy. Receipts should be issued for all payments. If there is any doubt about the validity of a check, the seller may ask for identification and may hold the papers and contract until the check has cleared. Many breeders have found it safest to ask for cash or certified checks.

Provisions for neutering pets should be spelled out very carefully. Written confirmation of the neutering by a veterinarian should be required before papers are released. The blue litter registration should bear the inscription, "This dog will not be bred" and initialed by both buyer and seller. AKC will not register litters from that particular dog as long as he is owned by the original purchaser.

FOLLOW-UP

Follow-up is so important. It lets you know if your dogs are in good homes, if the buyer is satisfied, and if the temperament and quality of the dog turned out as you had predicted. Sometimes, follow-up helps you learn from your mistakes— you thought that a puppy was better than it was, a pet turned into a lovely show animal that will

---

SALES CONTRACT FOR PET PUPPIES

_____ Kennels agrees to sell the following

to _____
_____ breed _____   name

of _____ phone _____

on_____ 19 ____ , for the sum of $ _____ .

Registration Number _____ Sex _____

Color _____ Whelped _____

144 Sire _____ Dam _____

Terms: ☐ Cash   ☐ Check   ☐ Time payments   Other _____

Registration papers: ☐ Supplied with contract
☐ Will be transferred upon their receipt from AKC
☐ Will be transferred when proof of neutering is supplied in the form of a veterinary certificate

Guarantee:
It is understood that at the time of sale this dog is not considered to be of show or breeding quality, but is representative of its breed and structurally and temperamentally suited as a companion and/or obedience dog. This dog is guaranteed for forty-eight hours against any health or temperament irregularities, and it is recommended that the buyer have the puppy examined by a veterinarian during this time period. A full refund will be given for any pup found unsatisfactory during the first forty-eight hours.

No other guarantee is given except in the case of a hereditary defect which develops to the extent that it renders the dog unsuitable as a pet within three years from the date of sale. In this instance, a replacement will be given as soon as one becomes available.

The buyer agrees that this dog will not be bred and neutering will be performed before the dog is one year of age.

Special provisions:

Signed: _____
                                         buyer
Signed: _____
                                        witness
Signed: _____
                                         seller
Address: _____

_____

never be shown, or a hereditary or temperament defect crept in where you least expected. You owe it to yourself and to your buyer to discover these things. It will be invaluable in planning future breedings and evaluating related puppies.

Your buyer may need assistance from time to time, and it is part of your responsibility as a breeder to provide this or guide him to another source. Many friendships, proteges, and new breeders develop from continued relationships between breeder and purchaser. Respect your buyers' right to their own opinions, however. My most rewarding experiences in the dog game have been seeing a rank beginner buy a promising puppy, learn from my advice and his own initiative, and take the dog to show or obedience victories. He may even establish a successful breeding program based on stock that I have bred and sold.

Ch. Jande Just Justin.

Right: Davealex puppies at home.

Bottom left: An Artisan puppy.

Bottom right: Hyfield Hyteeny (right), and daughter, Harrold.

145

Wishbone of Tambora, *Matthews*.

17 *Showing Off*

The elite of their breeds, groomed to perfection, trot through crowded aisles. A flurry of brushes, dryers, and people's voices all blend into one continuous rumble, topped occasionally by the roar of the crowd cheering on a favorite competitor. The air is filled with excitement and anticipation. There's no doubt about it—the atmosphere of a dog show is contagious! Many new owners purchase a purebred dog with no intention of showing until, out of curiosity, they enter their first show. From that point on, the competition, fun, and excitement continue to grow.

Dog showing originated many years ago in England, probably for the same reasons that we continue this pastime today. It gives the breeder a chance to prove the quality of his breeding stock, it provides social advantages by bringing together breeders from many areas of the country to discuss and compare, and, for the novice, it presents the ideal opportunity to learn about the breeds. Today, almost every major country in the world has a national kennel club responsible for the registration and record keeping of all recognized purebred dogs. The kennel club approves shows, licenses judges, and offers obedience degrees and championship certificates to outstanding canines. Each country has a different system for tabulating these awards. The prizes are based on a point system determined by the scores in various obedience exercises or by the number of dogs over which an individual wins in conformation.

All dog shows in the United States are held under the rules of the American Kennel Club, which has responsibility for licensing judges and superintendents and for keeping records of the points awarded at each show. The show is sponsored by a local all-breed club or by a specialty club whose members are fanciers of a particular breed. The management of the show may be handled by the members of the club or by professional show superintendents who supply the necessary equipment and are responsible for all arrangements.

HOW DOG SHOWS ARE ORGANIZED

Shows may be all-breed conformation only, all-breed obedience only, all-breed conformation and obedience combined, or "specialty" shows limited to one or a few related breeds. Most American shows are unbenched, meaning that the dogs may be brought to the show grounds just before their class and may leave immediately after showing. Larger American and most European shows are "benched." All dogs must remain in assigned benches (stalls) for all or for a specified part of the day on which they show, except, of course, for the time that they are in the ring. Benched shows provide spectators a chance to view the dogs close up before and after judging.

Each breed is judged against the Standard of perfection for that breed. There are a minimum of five regular classes: Puppy, Novice, Bred-by-Exhibitor, American-Bred, and Open. All of the males compete first in the five classes, after which a "Winners Dog" and a "Reserve Winners Dog" are chosen. These are the best of all males entered that day. Then, all bitches compete in a similar manner, and the top two bitches are selected. The "Winners Dog" and "Winners Bitch" must then compete with both male and female champions for the "Best of Breed" award. This is the win that everyone hopes for! A "Best of Opposite Sex" is then chosen, as well as the "Best of Winners." If a male receives the "Best of Breed" award, a female must be chosen for "Best of Opposite." She may be a champion, or she may be the "Winners Bitch." If one of the "Winners" is appointed "Best of Breed," that dog automatically takes "Best of Winners" as well.

Championship points are awarded to both "Winners Dog" and "Winners Bitch," but only the "Best of Breed" goes on to compete for "Best in Group" and then, possibly, "Best in Show" (*see chart*).

The Classes

Classes are divided by sex and are judged in a sequence from puppy to open.

Puppy—Puppies must be at least six months of age to be entered at a point show. At large shows the entry will be split into two groups—six to nine months, and nine to twelve months. Puppies may also be entered in any of the adult classes, but only a particularly mature Beardie will be able to compete successfully with adults.

Novice—A class for dogs that have won less than three blue ribbons and have won no points at licensed shows. This is a good class for a beginning handler, an unproven dog, or a "teenage" Beardie not yet ready for adult competition.

American-Bred—This class is open to any Beardie of any age bred in the United States. Amateur handlers may prefer this class because it is generally smaller. A dog that is not in peak condition will look better here.

Bred-By-Exhibitor—Any dog owned or co-owned and handled by his breeder can be entered in this class. Competition may be stiff, but numbers will be small. It is a class for which any breeder should be proud to qualify.

Open—A class for mature dogs and bitches in peak condition. *It is the only class in which an imported Beardie can be shown.*

Best of Breed—A class in which only champions may be entered. These dogs compete with the best male and best female chosen from the regular classes.

Non-Regular Classes—These are separately listed classes offered primarily at specialty shows. Included are brace, team, veterans, brood bitch, and stud dog classes. Classes for dogs from a particular area or club may also be offered.

Futurities—Classes offered at some specialty shows for puppies that were nominated before birth. Entry fees are generally divided into cash prizes for the winners.

The Groups

The dog chosen Best of Breed in each breed in a particular group go into the ring at the end of the breed judging to compete for group placements one through four. There are seven groups: Sporting, Hound, Working, Herding, Terrier, Toy, and Non-Sporting. The Bearded Collie is a member of the herding group, which also includes Australian Cattle Dogs, Bearded Collies, Belgian Malinois, Belgian Sheepdogs, Belgian Tervuren, Bouvier Des Flanders, Briards, Collies, Old English Sheepdog, Puli, and Cardigan and Pembroke Welsh Corgis.

New breeds are added as they are accepted by AKC. There is also a Miscellaneous Class at AKC shows, but these dogs do not compete for points, Group, or Best in Show. The Miscellaneous Class provides a class for exhibitors of rare breeds which have applied for AKC recognition but have not yet been granted full AKC status.

Best in Show

The winners of each of the six groups compete at the end of the day for the coveted "Best in Show" award. Beardies have proven that they are contenders for this award. In their first year of showing, two Beardies have already taken "Best in Show" honors (*see* Ch. 1).

Acquiring a Championship

Only two Bearded Collies will take points toward a championship at any one show. They are the "Winners Dog" and "Winners Bitch." The number of points awarded can range from zero to five and is determined by the number of Beardies of each sex that are entered on a given day. A different number of Beardies must be entered on the east coast as opposed to the west coast to make a three-point show because the country is divided into several regions, and the number of dogs needed to make a "major" in any one breed is tabulated on the basis of the number of that breed shown in a given region. These numbers are revised yearly by AKC.

In order for a dog of any breed to become a champion in the United States, he must win a total of fifteen points. Two of these wins must be majors (three to five points awarded at a single show), and the majors must be won under two different judges. A dog that wins fifteen points without any majors will not be awarded a championship, and continuing to show at nonmajor shows if points are not needed is generally considered unsportsmanlike.

As a general rule, it takes more bitches entered to make, for instance, a three-point win than it does males, because more females are being exhibited. If the show offers two points in males and three points in bitches and the male takes "Best of Winners," he will take three points instead of his two. In other words, the "Best of Winners" always takes the higher number of points.

How a dog show progresses.

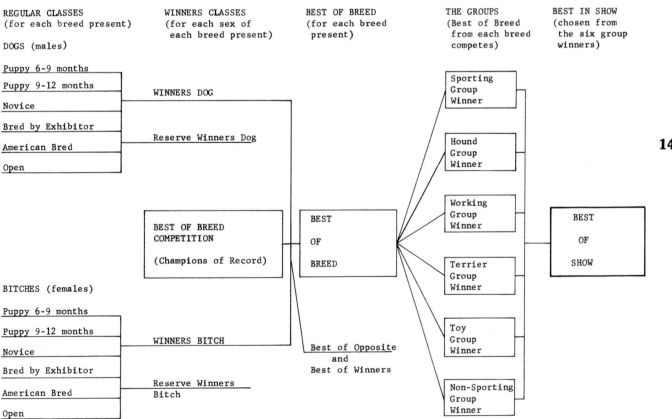

149

Obedience Trials

In conformation classes, the dogs are judged on looks and personality, and the judging is somewhat subjective due to personal opinion and individual interpretation of the Standard. In obedience trials, however, the dogs are judged solely on performance. Showing is more relaxed and fun for some people, and there is a definite sense of accomplishment from having trained a winner.

Any dog registered with AKC or possessing an ILP number (a number assigned to dogs that are obviously purebred but cannot be registered) may compete. Each class has specified exercises which are assigned points totaling a possible 200. To qualify, a dog must score a minimum of 170 points and at least fifty percent in each exercise. Each "qualifying" score is called a "leg," and when a dog has three legs won under three different judges, he is awarded an obedience degree for that level. There are three levels, varying in degree of difficulty. The Companion Dog (C.D.) degree is awarded to dogs competing in the Novice Class. A Companion Dog Excellent (C.D.X.) is awarded for completion of the Open Class legs, and a Utility Dog (U.D.) degree is given for three legs in Utility classes. Matches often offer two additional classes: Sub-Novice for dogs not ready to work off-leash as in Novice, and Graduate Novice for dogs training for the Open Class.

Novice Class—This class is divided into section "A" for dogs with owners who have never

150

The broad jump exercise.

handled a dog at an obedience trial, and "B" for professional handlers or anyone who has previously shown in obedience. The Novice exercises and scores awarded for correct completion are:

Heel on Leash	40 points
Stand for Examination	30 points
Heel Free	40 points
Recall	30 points
Long Sit	30 points
Long Down	30 points
	200 points

When a dog has received confirmation of his C.D. degree, he can no longer compete in Novice obedience classes.

Open Class—This class is also divided into sections "A" and "B," but this time "A" division is for all dogs that are owner handled and that have a C.D. but not a C.D.X. degree. Dogs that have three qualifying scores in the class may continue to compete in section "B" along with dogs shown by professional trainers or handlers. Exercises are as follows:

Heel Free (off leash)	40 points
Drop on Recall	30 points
Retrieve on Flat	20 points
Retrieve over High Jump	30 points
Broad Jump	20 points
Long Sit	30 points
Long Down	30 points
	200 points

Utility—This most advanced class is open to any dog that has a C.D.X. degree. Exercises include a signal exercise in which the dog performs a series of heeling maneuvers and other movements in response to hand signals with no verbal commands; a scent discrimination exercise in which the dog selects his handler's article from among many identical articles by scent alone; a directed retrieve in which the dog is signaled to pick up one of three gloves; a directed jumping exercise; and a group stand for examination. Utility dogs may continue to compete in both Open and Utility classes after they have qualified for the U.D. degree.

For more complete information on rules and regulations, write to the AKC for the free pamphlet, "Rules Applying to Obedience Trials."

Advanced Titles

In addition to the three basic degrees, the AKC offers a Tracking Dog degree (T.D.), Tracking Dog Excellent (T.D.X.), and an Obedience Trial Championship (O.T.Ch.).

While a dog must earn the C.D., C.D.X., and U.D. titles in sequence, he may compete for the Tracking Dog title at any stage of training. A dog trained in tracking may be useful in locating lost or missing people, lost objects or strayed livestock. He may also compete in AKC approved tracking tests.

The ultimate achievement for the obedience dog is the O.T.Ch., which is acquired by earning 100 points in obedience competition as determined by the chart below. The dog must already have his Utility degree. The dog must win at least three first places, one in Utility, one in Open B, and the third in either class. A dog may continue to compete in Open or Utility even after he has earned his Obedience Championship, but no further titles are available.

Obedience Championship Points

No. Dogs Competing	Open B Class Points for 1st Place	Points for 2nd Place
6-10	2	0
11-15	4	1
16-20	6	2
21-25	10	3
26-30	14	4
31-35	18	5
36-40	22	7
41-45	26	9
46-50	30	11
51-56	34	13

	Utility Class	
3-5	2	0
6-9	4	1
10-14	6	2
15-19	10	3
20-24	14	4
25-29	18	5
30-34	22	7
35-39	26	9
40-44	30	11
45-48	34	13

Some Beardies do it all! Ch. Windcache A Briery Bess O.T.Ch. is shown performing utility jumps and winning in the breed ring.

151

Junior Showmanship Competition

Junior showmanship classes are judged according to the handler's presentation, rather than the quality of the dog. Classes are: Novice Junior for boys and girls at least ten and under thirteen years of age who at the time entries close have not won three first places in a Novice class at a licensed show; Novice Senior for youths thirteen to seventeen years of age who have not won three first places in a Novice class; Open Junior for youths ten to thirteen years of age who have won three or more first places in Novice; and Open Senior for youths thirteen to seventeen years of age who have won three first places in a Novice class.

MATCH COMPETITION

Before a club is licensed to hold a point show, it must earn the privilege by holding several "matches." These matches are strictly for fun. They give both the exhibitors and the show committee a chance to practice. There are several types of matches. "Fun" matches do not meet AKC requirements and may be held by any club, including those not recognized by the AKC (such as small new clubs, 4-H groups, or humane societies). These matches often include classes such as best-dressed dog, team obedience events, and classes for puppies as young as eight weeks of age.

"B" matches are the beginning level contests approved by the AKC. Pre-entry is not always required, but the show is organized in the same manner as a licensed show. A three- to six-month-old puppy class may be allowed. An "A" match is run in the same way as a regular show, complete with pre-entry and even a catalog listing all competitors. Only standard regular and non-regular classes are allowed.

No championship points are awarded at any match, and champions may not compete.

Glen Eire's Charlie Brown with junior handler Jennifer Babineaux.

ENTERING A SHOW

You can learn about shows in your area by contacting a local kennel club or professional handler or trainer. You may also consult the list of upcoming shows published each month in *Purebred Dogs, The AKC Gazette* (see "Other Sources"). In order to enter an AKC licensed show, you must fill out an official entry form. Copies are not acceptable unless they also have the rules copied on the back of the form. Entry forms are obtained from the show superintendent, or blank forms may be obtained by writing the AKC office. After you have entered a few shows, you will be placed on that superintendent's mailing list for the following year. Addresses of some of the more popular superintendents include:

- Jack Bradshaw, P.O. Box 7303
  Los Angeles, CA 90022
- Norman E. Brown, P.O. Box 2566,
  Spokane, WA 99220

- Thomas Crowe, P.O. Box 22107
  Greensboro, NC 27420
- Ace H. Mathews, P.O. Box 06150,
  Portland, OR 97206
- Jack Onofrio, P.O. Box 25764,
  Oklahoma City, OK 73125
- Mrs. Dorothy Sweet, 2321 Blanco Rd.
  San Antonio, TX 78212

Show entries generally close two and one-half to three weeks prior to the show date, so send your entry in early. Entry forms must be completely and accurately filled out and accompanied by the entry fee (see sample form below).

SHOWS IN ENGLAND

English shows are very much like those in the United States, but the terminology and the point system are quite different. "Exemption" shows are practice events similar to our matches except that entries are small and dogs of different breeds compete together. One international judge must be among the judging staff.

"Limit" shows are those especially for the young and unproven dogs that have a limited number of wins to their credit. Wins do not count toward a championship. "Open" shows are for all breeds and are similar to championship shows except that no challenge certificates are awarded. However, these shows are considered prestigious because top-notch competition is judged by respected, knowledgeable judges.

"Championship" shows are the equivalent of our "licensed" or "point" shows. However, not every breed will be awarded a challenge certificate at every show. The Kennel Club allots only a specified number of challenge certificates to each breed each year, and these are parceled out among the various shows. As a breed becomes more popular, more challenge certificates are issued.

In order to win a championship in England, a dog must earn three challenge certificates, or "tickets," under three different judges. In a country as small as England, this is a difficult task; therefore, a championship means a great deal. Once a dog is "made up," or "finished," as we say when a dog becomes a champion, the dog can still continue to enter in the Open Dog or Open Bitch classes at championship shows and must be defeated before another Beardie can earn a C.C. There is no separate class for champions or "Best of Breed."

OFFICIAL AMERICAN KENNEL CLUB ENTRY FORM

ALL-BREED DOG SHOW AND OBEDIENCE TRIAL
ELECTRIC CITY KENNEL CLUB
SATURDAY, JUNE 24, 1978
North Montana State Fairgrounds - Great Falls, Montana

ENTRY FEES: First Entry of Each Dog (Except Puppy) $10.00; Puppy Class Only $5.00; Obedience Only $10.00; Junior Showmanship Only $5.00 (includes 25¢ A.K.C. Recording Fee). Obedience, or Junior Showmanship as an additional class $5.00.
ENTRIES CLOSE: 12 Noon, Wednesday, May 31, 1978 at the office of the Show Superintendent.
MAKE CHECKS AND MONEY ORDERS PAYABLE TO: COAST DOG SHOWS.
MAIL ENTRIES, WITH FEES TO: Dorothy G. Sweet, Show Superintendent, Coast Dog Shows. P.O. Box 429, 106 W. Hawthorne St., Fallbrook, CA 92028

I enclose $ 15 for entry fees.
IMPORTANT — Read Carefully Instructions on Reverse Side Before Filling Out.
PLEASE — TYPE OR PRINT PLAINLY ALL INFORMATION ON THIS ENTRY FORM.

| Breed: Bearded Collie | Variety: See Instruction No 1 - reverse side (if any) | | Sex Female |

| Dog Show Class Open Bitch | See Instruction No 2 - reverse side (Give age, color or weight if class divided) | Obedience Trial Class Open A |

If dog is entered for Best of Breed (Variety) Competition — See Instruction No 3, reverse side — CHECK THIS BOX | Additional Classes

If entry of dog is to be made in Junior Showmanship as well as in one of the above competitions, check this box, and fill in data on reverse side. | If for Junior Showmanship only, then check THIS box, and fill in data on reverse side.

Name (See Instruction No 4, reverse side) Actual Owner(s) Dawn G. and Barbara H. Rieseberg

Name of Licensed Handler (if any) [ ] Handler ●

Full Name of Dog: Parcana Silverleaf Betse Ros C.D. ●

| Insert one of the following: | Date of Birth 3-9-76 | Place of Birth ☐ USA ☐ Canada ☐ Foreign |
A.K.C. Reg. No. WD-440074 | | Do not print the above in catalog
A.K.C. Litter No. | | Breeder Mrs. R. S. Parker ●
I.L.P. No. | |
Foreign Reg. No. & Country | |

Sire Ch. Parcana Silverleaf Vandyke —

Dam Ch. Edenborough Parcana ●

Owner's Name Dawn G. & Barbara H. Rieseberg Phone No. 449-5442

Owner's Address 11316 Flatiron Drive

City Lafayette State Colo. Zip Code 80026

I CERTIFY that I am the actual owner of this dog, or that I am the duly authorized agent of the actual owner whose name I have entered above. In consideration of the acceptance of this entry, I (we) agree to abide by the rules and regulations of The American Kennel Club in effect at the time of this show or obedience trial and by any additional rules and regulations appearing in the premium list for this show or obedience trial and further agree to be bound by the "Agreement" printed on the reverse side of this entry form. I (we) certify and represent that the dog entered is not a hazard to persons or other dogs. This entry is submitted for acceptance on the foregoing representation and agreement.

SIGNATURE of owner or his agent duly authorized to make this entry. *Dawn Rieseberg*

A completed entry form.

153

SHOWING YOUR BEARDIE

You and your Beardie will have plenty to do in preparing for your first show. Winning may be fun, but it also requires hard work and discipline. Become familiar with the ring patterns and methods of handling, and work, work, work. Your Beardie should be well trained (*see* Ch. 18) and working smoothly on leash before you even consider entering a show.

But that day will come, and you will find yourself packing up for the first show-bound trip. You will need a kit of basic grooming tools (*see* Ch. 6), show leads, and a crate or exercise pen in which to confine your dog while you are waiting to enter the ring. A folding grooming table will make preshow preparations easier, but it is not a necessity. You will need, however, a grooming smock or coat to protect your clothing from dog hair, a supply of towels, and a damp washcloth. If it is to be an all-day affair, include some newspapers for the exercise pen, a bottle of drinking water, and a water bowl for the dogs.

Your own apparel is always a consideration. Most shows today are reasonably casual, but you will want to look neat. Select clothing that will not interfere with your own or your Beardie's movement and that will not show hair easily. Men usually choose slacks and either a sport shirt or sport jacket with tie, while women wear culottes, dresses, or pantsuits.

The show superintendent will mail confirmation of your entry several days prior to the show. Included in this form, which allows you admittance to the show grounds, will be a schedule telling the time and the ring number at which each breed will be judged. Following the breed listing will be three numbers representing, in this order, the number of dogs, bitches, and champions entered at this show.

Most exhibitors like to arrive at the show grounds at least an hour before their breed is scheduled for judging. This allows the dogs and their handlers to become familiar with the surroundings and to relax. After your last-minute grooming is finished, take advantage of any waiting time by going to your ring to watch the judge in action. Each judge works a little differently, so it helps to familiarize yourself with his or her favorite patterns, hand signals, and commands. You will be less confused and less likely to make a mistake when your turn to show arrives.

Get to the ringside as early as possible when your class is scheduled. No matter how well trained a Beardie may be at home, he will probably go absolutely bananas the first time he sees another Beardie. The love and excitement that these animals have for one another is totally amazing, so let them get their greeting capers over with outside of the show ring.

The dogs will enter the ring circling counterclockwise at a trot. Usually, they will be asked to continue around the ring until the judge signals for all handlers to halt, but some judges will prefer that you walk into the ring and stand in a lineup before moving. If you are a novice, try to allow a few experienced handlers in front of you and follow their lead. However, at some shows you will not have a choice, as you will be asked to enter the ring in the order of your armband numbers. The handler at the front of the lineup must be especially alert to the judge's commands.

All of the dogs may first be gaited simultaneously and then examined or gaited individually, or the individual examinations may be performed first, followed by group gaiting. Watch your dog as much as possible, not the judge, but always be aware of the judge's location and be attentive to his commands. Some judges, having large numbers of dogs to see in a day's time, get impatient if they have to repeat or explain instructions.

Good sportsmanship in the ring is the only other thing required of you. Show common courtesy to the judge and to the other exhibitors. Don't crowd or distract another handler's dog; treat co-exhibitors, as well as the judge, with respect; and don't make excuses if your dog is not up to par.

Handling in the Ring

Most judges prefer that any working breed, Beardies included, be shown on a loose lead and walked into a natural stance without stacking (placing the feet and holding the head). If you are handling a young or unsteady dog, you may want to place his feet and hold him a little more firmly than you would a more experienced Beardie. In England, it seems to be common practice to stack a Beardie and hold him in position, but we much prefer the more natural method that is commonly used in the United States. Temperament is more easily evaluated this way.

It is difficult for a judge to evaluate a dog that is moving in a jerky manner or that is weaving rather than moving at a steady tempo in a straight line. Be aware of your dog's best trotting speed and try to move him accordingly. If

Handlers set up their dogs for the judge to view.

Left: Bobbie Brie, *Sutter*, gaiting individually.

Right: individual examination by the judge.

Bottom: group gaiting at the Windsor show, England.

155

your dog breaks stride or begins to play in the ring, it is acceptable to stop him and repeat the part of the pattern that he performed badly. When coming back to the judge, be sure that the Beardie, not you, is directly in front of the judge. Slow your dog gradually to a halt about six feet away from the judge. He will want to see front stance and expression at this point. If mats are narrow, make certain that the dog is the one gaiting on them.

Four standard patterns are used for individual gaiting, and you should learn and practice all of them. The judge may call for you to move straight down and back (fig. a), in an "L" pattern (fig. b), in a triangle (fig. c), or in a "T" pattern (fig. d).

Your Beardie may be a perfect angel in the ring, but please don't count on it. Most Beardies love shows, and they like to have more fun by making a game of the situation. Don't be surprised if your "super dog" decides to eat the judge's carnation, pretends that he has never worn a leash, or rolls over to "play dead." Derek Stopforth, Davealex Beardies, recently wrote of a

Most judges will use one of these standard gaiting patterns when evaluating individual dogs.

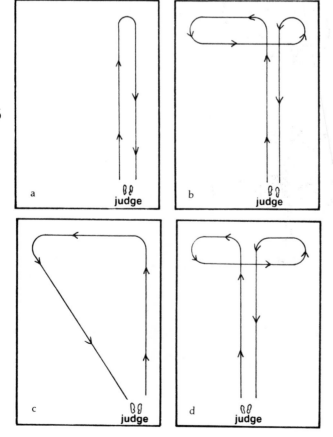

typical experience which he had with his first Beardie, Eng. Ch. Davealex Blaze Away at Osmart, "Charlie."

> "At his second show at just over six months, he (Charlie) decided to act up a bit, as puppies do. He wasn't too bad whilst the judge was examining the other dogs, but when it came to his turn, he decided he liked the judge so instead of standing, he rolled over on his back and put four paws in the air and invited the judge to tickle his tummy."

Nevertheless, Charlie (according to his owner) was one of the greatest showmen seen in the Beardie ring, and he enjoyed every minute of it.

Jenny Osborne also tells of moments when she would have liked to simply disappear into the ground. Her bitch, Eng. Ch. Blue Bonnie of Bothkennar, pulled some famous ring pranks. So, hold your head up and simply be proud that you own a breed with "character." You'll both enjoy the experience of showing much more than if you expect perfection!

Judges

Most judges are volunteers who may give up an entire weekend for nothing more than their transportation and lodging and the chance to be of service. They are generally on their feet all day, often in very uncomfortable environments. A considerate exhibitor, therefore, does everything he can to make the judge's work as easy and as smooth as possible.

Some judges are "all-rounders," licensed to judge all of the registered breeds, while others are licensed for only a few breeds. Some judges are themselves Beardie breeders. On the whole, they are knowledgeable, honest, and objective; but, being human, they may also at times put undue emphasis on one particularly favored trait or pet peeve, play politics, or behave discourteously. A sharp exhibitor observes as many Beardie judges as possible to determine their preferences and styles of judging. But even with a wide knowledge of individual preferences, it is trite to believe that you must win every time. There will be days when the competition is much different from the previous day, and the dog that has had a long winning streak may not even place. Other times, either you or your Beardie may simply not be mentally or physically "up."

Before you make rash judgements about the way in which a class was placed, remember that there are many small details that only the judge can know—bite, testicles, structural defects, and expression may not be visible to another exhibitor, much less from ringside. Also consider that while as a breeder you may see problems with the way in which a dog will develop, or potentials that *will* exist but are not there today, the judge cannot consider these. He must judge the dogs as he sees them at this time.

Finishing a Champion

Finishing a champion often requires three elements: patience, perseverance, and money. While some Beardies finish speedily with three five-point majors, others will need to be shown twenty times or more. This varies depending on the quality of the individual, the competition, the preferences and experience of the judges, and the number of points offered at each show. Entry fees at the time that this book is being written average about ten dollars per show, but like everything else, costs of showing continue to rise. Add these fees to the travel, lodging, and equipment required, and you will rapidly see the costs mount. Should you prefer to have someone else show your dog, you can hire a professional handler.

In order to finish your dog, you must first believe in him. Secondly, you must show wisely. Select judges who are known to like what your Beardie has to offer whenever possible. Try to show your dog in his prime. Puppies can rarely compete successfully with adults, and one- to two-year-old Beardies are usually in an awkward, teenage period. Thirdly, you must keep trying. Never give up without giving a good dog a really fair chance.

You will know that it is time to stop showing if the money you are spending begins to outweigh the dog's value, or if your Beardie is aging and is continually being defeated by younger dogs of lesser quality. Most Beardies have their peak winning period between three and six years of age, and it is during this period that your dog is most likely to capture that elusive "Best in Show," or simply "Best of Breed," win.

Right: you may get better results if you hold a puppy.

Bottom left: steady your Beardie as he is being examined.

157

18 *Beardie Be Good*

THE PSYCHOLOGY OF TRAINING

Training is accomplished by teaching a dog to associate a verbal command or signal with an action. Once he makes this association, more complicated exercises can be easily taught.

The dog reacts much like a very young child; he will choose the path of least resistance, especially if it is reinforced by approval of his superiors. In the case of the dog, the natural peck order is very pronounced, from the pack leader to the weakest member of the pack. In fact, only the most dominant animals are allowed to breed in the wild. The offspring are quickly relegated to their respective positions within the litter, and as they grow, they accept their placements within the adult community based upon their dominance and physical prowess. A submissive animal will not often challenge those above him in the peck order, even if he could effectively do so. A dog's rolling over onto his back is an indication of submissiveness in a particular situation. All dogs are dominant to some animals and submissive to others.

So it is with the domestic dog. However, if you want a successful relationship with your pet, you must establish yourself as a "pack leader" substitute. This allows you to have absolute authority in the eyes of the dog. This is especially important if you own a male Beardie, for if he feels that you are not assuming command, he will gladly challenge for the position. You must know what you want the dog to do and decide on a reasonable approach to achieve those results. A Beardie is extremely intelligent and capable of acting independently; however, he has also been selected for reasonable submissiveness which aids in trainability. Therefore, the dog will try to please you once he knows what you want.

The true pack leader is consistent, so you will get better results in your training if you behave predictably. A dozen half-hearted attempts at controlling a situation will never be respected, while a severe correction will only have to be given once. Always think before you react. If you are too emotional or inconsistent, your dog will become frustrated. Proper behavior for the Beardie conditioned by a particular stimulus must be reinforced by approval each time it occurs if training is to be effective.

A dog's attention span is short, especially when he is a puppy. Therefore, he responds better to short, fast-paced training sessions. About ten- to fifteen-minute sessions either once or twice a day are best. Once you lose his attention, he is no longer able to learn, and you will find yourself vainly fighting with him. Also, if you ever lose your temper, the dog has won the battle. Stay cool, calm, authoritative, consistent, and worthy of your position as the pack leader. Do not underestimate your dog's ability; he will never overestimate yours.

Training Guidelines

There are a few basic rules that apply to any form of training. Success is dependent upon careful attention to these details.

Be Consistent—Always use the same words for a particular command, and require the same response from the dog each and every time you use the words. Training is basically achieving a desirable conditioned response from the dog, and it takes repetition to condition him thoroughly. Eventually, his response to a particular command will become automatic.

Use Clear Commands—Keep your verbal commands short, make them distinguishable from other words, and give them in an authoritative (not loud) tone of voice. Allow a short but reasonable time for the dog to react. Say, "Dog, COME," not, "There's a good boy, wouldn't you like to come here?" If you are casual or uncertain, your dog's response will show these same attitudes.

Use Plenty of Praise—Obviously, you should praise your dog whenever he obeys. Even more important is to praise him immediately after you have corrected an incorrect action. Praise is the only way for the dog to recognize acceptable behavior. He cannot understand your words, so make your tone of voice or your touch show approval. If the dog is really uncertain, a few food treats may reassure him. Never substitute food for praise—the incentive to work is much higher if the dog is doing it to please you.

Use Proper Equipment—This need not be elaborate, but it must be functional. For most types of training, a medium-weight chain "choke" collar and a flat, six-foot-long leather or nylon leash are best. For herding or tracking, a fifty-foot "long line" (usually made of nylon webbing) is necessary. For tracking, the dog must also wear a properly fitted harness, and you will need a leather glove or wallet for him to find. Nylon choke collars or show leads may be used, or a light chain collar may be substituted for conformation showing of a well-trained dog or for leash breaking a very young pup. Rolled leather collars are fine for yard wear and are a safety precaution while traveling. These are excellent for use in attaching ID tags, but they are unsuitable for training. Chain leashes are worthless, perhaps even harmful. They cut the handler's hands and hit the dog's face as he works. For this last reason, the metal snap on any lead should be reasonably small.

160 Left to right: obedience lead and collars, nylon choker and lead, two styles of martingales, fine choke chain and leather lead, and nylon choker with web lead. The five styles on the right are suitable conformation leads.

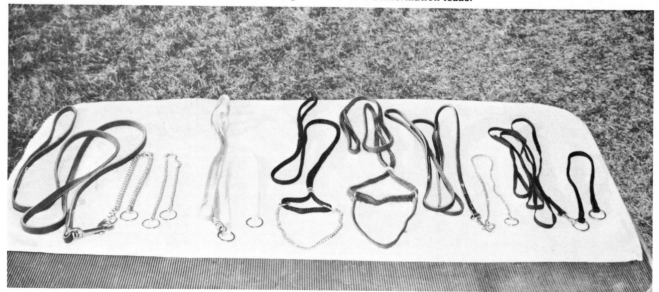

Use Aids Correctly—The choke collar must be put on the dog so that it tightens over the top of his neck when he is sitting at your left (*see* illustration). This allows the collar to release immediately after a jerk. If it is put on backward, the collar will remain tight, destroying its effectiveness as a training tool and perhaps choking the dog.

The lead should be held so that a slack loop appears at the collar. Fold the lead back and forth and hold the excess in your right hand. When you need to make a correction, quickly tighten and immediately release the pressure of the lead on the collar. Use a series of jerks if necessary, but never apply constant pressure to the collar.

When using a harness, however, keep your long line taut so that you can "read" your dog's responses to the track or livestock. Never allow a dog to lean into a collar. Correct him with quick jerks and praise. If you need a taut lead for any type of training, use the harness rather than the collar.

Never leave either a choke collar or a harness on a Beardie when you are not giving him a training lesson. He can easily hang himself if left unsupervised. Of lesser importance, but annoying nonetheless, is the fact that the collar will saw off the coat around the neck, leaving your Beardie with a short or bald area which can take months to grow back. If you must leave a collar on at all times, use a rolled leather one or a nylon choke collar with a snap connecting both rings so that it cannot tighten.

Give Release Commands—Never leave your dog on a "Stay" command without returning to release him. Many trainers use a separate command "Wait" if they intend to give additional instructions. The dog is not allowed to move even a foot on a formal "Stay." By not returning to the dog, you teach him to break whenever he is tired

There is only one correct way to put on a training collar.

The proper heel position. Note how handler holds leash.

161

of waiting. The dog cannot be blamed if you behave inconsistently in your demands on him.

Encourage the Dog to Challenge the Command—A dog that always performs perfectly does not truly know he must respect the command. He has no idea that he'll be corrected, and therefore may be unreliable under a stressed condition. A dog that has lost a disagreement with the trainer over an exercise will be less likely to break later. Vary your training enough so that the dog respects the command in any situation. Distractions are vital in testing a dog's training. The dog that will work only in a quiet, controlled environment is not really trained. He is only playing along because he has nothing better to do.

Vary Your Technique—If you experience continued problems with a specific exercise, go back to the beginning and retrain that exercise using a different approach which may be better suited to that individual dog. Seek professional advice if possible, or use some of the books listed in the bibliography for reference. Try to determine why your dog reacts as he does, and condition his responses accordingly.

Training Tips Specific to Beardies

Beardies can be independent creatures. They are usually self-assured and sometimes strong willed. To successfully train a Beardie, you must establish yourself as the dominant personality so that your Beardie will respect you. Be consistent, but get tough if necessary to get his attention. Respect his intelligence, but demand his obedience. Use praise lavishly when he responds to you. You may think that he's hopeless at first, but after a couple of lessons he will settle down and become much more manageable.

Beardies usually perform the worst on their "stay" exercises, which are taught first and require the dog to ignore distractions (nearly an impossibility for a Beardie on his first outing). Even if you are certain that your dog is the class dunce, keep working on this exercise (without losing your temper, or at least without letting the dog know that you've lost your temper) until he gives in. After that point, you will find him very quick to learn and rapidly passing his classmates in proficiency. The "stays" are very important for two reasons, so must be successfully mastered. First, they establish your dominance over the dog, a condition which is mandatory for any further training. Secondly, the "stay" is fundamental to many future exercises which cannot be taught

until the dog knows this step. It is the most useful tool in controlling the dog in everyday situations.

Beardies are very apt pupils, often learning their lessons as quickly as you demonstrate them. However, this same intelligence causes the dog to become easily bored and creatively defiant about performing by rote. You must work with enough speed and variety to keep the dog's interest, and whenever possible, show him a purpose for his actions. Alternate his lessons and create enough variations of each one to make them fun. You'll wind up with a better-trained dog that can perform all sorts of useful tasks.

What Every Beardie Should Know

A few basic concepts are necessary for every Beardie to learn for him to be socially acceptable. These are referred to by bird dog trainers as "yard manners" and constitute the very minimum of training that any conscientious owner should expect to do.

Leash Breaking—A young puppy can be started wearing a nylon choke collar or an English martingale. Older Beardies should be lead trained with a metal choke collar and leather leash. With the dog on your left side, start walking and encourage the dog to follow. Pat your leg and talk to him. This is not a formal "Heel," so don't use that command. If he follows along, stop after a few yards and pet him. Tell him how good he is, then resume walking. If he balks or runs the other way, give a snap on the lead, release pressure immediately, and in a light-hearted voice

Your Beardie may fight the lead at first.

162

encourage him to come with you. You may need to use several jerks in succession, each followed by praise. Don't stop walking if the dog screams or throws himself; just ignore him and keep talking happily to him. Do not drag him along on a tight lead; rather, move him with a series of jerks and immediate releases of the collar. When he starts walking willingly, don't make him go too far at a time. A food treat may be offered to encourage him. If the dog forges ahead, jerk him back to your pace, but do not be too severe. Keep the lesson to about ten minutes and repeat once or twice a day until the dog trots along freely on a loose lead.

Sit and Lie Down—Give the verbal command "Sit," pull up on the collar, and push down on the dog's rear. As soon as he's sitting, praise him lavishly. Wait until he knows how to sit before teaching him to lie down. Start with him sitting. Say "Down," and step on his leash, forcing him quickly to the floor. Hold him until he quits struggling. If he resists, kneel beside him with one arm over his body and grasp one of his forelegs in each hand. Give the command "Down," and pull his legs toward you, moving your body into him and forcing him onto his side. Do this a few times, then return to stepping on the leash. Remember to praise your Beardie immediately upon his response or your correction.

Stay—Sit your dog at your left side with the collar and leash on. Tell him to stay, and hold your open palm in front of his nose. Step in front of him and face him. If he moves, replace him and jerk up on the collar, repeating the command. Gradually increase the distance between you and the dog until you can walk across the room with the dog off lead. Always return and give a release command ("OK" or "Free") before you allow him to move.

Not Jumping on People—Bump the dog's chest with your knee every time he jumps, and say "No." This should discourage him if you are consistent and correct him *every* time. If you still have problems, grab the dog's front feet and run with him backwards like a wheelbarrow. Flip him backward after about ten feet. Pretend that you're having a great time, and he'll soon decide that he doesn't like your game.

I use the command "Feet" and grab the collar, pulling the dog off of anyone on whom he jumps. I began this because one dog minded me but felt that he had to try jumping on everyone else who came in. Most visitors encouraged him and made it worse, so I taught the command like an obedience exercise, with excellent results.

Stop Biting—No dog should *ever* be allowed to bite unless he is badly injured and in shock. Stress or fear are not adequate excuses. Some Beardies tend to be "mouthy"—they nibble or grab with their mouths at every excuse. This must be discouraged. A slap on the muzzle and a sharp "No" may be adequate, but if the dog actually snaps, grab him and run your hand down his throat. This renders him unable to bite, but will gag and frighten him. Use your advantage to scold him and exert your dominance. Once the dog backs down, reassure him that you are still friends.

163

Training the dog to stand for examination.

Come When Called — The biggest secret is to always praise the dog when he comes, regardless of how long it takes or what he has done. *Never* call him to you and punish him, or he will have second thoughts about coming the next time. He will think that he has been punished for coming and not connect the correction with any previous action. At three months of age he will run away, but given another month to develop emotionally, he should come eagerly. Make sure that he trusts you and that you don't grab or frighten him every time he comes within reach. If the dog does not come willingly, he must be insecure about your reaction or motives. Loosen up, and so will the dog.

If the dog continually runs away, attach a long lead and correct him every time he fails to come when called. Follow the correction with a great deal of praise and reassurance.

Coax the dog into show stance using bait.

164

SHOW TRAINING

Training a Beardie for conformation showing is simply a matter of keeping him under control. Most Beardies are cheerful extroverts and enjoy showing once they understand what is expected of them. Start training pups between ten weeks and five months of age. Puppies of this age are ready subjects and need to gain confidence in a show atmosphere before they enter adolescence.

The first thing the puppy needs to learn is to trot freely on a loose lead. He should move in a straight line without weaving or crabbing. Use quick jerks and talk to him to bring him back in line. Speed up a bit to help to get the dog moving with his body in a straight line. When the pup has learned to move smoothly both in a straight line and as you circle the ring, practice making smooth turns (*see* gaiting patterns, Ch. 17) and

The puppy should stand still, yet look alert.

walking smoothly into a stop as you face an imaginary "judge."

The puppy must also learn to be friendly and relaxed while being examined by a stranger. Kneel beside the pup and hold his collar with your right hand, steadying him with your left hand resting under his flank. This way you can talk to the puppy and hold him while the "judge" examines him. I try to keep the training casual and fun so that the puppy feels it is a game. Do not worry at this point if he does not position his feet properly or if he does not stand still for more than a few seconds, and always give him plenty of praise.

Practice is required if you hope to obtain perfection. If a conformation training class is held in your area, make use of it. If not, or for additional exposure, take your puppy to shopping centers, parks, or wherever people congregate. Ask people to pet your puppy while you stack him. They will generally be happy to oblige if you explain what you are doing.

As the pup gains proficiency, begin "stacking" him for more control. Lift your puppy by the chest (*see* illustration) and set him down so that his front feet are positioned squarely and naturally under his body. Hold him steady by placing your right hand under his chin. With your left hand, set his hind feet individually. Position them so that the metatarsus is vertical and slightly behind the line of the hip.

Some people continue to show adults in this manner. I prefer to walk an older dog into a natural stance and train him to stand squarely while he is "baited" to show expression. Of course, the dog must be constructed properly to be shown naturally, and many structural deficiencies can be minimized by clever stacking. However, any knowledgeable judge is aware of this. My own dog won a "Best In Show" because he was stepped forward several times at the judge's request and set himself up perfectly each time. His closest competitor required constant stacking, and in the final evaluation, the handler

Right: a Beardie should gait freely on a loose lead.

Bottom left: lift the dog to set the front legs.

Bottom right: steady the puppy with a hand on his flank.

165

had him slightly overstretched. I firmly believe that a good Beardie with correct temperament looks better in a natural, alert pose than he does if artificially stacked.

OBEDIENCE TRAINING

Obedience training begins with the same exercises used to teach yard manners but demands more precise reactions and continues into more advanced work. Each exercise has practical applications, and there are three levels of proficiency, each level adding new and more difficult exercises (*see* Ch. 17). The first stage can earn a degree called the Companion Dog (C.D.), which is indeed descriptive. Any obedience-trained Beardie makes a superior pet, and obedience lessons are highly recommended for any dog. They will enhance your relationship with the dog and benefit him in nearly any capacity. Obedience-trained dogs are often welcomed where other dogs are not allowed.

All obedience work is started with the dog in the "heel" position (i.e., sitting at your left with his front legs even with your legs). Once the dog is trained, he is expected to perform with each command spoken only once. A dog that has been formally trained will work in a precise, efficient manner which is exciting to watch.

Beardies are excellent workers as long as the routine is varied during training sessions so that they do not become bored. Most Beardies especially enjoy the advanced work if you can struggle through the initial stages of training. The sport of obedience is fun and constructive as it encourages individual achievement. Most communities offer training classes, at least on the beginning level. If you live where classes are not available, consult one of the many fine books on the subject. Be sure to work your dog where there are distractions so that he will be reliably trained for any situation.

TRACKING

A tracking dog follows a scent along a track until it leads to a person or an article bearing his scent. A well-trained dog can advance to search

and rescue work or find your lost car keys in heavy underbrush. Either task is infinitely useful and satisfying and is within the reach of any Beardie owner who pursues training his dog to track. AKC offers a "T" title for dogs that successfully complete a tracking test. An advanced degree is being considered. The first American Bearded Collie to win a tracking degree was Ch. Cannamoor Honey Rose. Several more Beardies are presently in training and the breed seems to excel at tracking.

A dog must be "certified" by a licensed tracking judge before he can enter a tracking test. The certification involves an informal test given to assure that the dog is qualified to compete. It helps to avoid unnecessary expense and time required to set up a test for dogs that are not ready. A great deal of space is needed, so most tracking tests have limited entries concerning numbers. The certification is usually somewhat easier than the actual tracking test, but individual requirements are at the discretion of the judge. Only one tracking test must be successfully completed to obtain a "T." Dogs may continue to compete in future events.

Complete rules concerning tracking tests may be obtained by writing to the AKC. Since these are periodically updated, I recommend obtaining a current set of regulations for either tracking or obedience before beginning training. Professionally supervised classes in training a tracking dog are held in many areas of the country, or you can attempt training on your own with the help of a good book on the subject (*see* "Other Sources").

Well trained dogs enjoy special privileges.

166

19 The Happy Herder

The Bearded Collie is a highly versatile herding dog, capable of working a variety of livestock in many situations. In its native Scotland, the breed is used in many ways, the most common being:

- as a "huntaway," casting out over vast mountain areas, barking as the dog runs, to flush out hiding or lost sheep (the barking moves sheep that cannot see the dog but can hear it), and then gathering them into a large flock and bringing the sheep into the fold;

- as a "drover's dog", driving cattle down lanes or from pasture to pasture;

- as a "hill" dog, casting out and gathering up sheep from the moors and bringing them in to their owner.

Because a variety of talents were needed for these many uses, there will be some Beardies (perhaps the majority) that are naturally gathering (fetching) dogs, while a few will naturally drive. Some will show varying degrees of "eye" while some will be loose-eyed and use barking.

While many "styles" of work are to be tolerated in the breed, owing to its many uses, all good Beardies should show a desire to keep the herd or flock well grouped and moving, exhibiting a clearly defined technique as well as a desire to conform to the wishes of its owner.

Working sheepdogs are still actively used in many areas of the world. In fact, it is not unusual to see them moving and tending sheep on summer pastures anywhere in the West. The art, or interest, in training sheepdogs is still very much alive, and with the growing interest in trials, even city dwellers are becoming involved. In the Denver area, a group of interested persons formed the Stock Dog Fanciers Club of Colorado. Members representing several breeds of stock dogs purchased a small herd of sheep and cattle, plus numerous ducks, and all members have access to the animals and facilities. The club offers training classes in various levels of achievement, sponsors local trials, and issues awards for completion of each level of training. Hopefully, similar organizations nationwide will encourage more novices to take up stock dog trial work as a sport and thus preserve an innate part of the working dog's heritage.

HERDING INSTINCT

The herding instinct is merely a divergence from the wild dog's instinct to hunt. Wild dogs lived and hunted in packs. The faster dogs ran ahead of the game and turned it back toward the pack, while the slower ones completed the kill. The forerunners of the pack were developed by man into herding dogs through careful selection and adaptation. The slower types evolved into hunting and trailing (particularly hound) breeds.

The strong "eye" exhibited by some breeds, notably Border Collies, is also an adaptation from the wild dog's instinct. Foxes and coyotes will "eye" (stare intently at) their prey before pouncing on it. Pointers and setters exhibit the same instinct in a more controlled way. Beardies sometimes show a strong tendency to eye, but this is of less importance than an attitude of intense concentration on the stock. In fact, a dog with too much eye may frighten the sheep with his fixed stare, **168** and the showing of the white part of the eye in a wild but intent fashion probably has little advantage whatsoever.

While it is possible to train almost any Beardie to herd, a *good* stock dog must possess strong herding *instinct*. It is this urge to herd that makes the dog a willing and eager worker. Forcing a dog to work stock is never really successful. When a young dog "starts to run," he does it instinctively. He is like a youth who suddenly develops an interest in the opposite sex—the time has come when nature's influence takes over.

In addition to the herding instinct, Beardies have a dominant/submissive nature. The instincts to herd and to submit need to be balanced. The stronger the herding instinct, the stronger the willingness to submit must be. Otherwise the dog becomes uncontrollable.

In their wild state, only a few dogs were pack leaders, while the majority followed them. The modern "pack leader type" is usually too independent to become a good herder. On the other hand, the submissive "follower" will accept his human master as a substitute pack leader. This submissive instinct is what makes the dog trainable. It is apparent in the young puppy that follows you around and licks your hand for attention. As the dog matures, the submissive instinct should diminish unless it is developed and directed by training. The overly submissive Beardie may never want to leave his handler to work independently.

Both the herding and the submissive instincts must be nourished and encouraged to become useful. Normal herding instinct can be discouraged or killed by harshly disciplining a puppy for showing interest in stock, chasing, or trying to herd pets or children. Instead, such behavior must be encouraged whenever possible. The submissive instinct, on the other hand, is developed through basic training and by praising the pup's responsiveness to requests and commands. A dog that is to be trained for herding should learn to accept discipline and restraint in the form of leash training and the teaching of basic household manners, and he should never be reprimanded for chasing or showing interest in livestock.

Puppies started in herding too young may simply want to chase.

TEMPERAMENT IN A HERDING DOG

Most Beardies are fairly "hard" with stock and will tend to rush in boldly and work the sheep or cattle too fast. A few dogs, however, may be "soft" or hesitant with the stock and generally also more sensitive to their trainer. The "hard" dog is perhaps easier to start with because he will always act boldly and aggressively, but he needs a tougher trainer to control him. The "soft" dog is generally more tractable and may make the better pet, but he may try to run away rather than deal with a frightening situation. It takes considerably more patience to train this dog.

Moderation is preferred so that the dog is neither too hard nor too soft; in addition, the dog's temperament must be compatible with his trainer's disposition. Some people can obtain marvelous results with a hard dog and accomplish nothing with the soft one, or vice versa.

Common sense is another important attribute of the herding dog. This is primarily apparent in the older puppy or adult dog and is developed with experience and exposure to various situations. A good stock dog is capable of thinking for himself and adapting to problem situations.

CHOOSING A HERDING DOG

The herding instinct is not always evident in a young puppy. It develops as the dog matures and usually becomes apparent somewhere between his sixth and eighteenth months of age. Occasionally, you will notice a puppy herding or eyeing his littermates almost as soon as they start playing. Just as common is the dog that refuses to look at sheep until well over a year of age. Either Beardie can become a superior herder if he develops an interest in stock.

It is usually advisable to choose a young puppy that you can raise to suit yourself. A partially trained adult may be spoiled or may have formed bad habits, and the professionally trained dog may perform admirably for his expert handler but not at all for a novice owner.

Choosing a puppy for herding is largely a matter of chance, but the odds may be improved slightly if you select a puppy from working parents, or if the puppy himself shows interest in herding. He may exhibit a tendency to circle or bunch other animals, or even a rubber ball. At three months of age, a few Beardies will actively approach stock. They are too young to under-

GreyPaul Milktray of Brackenwood herding sheep at Cedora College at the age of one year.

169

stand basic commands, and, except to demonstrate this interest, they should be prevented from working the stock. Pick the puppy up or confine him. Puppies that are allowed to work livestock of any kind too early will only learn bad habits or become frightened. Such puppies are not good risks as herding prospects. However, familiarity with livestock so the dog is not frightened is beneficial.

Do not choose a shy Beardie or an overly excitable or aggressive pup. Look for soundness and for the puppy that is quick on his feet. Poor angulation, crooked legs, weak pasterns, or other structural faults will inhibit free movement and cause the dog's structure to be too weak for the demands of hard work.

INTRODUCING THE BEARDIE TO STOCK

The dog's first reaction to stock is very important. As long as he does no real damage, any positive interest or action that the dog makes should be encouraged. The most favorable response is when the Beardie tries to circle or move the sheep. He may "grip" or bite them as well. This is normal in a young, inexperienced dog and should not be corrected at this time.

A good stock dog will not charge the stock but will work them gently. Puppies sometimes tend to be overenthusiastic, while an older Beardie that

has never seen stock may show no initial interest in herding. If this dog watches the sheep with an intense fascination, it is sufficient. After several introductions to the livestock, this dog's herding instinct will probably be awakened.

I find it best to cultivate the herding instinct and start the dog herding before initiating formal obedience training; however, it is imperative that the Beardie be leash trained and that he understand the meaning of the basic commands "Come" and "Down." An obedience-trained dog can become a good herder, but it may take longer because he will probably watch his handler rather than the sheep. The handler must have established dominance over the Beardie before stock dog training is attempted, and he must maintain this dominance in direct proportion to the dog's increasing aggressiveness with the sheep.

A puppy should never be introduced to "dog-wise" or mean livestock, or to ewes with young lambs. One kick from or butt by a sheep at this time may turn the Beardie off herding forever. The young pup that shows interest in herding will probably chase chickens, ducks, sheep, or anything else he can find to run. In the process, he is not only liable to be hurt, but he will develop many bad habits as well. The best way to prevent this is to pick up the puppy or snap a leash onto his collar whenever he is around livestock. Do not scold him for showing interest or chasing.

The Beardie is ready to work stock when he is full grown and fast enough to outrun the stock—

170

Introduce a young dog to docile sheep or lambs.

usually eight or nine months of age. Younger puppies may be started on lambs.

TRAINING POINTERS

There are as many ways to train a herding dog as there are trainers. Trial and error will determine your best results, but here are a few tips which helped me get started.

Most Beardies should be started on a long lead, thirty to fifty feet in length. This is attached to the dog's choke collar and kept on until he reliably goes "down" on command while around the sheep. After a while, he can be allowed to work free, but with the leash dragging behind him in case you need to regain control. Initially, you should let the dog sniff and test the sheep without interference from you. Once interested, most Beardies will circle the flock and attempt to bunch them into a corner. Each dog will show a definite preference to circle in one direction, either to the right or to the left. After he develops confidence, you will need to concentrate on training him to circle in the opposite direction so that he will go either way on command, depending on the situation.

You will need to establish some method of communication which direction the flock is to be moved, along with some basic commands. Some trainers use voice commands, while other whistle. Either method is acceptable. The dog must know the command "Down" and obey instantly. "Down" is used to stop a charging dog, to allow the stock to calm, or to get the dog's attention prior to giving further instructions. Some trainers use "Haw" and require only that the dog stop in his tracks. Other trainers use both commands, saving the "Down" for emergencies when the dog's bobbing up and down would startle the sheep. "Easy" usually means to slow down or hesitate. Commands are most effective if spoken in a low-pitched, steady tone. Decide which commands you want to use and be consistent.

In directing the dog to move the flock in a specific direction, commands will be needed for right, left, straight ahead, bringing the sheep toward the handler, going around the flock, and going around the handler. Traditional terms for directing the flock include "Walk On," meaning drive the sheep straight ahead, "Way to Me," indicating the dog to move counterclockwise, and "Go By," commanding the dog to move clockwise. You may prefer to improvise your own commands.

The shepherd's crook or stick, used as an extension of the trainer's arm, is a valuable training aid. It is easily seen at a distance and is used during early training to teach the dog directions and to encourage a wider outrun. If the dog

Beardies often prefer to circle one direction. O'Kelidon's Caledonia, *McHugh*.

Beardies naturally bunch the sheep. Ch. Silverleaf English Leather, *Bootleg*.

resists a command, he can be pushed gently with the crook in the direction toward which you wish him to move. Don't strike or frighten the dog or he may be afraid of coming close to you when necessary.

Actual Exercises

In the outrun, the dog leaves the handler and circles the flock to a point opposite the handler. This action is natural for most Beardies that fall into the category of "herding" dogs. (Those few that tend to be "heelers" will have to be taught the maneuver.) The Beardie's natural outrun may be too close to the sheep and may need to be widened with training so that no sheep are disturbed as the dog circles them.

With the Beardie on lead, send him toward the flock, but direct him with the crook so that he swings wide. Encourage him to keep going. Work only four or five sheep at first. As the dog circles around them, start running backward and encourage the dog to bring the sheep toward you. You will probably have to make many turns in order to slow the sheep enough to be easily handled. A large lot or small pasture should be used so that the sheep cannot get out of control.

If the sheep run past you, make an about-turn and back up. The dog will naturally circle around in front of them again and can be encouraged once more to bring the flock toward you. As the dog comes toward you around the flock, hit the ground with your stick as he approaches and command him back in the other direction. This will keep him on the opposite side of the flock. As he returns from that direction, send him around behind the sheep again, creating the zig-

Train the dog to bring the sheep toward you.

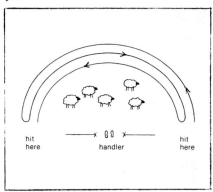

The dog circles the flock.

Use the crook to turn him back.

172

Keep the dog behind the flock.

Now he can move the flock in your direction.

The dog must learn to move the sheep away from the fence.

Left: keep the dog behind the sheep to teach the "walk on."

Right: as the dog progresses, control him from a greater distance.

Bottom left: the dog approaches the sheep in a straight line for the "walk on." He may do an outrun to reach this position.

Bottom right: a dog that has learned the "walk on" can drive the sheep as well as herd them. Ch. Parcana Silverleaf Vandyke, *Parcana.*

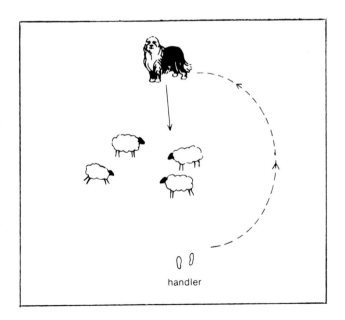

handler

zag herding pattern (see illustration). The Beardie will constantly be bunching the sheep but will also be moving them toward you. If the dog tries to circle around behind you, move in front of him, continually forcing him to reverse his direction and go back around the stock.

Once this routine becomes familiar, lead or direct the dog between the sheep and a fence to teach him to move them out of a corner. Then work on teaching him to move the flock in a certain direction. Eventually, your Beardie should be able to change speed on command, drive the sheep in any direction you want, drop anywhere that you ask, and come on command. Give lots of encouragement, and allow the dog plenty of time to build up his confidence as he masters each step of the training. It usually takes three to six months of training once or twice weekly, or two months of daily work, to develop proficiency in the basics.

You will then be ready to teach the "walk on" or drive, which goes against most Beardies' natural instincts. Put your dog back on lead. Teach him to move the sheep straight ahead,

COMMONLY USED HERDING TERMS

GATHERING	A style of bringing animals to the owner, sometimes called "fetching" or (in Australian usage) "heading."
DRIVING	Taking the livestock away from the owner, or from side to side, either naturally or upon direction from the owner to do so.
"EYE"	An intense, unblinking gaze used by the dog to control the stock often accompanied by a creeping or crouching approach to the animals.
STRONG-EYED	A dog showing the above qualities to a marked degree.
MEDIUM-EYED	A dog showing "eye" but without the crouching approach.
LOOSE-EYED	A dog that does not show an intense gaze at all times on the stock, such dogs may glance around or at the owner from time to time—*most dogs that bark while working are loose-eyed.*
HEADING	A dog that nips at the heads of livestock to turn them.
HEELING	A dog that nips at the lower part of the hind legs of livestock to move them forward.
WOOL-PULLING	A dog that nips or grips at the bodies of sheep, marking the flesh by tearing out of wool—called "body biting" on cattle. Biting at the body of sheep, cattle, ducks or goats is a fault.
WEARING	The pendulum motion, in a half circle, the dog makes to keep the herd or flock grouped.
POWER	A dog that, by virtue of its strong self-confidence, can move stubborn or fighting animals, often without nipping.
WEAK	A dog lacking the confidence to stand up to stubborn animals, such dogs often "turn tail" (run away) when confronted with a challenge from the stock.
WIDE RUNNING	A dog that runs out very wide off the stock, making wide passes going around, naturally keeping a good distance from the stock.
CLOSE RUNNING	A dog that runs in very close to the stock, trying to get as close as possible as it passes around.
FORCE BARKING	A dog that works quietly, except in situations where the stock challenges the dog, and the dog barks as a precurser to a nip.
APPROACH	The manner in which the dog comes in to the stock, a "smooth" approach being most highly prized—that is, a dog moving in very steadily and surely without bouncing around, weaving, or jumping in aggressively.

driving either toward you or away from you. With experience, the dog will work farther and farther distances from his trainer. Since many trials include a water obstacle, it may be helpful to train your Beardie to drive ducks or sheep from a pond by working around them. Portable panels are easily constructed to form gates through which the sheep can be driven.

BCCA WORKING PROGRAM

A new Working Program is available to all purebred Bearded Collies through the Bearded Collie Club of America.

This exciting new program, which passed unanimously at the Board meeting held Feb. 21, 1983, was a long time in planning. It has two separate functions. One is to reward and establish by an impartial system those dogs who demonstate natural herding instinct. This part of the program will be called the "Herding Certificate" program, and dogs which pass at herding tests will receive a parchment certificate stating that each dog has passed such a test and will be entitled to use the intials "H.C." *after* its name as evidence of natural herding ability. The great advantage of this part of the program is that the dogs being tested need not have any training for herding—in fact, many will be seeing livestock for the first time in such tests. Thus city owned dogs may be tested and instinct be preserved.

The second part of this program is the Herding Championship. This is for dogs that are trained on livestock and are competing in herding trials. This championship system is based on a set number of points, and a sliding point scale (similar to that used by the A.K.C.) based on the number of dogs in competition. Dogs that earn the required points in the approved manner will be issued certificates of Herding Championship and will be entitled to use the title of Herding Champion *preceeding* the dog's name. Thus we expect to see Dual Champion Bearded Collies competing not only in conformation but in herding as well.

Certificates will be issued as they are earned, and we encourage you to read and study the rules of this program to avoid any confusion. A modest filing fee is under consideration to help pay for the costs of postage and printing for those dog's submitting certificate forms (such as from herding tests and trials).

Other breed clubs of A.K.C. herding breeds including the Belgian Tervuren Club of America and the Bouvier De Flanders Club have requested copies of the B.C.C.A. program to use as models for their own programs in herding.

ELIGIBILITY

1. These programs and titles shall be open to all purebred Bearded Collies six months of age and older.

2. As proof of pure breeding, all eligible dogs must be litter or individually registered with the American Kennel Club through normal registration, or registered through the American Kennel Club under Indefinate Listing Privilege (I.L.P.), or registered with the valid registry of a foreign country.

3. Spayed bitches, neutered dogs, and dogs with faults according to the breed standard *shall* be eligible to participate.

4. Dogs that have been in previous tests and not passed shall be eligible to test again on another day.

5. Owners of participating dogs need not be a member of any club or organization.

6. Dogs need not have had any training to participate in herding tests.

HERDING CERTIFICATE PROGRAM

1. Tests for Herding Certificates may be held at any Bearded Collie Club function, including local and national clubs, at events such as shows, meetings, picnic days, etc. or in conjunction with any other working dog group, providing the local or national club acts as co-sponsor.

2. In the event that a person or persons wish to have their dogs tested, but there is no local club in their area, they may write the Working Committee giving all information on the test requested, and such tests may be approved at the discretion of the Working Committee.

3. Test may be held on ducks, sheep, cattle or goats, with a minimum of three (3) head of

stock per dog. Groups of animals may be re-used, providing a lengthy rest period is provided for the stock.

4. Testers must be approved prior to the test by the Working Chairperson. (See Testers for Herding Tests.)

5. Tests are run on a pass, not pass system, and the decision of the tester on that day shall not be subject to dispute.

6. Each dog shall be allowed a maximum of fifteen (15) minutes in each test to show instinct.

7. Dogs must be tested off-lead or with lead dragging, and not held or directed by any person or tied to any object.

8. Dogs that are tested will have forms filled out in full by appropriate parties and one copy shall remain with the owner. The host club (or individual) shall submit all other forms to the Working Chairperson.

9. Dogs that pass herding certificate tests shall be issued a Herding Certificate by the Bearded Collie Club of America and shall be entitled to use the initials "H.C." after the dog's name.

10. Sponsoring clubs and individuals shall request test forms and approval from Working Chairperson at least 30 days before their test.

11. It shall be the duty of the club representative or sponsoring individual to see that all forms

176

HERDING CERTICATE TESTING FORM

On the day of _____, I, _____
did test the Bearded Collie (please give registered name): _____
Registration number: _____, for herding instinct using:

Ducks _____   Sheep _____   Cattle _____   Goats _____

This dog, on this day:

_____

PASSED   _____

DID NOT PASS   _____ (Re-testing is recommended)

_____

With regard to working style and characteristics, the following best describes this dog's herding instinct: (circle applicable)
STYLE: Dog shows gathering (fetching) instinct, dog shows driving instinct, dog shows no clear style preference
APPROACH: Dog runs wide, dog runs wide through training, dog runs close
WEARING: Dog shows "wearing" to keep herd grouped, dog shows a little wearing, dog shows no wearing
BARK: Dog worked silently, dog forces barks, dog barks a good deal
EYE: Dog shows strong eye, dog shows medium eye, dog does not show eye
AGGRESSIVENESS: Dog was forceful without excessive aggression (on ducks, forceful without nipping), dog nips excessively for the circumstance
TEMPERAMENT: Dog appears readily adjusted, dog is easily distracted, dog is frightened of new situations

Signed (Tester) _____ Test Location _____
Name of Sponsoring Club _____
Signature of Club Representative: _____
Name and address of Owner: _____
_____

Send this form to current Working Chairperson for recording. One copy remains with owner of dog being tested.

are completed in full before submission to the Working Chairperson.

12. Application to hold a herding certificate test may be made in regular letter form.

TESTERS FOR HERDING CERTIFICATE TESTS

1. Testers shall have owned and trained a Beardie to a Herding Championship.
2. Testers who do not complete the requirements of #1 must be an experienced member-trainer of North American Sheepdog Society.
3. All other testers will be considered and approved on a case by case basis.
4. Suggestions for herding testers in some areas may be obtained from the Working Chairperson.
5. If testers are paid, they should be paid by a designated person or club representative.
6. Testers shall be provided a copy of these rules prior to the test to familiarize themselves with its provisions.

JUDGES FOR HERDING TRIALS

1. Judges for North American Sheepdog Society, Australian Shepherd Club of America, and local or state sheepdog societies shall be eligible to judge trials.
2. Local judges will be approved on a case by case basis.
3. If judges are paid, they should be paid by a designated person or club representative, and not by each contestant.

PASSING QUALIFICATIONS

A dog who, after a period of introduction, shows sustained interest in herding livestock, either circling or attempting to gather them or following them about to drive them.

A dog who barks (either a lot or a little), a dog who shows "eye" (either a lot or a little), one that works quietly, a dog that may feint as though to nip (or actually nips if on larger animals) *providing it is not a threat to the health or safety of the livestock*, are all passable. It is to remembered that many dogs, through simple inexperience will make mistakes in their first exposure to livestock, but at all times the tester must see clear cut evidence of herding instinct.

NOT PASSABLE

A dog who, after a period of introduction, fails to show sustained herding interest in livestock, a dog that leaves or makes attempts to leave the working area, a dog whose interest is not strong enough to show a definable style, as determined by the tester.

A dog who shows aggression toward the livestock so strong and of a nature to be considered a threat to the health or safety of the livestock. Any dog that repeatedly splits the herd and attacks one or several animals with its teeth, or who grips any animal and holds on.

Any dog that, for whatever reason, cannot be tested off lead or with lead dragging in a fenced area.

Any dog that shows fear of the livestock in such a fashion that the dog cannot demonstrate herding interest.

HERDING CHAMPIONSHIP PROGRAM

1. Rules # 1, 2, 3 and 5 from Herding Certificate Tests also apply to Herding Championships.
2. Dogs may compete in any herding trials, whether sponsored by B.C.C.A. or other clubs or organizations approved by the B.C.C.A. for points.
3. Point sanction may be applied for any person, whether contestant or club representative.
4. Requests for point sanction may be made in regular letter form to the Working Chairperson at least 30 days prior to the trial in question.
5. Requests for point sanction must include name and date of trial, judges, location, sponsoring club, and a description of the course to be used.
6. Upon approval for points, the Working Chairperson shall send trials forms to the

person requesting such forms, and these forms MUST be signed by the judge and the trials secretary before submission to the Working Chairperson.

7. When a total of fifteen points have been earned, providing all other requirements have been fulfilled (See point system information) an Award of Herding Championship shall be issued.

8. Herding Championships may be used to precede the dog's name.

9. Points cannot be recorded unless required forms are submitted from each trial by the owner of the dog.

POINT SCHEDULE FOR HERDING CHAMPIONSHIP COMPETITION		
A (20 or more dogs in class or, if no classes, in trial)	B (10-19 dogs in class or, if no classes, in trial)	C (Less than 10 dogs in class, or, if no classes, in trial)
FIRST 5 points	4 points	3 points
SECOND 4 points	3 points	2 points
THIRD 3 points	2 points	1 point
FOURTH 2 points	1 point	0
FIFTH 1 point	0	0

POINT SYSTEM INFORMATION

1. A herding Championship shall be completed when fifteen (15) points have been earned, and have been recorded by the Working Chairperson.

2. Points may be earned from any class. Any dog competing in more than one class at a trial may earn points from any and all classes the dog places in.

3. Dogs competing for points must be worked off-lead.

4. For points to be earned, the dog in question must have defeated at least one other dog, either in the class, or, if no classes, in the trial, i.e. first in a class of one would not qualify for points, but first in a class of two would.

5. Points must be earned under at least two different judges.

6. Dogs that earn High in Trial shall count the total number of dogs defeated in the trial, and not just the number of dogs in the class, for their points, i.e. if the dog wins a class of fifteen, but also takes High in Trial over all in an entry of 30, then the points awarded would be for 30 dogs.

BEARDED COLLIE CLUB HERDING TRIALS RULES

1. These rules shall apply only to those trials held by local or national Bearded Collie clubs. Trials held by other organizations shall not be required to conform to these rules.

2. Any Bearded Collie Club may hold a herding trial in conjunction with a show, picnic day or other event, or clubs may hold trials as a separate function.

3. Trials may utilize classes in any, or all, of the following types of livestock: ducks, sheep, goats, cattle.

4. If classes are offered, they shall be divided by type of stock and may be further divided into a Started Class (for beginning dogs) and an Open Class (for trained dogs and Herding Champions in that type of livestock.)

5. The area size for trials held by Bearded Collie clubs shall be 80′ x 80′ or more for duck classes, and 250′ x 250′ or more for larger stock.

6. If a club has access to an irregular sized field, they may request special approval to hold a trial there from the Working Committee.

7. No set course shall be prescribed, but all courses should utilize an outrun, lift and fetch, along with some form of gates or obstacles and a pen.

8. Trial giving clubs may limit their entries to Beardies only, or may make them open to all breeds.

9. Applications to hold trials must be made 60 days prior to the date of the trial. Such applications must be sent to the Working Chairperson.

10. Applications to hold working trials may be made in regular letter form by the sponsoring

club, and shall include such details as score-sheet, names of judges, location and size of herding trial area, type of stock to be used, course design, etc.

11. All classes of livestock shall utilize a *minimum* of three head of stock per dog.

12. Dogs who earn herding championships on one type of livestock must always compete in the Open Class on that type of stock, but may compete in Started Classes on types of stock for which the dog has not yet earned its championship.

NATIONAL SPECIALTY WORKING TRIAL

1. *At the option of the host club,* a National Herding Trial may be held in conjunction with the National Specialty Show.

2. If such trial is held, the entry shall be limited to Bearded Collies.

3. All rules except #8 under Bearded Collie Club Trials Rules shall apply.

4. At the option of the host club, the herding trial may be held the day preceeding, the day following, or the same day as the National Specialty Show.

WORKING COMMITTEE CHAIRMAN GUIDELINES

The Chairman shall receive the results of all Herding Tests and forward the names of the dogs who pass to the Awards Chairman.

The Chairman shall record the points won by Beardies competing in herding trials and when the points necessary for a Herding Championship are acheived, this information shall be forwarded to the Awards Chairman.

The Chairman shall make regular reports to the President and the Board. The Chairman shall be the contact for B.C.C.A.

TRIALS FORM FOR HERDING CHAMPIONSHIP PROGRAM

Date:_____

Place of Trial:_____

Sponsoring Club:_____

Class or Division (if any):_____

If more than one class, list additional classes:_____

Number of dogs in each class or Division, or, if no classes or Divisions, in trial, (add each class dog places in separately):

_____

_____

I hereby certify that I did judge the Bearded Collie:_____

on this day at this trial and that this dog placed:_____

_____

Signed: _____   Date:_____

(officiating judge(s))

I hereby do certify that the number of dogs as listed in each class or division, or, if no classes or divisions, in this trial, is true and correct.

Signed:_____   Date:_____

(trials secretary)

Address:_____

Registered Name of Dog:_____

Name of Owner:_____

Address of Owner:_____

Sumit this form when signed to the Working Chairperson for recording.

WORKING COMMITTEE GUIDELINES

Two persons shall comprise the Working Committee, who will work with the Chairman to recommend changes that may be needed in this program, and to formulate new rules or instigate new programs.

Any changes to be made or new programs must have the unanimous approval of the Working Committee and the Working Chairman before being presented by the Chairman to the Board.

HERDING TRIALS

At this time, the American Kennel Club does not award herding degrees or sanction herding trials. Numerous local organizations hold trials, each with its own rules and awards, and the North American Sheepdog Society provides standardized trials. The Denver Stock Dog Fanciers club devised four progressive degrees to give encouragement to beginning herders as well as to

A standard pattern used at herding trials.

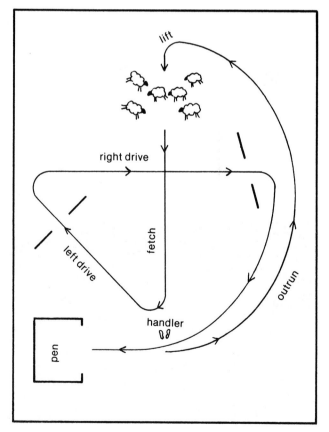

experts. The first degree, Stock Dog I, is awarded when the dog demonstrated interest and will dependably "Down" on and off the stock, making him safe to work off lead in any situation. Stock Dog II requires that the dog show herding ability and obey commands to move to a specified direction around the sheep. Stock Dog III tests the dog's proficiency in either herding or driving, whichever is natural to the dog. Stock Dog IV includes tests for both driving and herding much like a competitive trial. The first Beardie to earn a herding degree with this club was Ch. Parcana Silverleaf Vandyke. Others show considerable promise as stock dogs.

Competitive formal trials sponsored by the North American Sheepdog Society test the fully trained dog's ability to control a flock of sheep. Although most competitive trials are dominated by Border Collies, we believe that Bearded Collies will perform exceptionally well in them. Formal trails are usually conducted in a set "run" or pattern. Each part of the run counts a specified number of points, but a great deal of interpretation is usually allowed the judge. Penning is considered the most important exercise, and a dog that fails this exercise will only be allowed two-thirds of the points that he has accumulated in the other exercises. Since penning is the last exercise in the run, a handler may opt to skip one of the other, less important, exercises so that plenty of time is allowed for the dog to pen the sheep. The judge is the final authority at a trial and can stop a run that he feels does not meet his standard or that endangers the stock.

The dog works on his own at some distance from the handler, who is confined to a circular area at the starting point. The handler cannot step out of the area except during the penning exercise, when he is allowed to go to the gate of the pen. Here, he is again confined to a certain radius of the gate.

During the trial, the dog is expected to move the sheep without unduly disturbing them, biting, or otherwise handling the sheep roughly. The outrun should be wide so as not to start the flock running before the dog has control. The dog should never cross from one side of the flock to the other during the outrun. The dog should maintain control of the flock while keeping them as quiet as possible at all times.

A good herding dog is a joy to behold, and watching a Beardie working stock just as he was bred to do hundreds of years ago sends chills up my spine. I have been fascinated and challenged by herding since the day my first Beardie started to run, and I hope many of you will join in this rewarding sport.

The general rules are:

Outrun—10 points—In starting each run, the contestant and his dog shall take position at any point in the handler's circle—this same position to be the "fixed" position for all work during the "Gather and Drive." With the sheep in place, and upon signal from the course director, the run for each dog begins. On the outrun, the dog may be directed to go either "right" or "left," and each dog shall carry along on this given line until beyond the sheep. Cross-over shall cause deduction of points according to the judge's decision. The dog shall go "wide" and "beyond" the sheep before circling in so as to come upon the sheep from the "far side" in preparation for the "lift."

Lift—5 points—The lift should be cautious, the dog well balanced on the flock, the sheep not unduly startled, held quietly and firmly, and moved off steadily with the dog in full control.

Fetch—10 points—The fetch should be on a near straight line from point of contact and lift to the handler; swerving, zig-zagging, or other deviation from the near-straight line involves loss of points. The nature of the work and the condition and handling of the sheep are the foremost considerations. The fetch ends when the sheep enter the designated area.

Driving—15 points (7½ each)—From the handler's position in the back half of the handler's circle, the dog is required to drive the sheep away on a diagonal to the left, toward and through gate no. 1; thence horizontally across the field toward and through gate no. 2, each drive to be a near straight line. If either gate is not negotiated on first try, no re-try will be allowed. Failure to negotiate either gate will involve a loss of points or not, according to the decision of the judges under each circumstance. The drive ends when the sheep are through gate no. 2.

Penning—15 points—Penning begins immediately after the second drive through gate no. 2. The sheep are to be brought in a near straight line from the gate to the pen. The contestant shall open the gate of the pen, either to the right or to the left, so that it continues in a straight line along the side of the pen to which it is fastened. This opening shall not be changed until the sheep are confined. When the gate is opened, the contestant shall grasp the end of a rope six feet long, tied to the open end of the gate, and shall confine his movements to the limit fixed by this rope. Each dog shall work its assigned sheep into the open pen, unassisted in any way by the handler except for directions given by spoken, whistled, or otherwise imparted commands. Any dog that fails to pen the assigned sheep shall not be awarded more than two-thirds the total points for the work he has accomplished.

Right: the outrun can be widened with training.

Bottom left: a trained dog can control his sheep quietly.

Bottom right: the real thing is more of a challenge.

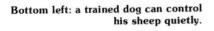

181

182

Ch. Parcana Silverleaf Vandyke, *Parcana*, "doing his thing."

20 History in the Making

The first Bearded Collie on record to be imported to the United States was Brand X of Bothkenner, imported by Mrs. Ralph Stone, Cross River, New York, in 1962. Others followed, and in November, 1967, the first American-bred litter was whelped and registered to Mr. and Mrs. Lawrence Levey. The litter was sired by Cannamoor Glencanach out of Cannamoor Carndoonagh.

In 1969 the Levey's and several other breeders, Mrs. Irving Beitel, Dr. Jessie Davis, and Mrs. Mary Wright, met in Long Island, New York, to found the Bearded Collie Club of America (BCCA). The club worked hard for AKC recognition, and in 1975 the Bearded Collie was admitted to AKC shows in the Miscellaneous Class. Barely two years later, in February 1977, full AKC status was granted. The first Beardie to finish was Ch. Brambledale Blue Bonnet C.D., who also was the first Beardie to earn a Companion Dog degree.

The BCCA held annual matches as a part of the requirement for AKC approval to hold a licensed specialty show. The first National Specialty Match was held May 31, 1970, at Mrs. Stone's home in Cross River, New York. Ken Henry, a Collie breeder, judged approximately forty entries. Nine years later, August 19, 1979, the first AKC licensed National Specialty Show was held in Medina, Ohio. Best of Breed went to a Canadian bitch, Eng. and Can. Ch. Edenborough Kara Kara of Josanda.

The Canadian Kennel Club had been much quicker to recognize the Bearded Collie, with championship status granted in August 1970. The first Canadian champion, Ch. Wishanger Marsh Pimpernel C.D., also became the first North American champion when she finished in the fall of 1970.

Since that first litter was whelped in 1967, many American breeders have entered the scene—some for only a fleeting time in the early days of AKC recognition, while others remained to make a lasting mark on the Bearded Collie in America. We will try to cover the major lines and breeders, (although some who did not respond have been omitted).

GLEN EIRE

Anne Dolan was raised in Scotland, where she owned a Beardie from childhood. One of the earliest breeders to import stock to the U.S., she is still very active in the breed. Imports over a span of fifteen years have included Ch. Luath Bonnie Blue Bairn ROM, Ch. Bunwells Springfields, Ch. Willowmead Something Super ROM, Ch. Willowmead Midnight Black, and Ch. Attleford Brown Bess. Although Glen Eire has bred only one or two litters per year, the kennel has produced twenty-nine champions to date. Most stem from the kennel's two foundation bitches, Ch. Glen Eire Molly Brown ROM and Ch. Luath Bonnie Blue Bairn ROM.

Ch. Glen Eire Willie Wonderful ROM with 14 champion offspring is currently tied for third top producing sire, but he is the top *American bred* stud dog. The Glen Eire Beardies are raised as house dogs and family friends.

RAGGMOPP

Raggmopp got its official start in England in 1968, when, after two years of intense Beardie- studying there and much serious searching for the right Beardie, Wishanger Marsh Pimpernel came into the life of Carol Gold. "Gael" was only five days old when Carol first saw her curled in Mary Partridge's palm; when she came home to Toronto with Carol she was only the second Beardie in Canada. (The first was a pet bitch in Montreal.)

Together, "Gael" and Carol laid the groundwork for getting the breed recognized in Canada. They appeared on the educational program of every dog club that would invite them, as well as on TV, were interviewed in newspapers, performed with an obedience club drill team, and Gael herself charmed a young, dogless couple into agreeing to import a male Beardie as a prospective husband. When he grew up, this male,

Left: Ch. Glen Eire Molly Brown R.O.M. (center) with daughter, Ch. Glen Eire Good Gracious R.O.M. (right), and granddaughter Glen Eire Dendarea Charity.

Below left: Ch. Luath Bonnie Blue Bairn R.O.M. with Ch. Glen Eire Willie Wonderful R.O.M. as a puppy.

Below right: Ch. Glen Eire Willie Wonderful R.O.M. (by Ch. Misty Shadow of Willowmead ex Ch. Luath Bonnie Blue Bairn R.O.M.). Willie has made his mark in the show ring and is in the top sires list.

184

Osmart Brown Barnaby, sired Gael's (and Canada's) first Beardie litter.

From that litter came Ch. Raggmopp First Impression Can. & Am. C.D., foundation of Alice Clark's Bedlam Beardies; Ch. Raggmopp First Lieutenant C.D., foundation stud for Barbara and Colin Blake's Colbara Beardies; Ch. Raggmopp First Chance, foundation stud for Culzean Beardies and the sire of Ch. Shaggylane's Beaming Teak; plus three other champions.

Gael had two other equally successful litters, one by Ch. Bronze Javelin of Tambora, whose best-known member was Ch. Raggmopp Bellarmine C.D.X., a multiple group winner, specialty Best in Show winner, and reserve BIS at the New Delhi, India, championship show. The third litter, sired by Worthing Memorie, produced specialty winning Ch. Raggmopp Gaelin Image.

Gael also took time for a show career, and when the Canadian kennel club recognized Beardies in August 1970, she quickly became Canada's first Beardie champion and the first Beardie with a C.D. A multiple group placer, she was twice Top Beardie of the Year in Canada, a specialty Best in Show winner, and she put Raggmopp solidly on the map as a leading kennel.

Now into its seventh generation of Beardies, Raggmopp is responsible for several strains, all going back by different routes to Gael. From her has sprung an identifiable Raggmopp look, based on the Wishanger type. The line is noted for flat skulls and strong forefaces with good underjaw, expression, good bodies, and flat, hard coat, as well as good temperament—another Wishanger legacy.

Top left: Ch. Raggmopp Gaelin Image (by Worthing Memorie Ex Ch. Wishanger Marsh Pimpernel C.D.).

Top right; Ch. Wishanger Marsh Pimpernel R.O.M. (by Wishanger River Humber ex Wishanger Creeping Tansy), foundation of Raggmopp.

Bottom left: Am. Can. Ch. Banacek Fawn Fabric ROM both U.S. and Canada (by Ch. Osmart Bonnie Blue Braid ex Banacek Black Bobbin).

Bottom right: Ch. Raggmopp Jamoca Fudge (by Ch. Banacek Fawn Fabric ex Ch. Bedlam's Echo Ere Raggmopp).

RICH-LIN

Richard and Linda Nootbaar founded Rich-Lin in 1970 with the arrival of Edenborough Full O Life ("Shag") and Edenborough Loch Ness ("Sanford"), from England. Shag was a love. The Nootbaar's children used her for a pillow, where she would lay for hours. Recognition for the breed came when she was seven and she was spayed shortly thereafter, so she never acquired her championship, but left her mark on the breed nevertheless with daughters Ch. Rich-Lins Royal Shag and Ch. Rich-Lins Molly of Arcadia. Shag's then unknown littermate, Edenborough Blue Bracken, became the top winning Beardie in the world.

"Sanford," on the other hand, was independent and unruly and prone to escaping to look for bitches in season. At times he would be gone for months, during which time he fit into all types of lifestyles, even herding sheep and cattle. He was always home within the year, and spent his last four years safely in Rich-Lin.

Next, Ch. Jaseton Princess Argonetta ROM, "Dusty," a Blue Bracken daughter, joined the kennel. An ambassador for the breed during pre-recognition, she became No. 1 Miscellaneous Class Dog in 1972. Ch. Edenborough Adventure ROM, also imported, was No. 3 Miscellaneous Dog that same year. The two were eventually bred to produce Ch. Rich-Lins Pride of Jason ROM. He in turn was bred to Ch. Rich-Lins Royal Shag ROM to produce the top winning Ch. Rich-Lins Mister Magoo ROM, No. 1 Beardie in 1978 and still among the top ten.

Rich-Lin is now into their fifth generation, producing only blues and blacks. In 1983 they had the thrill of seeing Ch. Rich-Lins Outlaw become the first American bred Best in Show Beardie.

186

Top left: Ch. Rich-Lins Royal Shag R.O.M.
Bottom left: Ch. Rich-Lins Outlaw.
Below: Am. Can. Ch. Rich-Lins Mister Magoo R.O.M.

HA'PENNY

The first Bearded Collie came to Ha'Penny in 1972 after a long search in England for the ideal specimen. Two littermates were imported, Ch. Brambledale Black Diamond and Ch. Brambledale Blue Bonnet. Bonnet became the first American Bearded Collie Champion and was top winning Beardie in 1977 and 1978. Her show record was surpassed by her daughter, Ch. Ha'Penny Blue Blossom, top winning Beardie in 1979 and 1980. Blossom and her sisters provided a rich genetic bank for Ha'Penny, but J. Richard Schneider decided to search once more in Britain for the perfect mate for Blossom. In 1980 the Schneiders imported English Ch. Chauntelle Limelight. He quickly finished in the U.S. and is the top winning Beardie in 1983.

Ha'Penny Beardies combine Brambledale and Bothkenner lines. The kennel has produced a Best of Breed winner at Westminister, plus group and Best in Show winners.

LOCHENGAR

As happens with most breeds, one dedicated breeder disciples another, and from one foundation may spring many top lines. So it is with Lochengar. James and LaRae Conro acquired their first Beardie Rich-Lins Honey Bear ROM in 1975, and later that year added Am. Can. Ch. Rich-Lins Mister Magoo ROM. Magoo, who is co-owned with the Nootbars, was owner-handled by LaRae to both his championships in a total of seven shows, and later to 89 Best of Breeds and 20 working group placements.

Right: Ch. Lochengar Never Surrender, "Jennie," with LaRae Conroe.

Below, left to right: Ch. Ha'Penny Blue Blossom (by Ch. Brambledale Bet ex Ch. Brambleadale Blue Bonnet), dam of 9 champions and top winning bitch.

Ch. Brambledale Black Diamond, littermate of Blue Bonnet.

Lochengar Old Curiosity Shop R.O.M.

In 1976 the Conroes imported Ch. Edenborough My Fair Lady and in 1977 they acquired Ch. Excellent Outfit Queen, also from Edenborough. Now into the third generation, Lochengar has produced eleven champions with six group placers.

A small kennel, they raise only one litter per year. Males are at stud by private treaty only, which may limit the mark they make on the list of all-time producers, but Lochengar dogs, nevertheless, are making a mark on the U.S. Beardie scene.

SILVERLEAF

Silverleaf Beardies began in 1973 when, with the help of Margaret Osborne, international judge, the Riesebergs obtained BIS Am. Can. Ch. Shiel's Mogador's Silverleaf C.D. ROM HC, and Ch. Shepherd's Help from Shiel C.D. ROM HC. "Kent" and "Sheila" totally sold the Riesebergs on

Bearded Collies, and soon the Shelties and Elkhounds were phased out in favor of the new breed.

Later more imports were added, including Am. Can. Ch. Osmart Silverleaf Goldmine ROM, ("Fawnzie"), Parcana Possibility ROM, ("Risky"), and Ch. Osmart Blueprint of Braid, ("Jenny").

Silverleaf combines the lineage of Cairnbohn and Blue Braid and other top English lines, and has been influencial in the founding of a number of U.S. and Canadian kennels. Now into the third and fourth generations, Silverleaf has produced sixty-four champions, breeding only two or three litters per year. As many as possible of the dogs are tested for herding, and soundness and preservation of the original herding instinct and temperament are important considerations in the breeding program. Bitches are bred no more than once a year, and although used only limitedly at stud, Kent is the second top producing sire to date with twenty-eight champion offspring.

Left: Ch. Lochengar Kernel Pikering (by Ch. Rich-Lins Mr. Magoo ex Ch. Excellent Outfit Queen).

Below left: Am. Can. Ch. Thaydom Silverleaf Cinnamon
Below right: Ch. Silverleaf Barbara's Girl (Am. Can. Ch. Osmart Silverleaf Goldmine ROM ex Am. Can. Ch. Silverleaf Kashmere Lynn ROM).

PARCANA

After breeding Shelties for twenty-five years, Jo Parker turned to Beardies in 1974. The original stock was chosen to meet Parcana standards of equal emphasis on type, soundness, intelligence and temperament. Believing that three lines—Osmart, Edenborough and Davealex—each had distinct qualities that would complement each other, Jo chose as foundation stud Ch. Parcana Silverleaf Vandyke ROM HC, a "Kent" son going back to Osmart through Sunbree. Vandyke is currently sire of ten champions, with other youngsters just coming up.

Foundation bitches included Ch. Edenborough Parcana ROM, dam of seven champions, (a daughter of Eng. Ch. Edenborough Blue Bracken ROM out of a Davealex bitch); Ch. Osmart Smoky Blue Parcana ROM, dam of five champions, (by Eng. Ch. Osmart Bonnie Blue Braid ROM). From these, Jo has retained Ch.

Parcana Portrait ROM HC, dam of six champions, Ch. Parcana Heart Throb HC, sire of four champions, and the young Ch. Parcana Jake McTavish. Parcana Beardies have included three who have been in the top ten nationally, and others with multiple BOB wins or group placements. Parcana dogs were among the first Beardies to be herding certified—six dogs covering three generations. Some of these are currently in training for sheepdog trials.

JANDE

Jande was founded in 1973 by Janice and De Arle Masters. At first the Masters concentrated on rough Collies, but for the past several years have focused exclusively on Bearded Collies. Foundation stock was imported from Australia, Wales, and England, incorporating Edenborough,

Right: (L to R): Am. Can Ch. Jande's Just Dudley, Am. Can. Ch. Jande's Oxford Knight in Blue, Ch. Jande's Lucky Tri, and Ch. Jande's Lucky Mary.

Below left: Aust. Am. Can. Ch. Beardie Bloody Mary ROM.

Center: Ch. Osmart Smoky Blue Parcana ROM.

Right: Ch. Parcana Portrait ROM HC, dam of six champions.

Willowmead, and some Brambledale bloodlines. International Champion Beardie Bloody Mary ROM, imported from Australia, quickly gained her U.S. and Canadian titles and was the 1981 BOS winner at the BCCA National Specialty.

Descendents from Mary who have received special recognition in the show ring include Am. Can. Ch. Jande's Just Dudley, Am. Can. Ch. Jande's Oxford Knight in Blue, both Top Ten winners; Ch. Jande's Lucky Mary, Ch. Jande's Lucky Tri C.D., 1983 BCCA National Specialty BB winner. This "Lucky-Mary litter," (Ch. Edenborough Happy Go Lucky and Int. Ch. Beardie Bloody Mary) also included Ch. Jande MaryJane and Ch. Jande's Shawn the Fawn.

While Jande is interested in a glamorous show type Beardie, they breed first for soundness, substance, temperament and movement.

ARCADIA

Jim and Diane Shannon started Arcadia Beardies in 1974 with the purchase of Rich-Lins Rising Son. Later they added Ch. Rich-Lins Molly of Arcadia ROM as foundation bitch. She went on to become All Time Top Dam with twenty-five champion offspring, including a Best in Show winner, multiple group winners and several ROM. In 1979 Molly was Top All Breed Dam with nine champions finishing that year, eight from the same litter.

Ch. Rich-Lins Whiskers of Arcadia ROM was number one American bred Beardie in 1977, and bred to Molly he produced Ch. Arcadia's Midnight Munday ROM, top brood bitch in 1980.

In 1977 the Shannons imported Ch. Edenborough Happy Go Lucky ROM, now the All

Left: Ch. Edenborough Quick Silver R.O.M. (by Heyescott Tar ex Tambora's Penny Black R.O.M.), dam or ten champions.

Bottom left: Ch. Rich-lins Whiskers of Arcadia ROM (by Ch. Rich-lins Rising Son ex Am. Can. Ch. Hootnanny of Bengray ROM).

Bottom right: Ch. Rich-Lins Molly of Arcadia R.O.M. (by Rich-lins Rising Son ex Edenborough Full of Life R.O.M.), all-time top dam with twenty-five champion offspring.

Time Top Sire with thirty-seven champion get. "Lucky" was also a Top Ten Show winner in two different years.

An imported bitch, Ch. Edenborough Quick Silver ROM gave Arcadia ten champions and became top producing Beardie bitch for the year in 1981.

Although a small kennel, Arcadia has bred or owned over sixty-five champions.

GAYMARDON

Gail Miller became interested in dog showing while living in England. After a brief experience with West Highland White Terriers, the Millers met that wonderful fellow, Eng. Ch. Wishanger Cairnbahn, known as Colin, and the Beardies "stole their hearts forever." They soon acquired Ch. Gaymardon Chesapeake Mist and her littermate, Ch. Gaymardon Yorktown Yankee, which they showed a bit in England as youngsters before returning to the U.S. "Misty" took BOB at Westminster in 1981, and BOB at the 1982 National Specialty from the Veteran's class. She was Top Beardie Dam for 1982, in the Top Ten All Time Producer list with seven champions to her credit, and No. 10 All Time Top Winning Bitch.

A Misty son, Gaymardon Bouncing Bogart is also among the All Time Top Winners and is the sire of four champions in very limited breeding. His littermate, Ch. Gay Baron of Bramel, is a multiple group placing Beardie, and Ch. Gaymardon T is for Toby is a third champion to finish from that same litter, sired by Am. Can. Ch. Brisles Mouffy Mister ROM.

Gaymardon Beardies, of which there have been only twenty-nine old enough to show, have totalled over four hundred Best of Breed wins and forty group placements, including three generations.

Right: Ch. Gaymardon's Baron of Bramel.

191

Below left: Ch. Gaymardon Chesapeake Mist, dam of seven champions.
Below right: Ch. Camshron Babs, the only white champion to date.

SNO-BERRY

Jerald and Maria Jozwiak purchased their foundation bitch, Ch. Camshron Babs ROM in Scotland in 1971. Calbrae's Tunes of Glory joined them in 1974 and the first Sno-Berry puppies arrived that fall. The name "Sno-Berry" came from these two foundation dogs—Babs, better known as "Winnie," was white as snow, while "Bandit" was black as a berry!

The breeding of Winnie and Bandit produced the group placing Ch. Sno-Berry's Black Lad and multiple Best of Breed winning Ch. Sno-Berry's Chrysanthemum. Bred to Can. Ch. Happy Hooligan of Bengray ROM, Winnie produced Ch. Sno-Berry's Black Wizard. These dogs combine the Wishanger, Tambora, and Osmart lines.

Later two more imports, Brambledale Bala and Ch. Brambledale Blaise, both sired by Eng.

Ch. Brambledale Balthazar, a Blue Braid son, were added to the kennel.

Other breeders who have made their mark in the early days of the breed in this country include Moira and Ian Morrison's Caldbrae Beardies, the Lachmann's Crickett Beardies, and Pam Gaffney's Unicorn Kennels in California.

HISTORY MARCHES ON

A number of newer breeders are coming to the forefront of the show scene. Some of them, perhaps, will be the trendsetters of the future. Many could be included. Only those kennels exhibiting current top winners and on whom we were able to obtain photos and information are listed.

Ch. Shaggylane's Beaming Teak has both U.S. and Canadian Best in Show wins on his record.

SAMMAMISH KENNEL CLUB

192

Shaggylane

Barbara Niddrie purchased her first Beardie in England in 1970 and soon was totally in love with them. Imported Ch. Yager Gigue, a Davealex Royal Brigadier daughter, was her choice. She was bred to Ch. Raggmopp First Chance, and the rest is history. From that litter came the first (and so far only) Beardie to win Best in Shows in both Canada and the United States, Ch. Shaggylane's Beaming Teak. Teak took his first Canadian group win at just fifteen months of age and went on to win thirteen Best in Shows. He was top Beardie in Canada, 7th All Breed, in 1978; Top Beardie and 6th All Breed in 1979; Top Beardie in Canada, 1980; Top Beardie in the U.S. Phillips System, 1979.

Teak is beginning to make his mark as a sire as well, with several champions to his credit.

Stonybrook

Stonybrook had it's beginnings with a brown bitch, Stonybrook's Mountain Lady, who goes back to Caulbrae lines. Mike Larizza has owned a Beardie since the breed was recognized. Breeding is on a very limited basis, with an emphasis on soundness, type, and temperament.

"Mountain's" first litter was by Am. Can. Ch. Glen Eire Willie Wonderful began the Stonybrook line. From that litter came Stonybrook's Wind Chime. She was bred to Ch. Copper Clarence at Beagold, who was imported from England and became All Time Top Winning Beardie in the U.S. "Chime" and "Copper" produced Ch. Stonybrook's Fantasia, a multiple breed winner and group placer, and Ch. Stonybrook's Hampton T, "Dancer."

BIS Ch. Copper Clarence at Beagold has one-hundred-eighty-one Best of Breed wins to his credit at the end of 1983.

Braemar

Don and Marily Thomas fell in love with Beardies when they saw them at a San Francisco show in 1976. Four months later they acquired their first bitch, Ch. Thomas' Day-Zee of Silverleaf. Later they obtained Am. Can. Ch. Silverleaf Virginia Reel and Ch. Parcana Braemar's Golddigger. Their first male was Am. Can. Ch. Glen Eire Red Button, "Rusty," later followed by a second male, Ch. Ha' Penny Blue Max at Braemar. "Max," sired by Eng. Am. Ch. Chauntel Limelight ROM, has become a multiple group placer.

Artisan

Artisan Beardies was founded in 1976 with the acquisitions of Am. Can. Ch. Silverleaf Gifted Artisan, A Ch. Shiel's Mogador Silverleaf son. He was joined a year later by Am. Can. Ch. Artisan Silverleaf O' Parcana, "Bonnie." The only breeding of Charlie and Bonnie produced a litter of nine, of which only one male survived. This puppy became Am. Can. Ch. Gaelyn Copper Artisan ROM, a top winner and producer that has accumulated 90 Best of breed wins and numerous group placements.

"Charlie" was next bred to Artisan Burnish'd Silverleaf, a "Kent" daughter, to produce Am. Can. Ch. Artisan The Sorcerer C.D., Am. Can. Ch. Artisan Sorcerer's Apprentice, and Ch. Artisan Sorcery at Greysteel.

Not to be outdone by his sire, "Cooper" has already produced several champions, including Ch. Briardale's the Blacksmith, Ch. Briardale's Summer Fantasy, and at home, Ch. Artisan Copper Breagan, Ch. Artisan Copper V V Loscann, Ch. Artisan Sir Winston Copper, and Ch. Artisan Copper Sileen.

Left: Am. Can. Ch. Gaelyn Copper Artisan, sire of nine champions and a top winner.

194

Below right: Ch. Ha'Penny Blue Max at Braemar.

Dunwich

'Thomas Davis' Dunwich Kennel was founded in 1967, but the first Beardie was not acquired until 1969. In the early days of the Club the Davises actively worked for breed recognition and were more heavily involved in this than in breeding. Their first litter was whelped in 1971, and the first American bred BCCA Specialty match winner was their Dunwich Dudley Dustmop in 1973.

Dunwich is now the home of top winning Eng. Am. Ch. Chauntelle Limelight.

Penstone

Jean Jagersma imported her first Beardie, Ch. Lovelace of Tambora, from Tambora in 1971, and later that year obtained a Cairnbahn son, Can. Ch. Misty Shadow of Willowmead from Suzanne Moorhouse. Misty Shadow became Top Beardie in Canada in 1974, BCCC Top Beardie in 1974 and 1977, and is Register of Merit in both the U.S. and Canada.

Several other imports followed, including Can. Am. Ch. MacMont MacKintosh. "Mac" won the BCCC Specialty three consecutive years, 1980-82, and was Top Beardie in Canada in 1982.

While Jean's career does not give her time to do much breeding, she has succeeded in establishing an impressive stud force in Canada and she has been active in the BCCC and BCCA since their earliest days. An active exhibitor in both countries, she has also made frequent visits to England (her parents home) where she had the opportunity to see many of the great Beardies over the years.

Right: Eng. Am. Ch. Chauntelle Limelight.

Below left: Can. Am. Ch. Misty Shadow of Willowmead.
Below right: Can. Am. Ch. MacMont Mackintosh.

195

ALL TIME TOP WINNERS

(Statistics compiled from the May, 1977 AKC
Gazette through March, 1983, ending with the
last shows in December, 1982)

		Breeds	Points				Groups	Points
1.	Ha 'Penny Blue Blossom	149	944		1.	Chauntelle Limelight 2 BIS	44	15858
2.	Brambledale Blue Bonnet	143	928		2.	Copper Clarence at Beagold	40	14548
3.	Copper Clarence at Beagold	158	878		3.	Shaggylanes Beaming Teak 3 BIS	37	13928
4.	Chauntelle Limelight	134	873		4.	Brambledale Blue Bonnet 1 BIS	43	12494
5.	Unicorns The Mighty Quinn	64	734		5.	Ha 'Penny Blue Blossoms	26	8030
6.	Rich-Lins Mister Magoo	89	569		6.	Rich-Lins Mister Magoo	20	5756
7.	Criterion Weiser O'Mellowitt	95	489		7.	Shiels Mogador Silverleaf 1 BIS	15	5323
8.	Gaymardons Chesapeake Mist	87	488		8.	Unicorns The Mighty Quinn	9	3699
9.	Shiels Mogador Silverleaf	55	476		9.	Gaymardons Bouncing Bogart	12	3426
10.	Shaggylanes Beaming Teak	115	460		10.	Gaymardons Chesapeake Mist	11	2995
11.	Edenborough Happy Go Lucky	54	453		11.	Jandes Oxford Knight in Blue	10	2640
12.	Bon Di Parcana The Patriot	80	428		12.	Osmart Smoky Silver Starter at Chaniam	10	2492
13.	Colbara Blue Spruce	52	339		13.	Rich-Lins Whiskers of Arcadia	6	2177
14.	Jandes Oxford Knight in Blue	40	321		14.	Mistiburn Merrymaker	7	2125
15.	Gaelyn Copper Artisan	64	316		15.	Bon Di Parcana The Patriot	4	2018
16.	Rich-Lins Whiskers of Arcadia	46	313		16.	Gaymardons Baron of Bramel	8	1818
17.	Mistiburn Merrymaker	24	312		17.	Davealex Larky McRory at Linchael	5	1624
18.	Osmart Smoky Silver Starter at Chaniam	98	280					
19.	Gaymardons Baron of Bramel	46	278					
20.	Parcana Heart Throb	31	244					

Eng. Am. Ch. Chauntelle Limelight, top winning Beardie.

THE ALL TIME TOP PRODUCERS

Sires	No. of Champion Offspring
Edenborough Happy Go Lucky	30
Sheils Mogador Silverleaf	28
Glen Eire Willie Wonerful	14
Cauldbraes Brigadoon	14
Brambledale Boz	11
Brisles Mouffy Mister	11
Banacek Fawn Fabric	9
Davealex Rhinestone Cowboy	9
Misty Shadow of Willowmead	9
Glenhys Marshal Silverleaf	8
Osmart Silverleaf Goldmine	8
Chauntelle Limelight	7
Bon Di Parcana The Patriot	6
Shaggylanes Beaming Teak	6

Dams	
Rich-Lins Molly of Arcadia	21
Parcana Possibility	12
Garmardons Chesapeake Mist	9
Shepherd's Help from Shiel	7
Edenborough Quick Silver	7
Wyndcliff Unicorn Sterling	6
Ha'Penny Blue Blossom	5
Beardie Bloody Mary	4
Pepperland Liberty Bell	4

Register of Merit

Each club sets up their own rules for the Register of Merit award as this is not a recognized award from the AKC. The Bearded Collie Club of America requires that an ROM sire must have produced five champions and dams three champions. The sire and dam themselves do not have to be a champion, as for many reasons they are not shown, but are able to produce champions in the conformation ring. Basically, a Register of Merit means that you are breeding top quality dogs that are shown to their championship and are as close to the standard as possible.

Each year the list of top ROM's are listed in the Bearded Collie magazine published by the parent club and a certificate is given by BCCA to the owners of all new ROM's for the year. This is a honor to the dog/bitch and their breeders.

In Canada the requirement for a sire are a minimum of seven champions which includes the progeny of at least three bitches. Bitches must produce a minimum of five champions which include the get of at least two dogs.

197

Ch. Edenborough Happy Go Lucky R.O.M. (by Ch. Edenborough Blue Bracken ex Davealex Dawn Reign R.O.M.).

INTERNATIONAL GALLERY

Beardies have become popular the world over. The first Bearded Collies were bred in Holland in 1959 by Windmill Hillway Farm ex Lonecharm of Willowmead. From 1962 to 1972 thirteen litters were whelped, of which five were by Elderberry of Tambora. Between 1972 and 1983 Oliver Black of Tambora sired about twenty litters. His successor was Osmart Black Lace with more than three hundred puppies in most European countries and even Canada. Today's leading sires in Holland are Davealex Willie Wumpkins and Beagold Bruin Scott.

The Dutch Bearded Collie Club was founded in 1966, and by 1983 their membership has risen to 466.

In Germany, Penny Bank Brown Derby of Padworth has done well, and Midnight Cowboy zum Gronegau is a promising Beardie with his name already on may pedigrees.

Denmark has also produced a number of top Bearded Collies. Tambora's Peggy Brown (Pictured on page 77 at ten months) is the foundation bitch of one of the first Beadie kennels in Denmark, Daisy Belle. Among her offspring are four Danish champions.

Dk. Ch. Daisy-Belles Black Goodie-Lass (by Int. Ch. Osmart Black Lace ex Int. Ch. Tambora's Peggy Brown). Owner, Birgit Gunner, Denmark.

198

Int. and Dutch Ch. Robdave Melody Maker (by Edward Black from Osmart ex Taffetta of Willowmead). Breeder, Bob Hinton. Owners, Joop and Dea Hartman, Holland.

Int. German Austrian Swisse Ch. and VDH Sieger Penny Bank Brown Derby of Padworth (by Tambora's Tamarind of Padworth ex Pepperland Lucy in the Sky). Breeder, Mrs. Crummark. Owner, Marianne Husmert, Hagen.

Int., German, Austrian, Suisse Ch. and VDH-Sieger Barbie von Trenkelbach (by Ch. Nigella Gloaming ex Blaze Acclaim at Deanfield). Breeder, R. Gross, Reinsfeld. Owner, Marianne Husmert, Hagen.

Pennybank Brown Lady of Padworth (by Tambora's Tamarind of Padworth ex Pepperland Lucy in the Sky). Breeder, Mrs. Crummark. Owner, Ellen Wehrspann, E Germany.

Int., Dutch Ch. Osmart Black Lace, a top Beardie in Holland (by Ch. Osmart Bonnie Blue Braid ex Glenwhin Kirstin). Breeder, Jenny Osborne. Owner, Fred Kreugel, Holland.

Braelyn Broadholme Crofter (by Ruairidh of Willowmead ex Bobby's Girl of Bothkennar). Breeder, Mrs. D. Hale. Owner, Suzanne Moorhouse, England.

199

Three generations of Daisy Belle Beardies, right to left: Int. Dk. Ch. Tamboras Peggy Brown (by E. Blue Bracken); Dk. Ch. Daisy Belle's Black Goodie Lass (by O. Black Lace); and Daisy Belle's Black Lucy-Lass, (by D.B. Challenge Cut) at seven months.

Willowmead Super Honey (by Wishanger Cairnbahn ex Broadholme Cindy Sue of Willowmead). Breeder-Owner, Susanne Moorhouse, England.

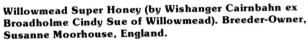

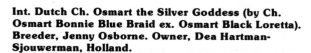

Int. Dutch Ch. Osmart the Silver Goddess (by Ch. Osmart Bonnie Blue Braid ex. Osmart Black Loretta). Breeder, Jenny Osborne. Owner, Dea Hartman-Sjouwerman, Holland.

Sunday Morings Genial Lennon, Daughter of Beagold Bruin Scott, Breeder, A. Cornelis, Owner, I. Hectors, Belgium.

200

Dutch Int. Ch. Beagold Bruin Scott (by Edenborough Star Turn at Beagold ex Beagold Pennyroyal. World Ch. 1980, 81, and 82, Eurocup winner 1978-1981. Breeder, J. Collis. Owner, Ben Scholte, Holland.

Appendix

COAT COLOR IN BEARDED COLLIES

For a long time, Beardie breeders could only say "anything is possible" when asked about color inheritance in Beardies. Now we can say the same thing and have facts to back it up! Dr. D. Johnson of the Dept. of Animal Genetics, University College, London, England, sorted out coat color inheritance for the English club and here are his findings:

The greying effect—that is, the gradual lightening of coat color as the dog grows from puppy to adult— is the result of the gene Greying G which is also found in Kerry Blues and Silver Poodles. This accounts for those black and white Beardies who turn slate or grey and for the brown who fade to cream.

There are four basic colors that puppies are born—black, blue (a smoke/steel grey shade), brown, and fawn (a biscuit shade). Puppies can also be tricolor but the tan always fades to a yellow/white at adulthood.

Leaving aside greying and tricolor, we have a two gene pair situation.

1. A black "B" versus brown "b." Any dog having one "B" will be black. Any dog having no "B" will be brown, i.e. BB or Bb will be black; bb will be brown.

2. Full color "D" will be dilute. An animal bbdd is both brown and dilute and this comes out as fawn.

Obviously, there are many combinations of these alleles, but each dog must have 2 at each locus, i.e. BdDd or BBdd, never bDD or Bdd. As an example, consider BBDD, a homozygous black crossed with bbdd, a homozygous fawn. All pups get a "B" and "D" from one parent and so must be BdDd. As they have a "B" and a "D", they are black full color.

If we cross two of these BdDd x BdDd, we can get a whole range of genotypes and appearances. This is because the offspring have received different B's and D's from each parent. From the BbDd parent they may receive BD, Bd, bD or bd.

A rainbow of coat colors in one litter! Left to right are: Jande LeRoy Brown (a brown); Am. Can. Ch. Jande's Oxford Knight in Blue (blue merle); Jande Sweetwater Jack (black); Ch. Jande's Shawn the Fawn (fawn); Jande Chocolate Frost (brown); and Ch. Jande's Lucky Tri (tricolor). Breeder, Jan Masters, Jande.

Here are the genotypes that make up the four different coat colors of pups at birth (omitting the greying gene)

Black	Brown	Blue	Fawn
BDBD	bDbD	Bdbd	bdbd
BDbd	bDbd	BdBd	
BDbd			
BDbD			

Below is a table showing all the possible combinations of matings between dogs of different colors and the ratio of colors to be expected from those matings. Excluded, as in the last issue, are the Greying gene "G" and the tricolour and white "Collie" patterns. The results of crosses are in ratio, of course, not actual numbers expected.

Black x Black
BDBD	x	BDBD	= all black
BDBD	x	BDBd	= all black
BDBD	x	BDbd	= all black
BDBd	x	BDBd	= 3 black; 1 blue
BDBd	x	BDbD	= all black
DBd	x	BDbd	= 3 black; 1 blue
BDbD	x	BDbD	= 3 black; 1 brown
BDbD	x	BDbd	= 3 black; 1 blue
BDbd	x	BDbd	= 9 black; 3 brown; 3 blue; 1 fawn

Black x Brown
BDBD	x	bDbD	= all black
DBd	x	bDbD	= all black
DbD	x	bDbD	= 1 black; 1 brown
Dbd	x	bDbD	= 1 black;1 brown
BDBD	x	bDbd	= all black
BDBd	x	bDbd	= 3 black; 1 blue
DbD	x	bDbd	= 1 black; 1 brown
BDbd	x	bDbd	= 3 black; 3 brown; 1 blue; 1 fawn

Black x Blue
BDBD	x	Bdbd	= all black
BDBd	x	Bdbd	= 1 black; 1 blue
BDbD	x	Bdbd	= 3 black; 1 brown
Dbd	x	Bdbd	= 2 black; 4 blue; 1 brown; 1 fawn
BDBD	x	BdBd	= all black
BDBd	x	BdBd	= 1 black; 1 blue
BDbd	x	BdBd	= all black
BDbd	x	BdBd	= 1 black; 1 blue

Black x Fawn
BDBD	x	bdbd	= all black
BDBd	x	bdbd	= 1 black; 1 blue
BDbD	x	bdbd	= 1 black; 1 brown
BDbd	x	bdbd	= 1 black; 1 fawn

Brown x Blue
bDbD	x	Bdbd	= 1 black; 1 brown
bDbd	x	Bdbd	= 1 black; 1 brown; 1 blue; 1 fawn
bDbD	x	BdBd	= all black
bDbd	x	BdBd	= 1 black; 1 blue

Brown x Fawn
bDbD	x	bdbd	= all brown
bDbd	x	bdbd	= 1 brown; 1 fawn

Blue x Fawn
Bdbd	x	bdbd	= 1 blue; 1 fawn
BdBd	x	bdbd	= all blue

Fawn x Fawn
bdbd	x	bdbd	= all fawn

Brown x Brown
bDbD	x	bDbD	= all brown
bDbD	x	bDbd	= all brown
bDbd	x	bDbd	= 3 brown; 1 fawn

Blue x Blue
Bdbd	x	Bdbd	= 3 blue; 1 fawn
BdBd	x	Bdbd	= all blue
BdBd	x	BdBd	= all blue

This article has been reprinted from the *English Bearded News*, May 1970, with thanks to Wendy Boorer and Dr. D. Johnson.

Other Sources
of Information

OTHER RECOMMENDED BOOKS

Breeding

Brackett, Lloyd C. **Planned Breeding.** Westchester, Illinois: Dog World Magazine, 1961

Burns, Marca; and Fraser, Margaret N. **Genetics of the Dog.** Edinburgh and London: Oliver and Boyd, 1966.

Harmer, Hilary. **Dogs and How to Breed Them.** Jersey City, New Jersey: T.F.H. Publications, Inc., 1968.

Judy, Will. **Dog Breeding Theory and Practice.** Chicago: Judy Publishing Co., 1958.

Onstott, Kyle. Revised by Phillip Onstott. **The New Art of Breeding Better Dogs.** New York: Howell Book House, Inc., 1970

Prine, Virginia Bender. **How Puppies Are Born.** New York: Howell Book House, Inc., 1974

Rutherford, Claire, and Neil, David H. **How To Raise A Puppy You Can Live With.** Loveland, Colorado: Alpine Publications. 1982.

Feeding

Collins, Donald, D.V.M. **The Collins Guide to Dog Nutrition.** New York: Howell Book House, Inc., 1972.

Gaines Dog Research Center. **Basic Guide to Canine Nutrition.** New York: General Foods Corp., 1965.

Whitney, Leon F., C.V.M. **How to Feed Your Dog.** Jersey City, New Jersey: T.F.H. Publications, Inc., 1960.

Gait

Elliott, Rachel Page. **Dogsteps-Illustrated Gait at a Glance.** New York: Howell Book House, Inc., Rev. 1983.

Lyon, McDowell. **The Dog in Action.** New York: Howell Book House, Inc., 1971

Lanting, Fred L. **Canine Hip Dysplasia and Other Orthopedic Problems.** Loveland, Colorado: Alpine Publications, Inc. 1982.

General Dog Books

Dennis, Sue; and Rowe, Sharon. **Pups n' Stuff.** Broomfield, Colorado, 1973

Dog Standards Illustrated. New York: Howell Book House, Inc., 1971.

The Complete Dog Book. New York: American Kennel Club, 1972.

Whitney, Leon F., D.V.M. **The Complete Book of Dog Care.** Garden City, New York: Doubleday and Company, Inc., 1953

Herding

Hartley, C.W.G. **The Shepherd's Dogs.** Christchurch, New Zealand: Whitcombe and Tombs, Ltd., reprinted 1972.

Holmes, John, **The Farmer's Dog.** London: Popular Dogs Publishing Co., Ltd., revised 1970

Little, Maryland E. **Happy Herding Handbook.** Wheel-A-Way Ranch, P.O. Box 2404, Riverside, California 92506. 1975.

Longton, Tim; and Hart, Edward. **The Sheepdog: It's Work and Training.** London: David and Charles, Ltd., 1976.

Mills, A.R.; McIntyre, W.V.; and Herbert, S.F. **A Practical Guide to Handling Dogs and Stock.** Wellington, Auckland, Sydney, and Melbourne: A.H. and A.W. Reed, 1964

Training

Davis, L. Wilson, **Go Find! Training Your Dog to Track.** New York: Howell Book House, Inc., 1974.

Johnson, Glen R. **Tracking Dog—Theory and Methods.** Rome, New York: Arner Publications, 1975.

Pearsall, Margaret E. **The Pearsall Guide to Successful Dog Training.** New York: Howell Book House, Inc., 1976

Pearsall, Milo D. and Verbruggen, Hugo M.D. **Scent: Training to Track, Search, and Rescue.** Loveland, Colorado: Alpine Publications, Inc. 1982

Pfaffenberger, Clarence J. **The New Knowledge of Dog Behavior.** New York: Howell Book House, Inc., 1963.

Saunders, Blanche. **The Complete Book of Dog Obedience.** New York: Howell Book House, Inc.

PERIODICALS, DOG SUBJECTS OF GENERAL INTEREST

Dogs In Canada. Apex, Publisher. 59 Front Street E., Toronto, Ontario, Canada. (Monthly. Official Publication of the Canadian Kennel Club. Newspaper format.)

Dog World Magazine. Helen Nowicki, Editor. Maclean Hunter, 300 W. Adams St., Chicago, Illinois 60606.

Dog World. (England.) The Dog World Ltd., 32, New Street, Ashford, Kent, England. (Weekly. Newspaper format.)

Front and Finish—The Dog Trainer's News. P.O. Box 333, Galesburg, Illinois 61401. (Monthly. Obedience news and articles.)

Off-Lead—The Dog Training Monthly. Arner Publications, P.O. Box 307, Graves Road, Westmoreland, New York 13490. (Monthly. Obedience subject matter.)

Purebred Dogs, American Kennel Gazette. Henry R. Bernacki, Editor. The American Kennel Club, 51 Madison Avenue, New York, New York 10010. (Monthly. Official publication of AKC.)

The Kennel Review. Dick Beauchamp, Editor. B. and E. Publications, Inc., 828 No. LaBrea Avenue, Hollywood, California 90038. (Monthly. geared to the professional handler and active shower. Excellent articles.)

ORGANIZATIONS

The American Kennel Club. 51 Madison Avenue, New York, New York 10010. All breed registry. Write to AKC for information on any breed, breed club, address of show secretaries and regional kennel club secretaries, and for rules and regulations for any AKC sanctioned event.

The Bearded Collie Club of America. The national, official organization for Beardie breeders and enthusiasts. Obtain address of current secretary or regional representatives from AKC.

Regional Bearded Collie Clubs. Obtain address of current secretary from BCCA. If you don't find a club listed for your area, write AKC or BCCA as new clubs are forming all the time.

Bearded Collie Club of California. San Francisco area.
Bearded Collie Club of Greater Dayton. Dayton, Ohio.
Bearded Collie Club of Greater New York.
Bearded Collie Club of Greater Long Island.
Bearded Collie Club of Southern California.
Berkshire Bearded Collie Club. New York area.
Chicagoland Bearded Collie Club. Chicago, Illinois.
Delaware Valley Bearded Collie Club.
New England Bearded Collie Club.
North Shore Bearded Collie Club. Illinois.
Queen City Bearded Collie Club. Denver, Colorado.
Tri-State Bearded Collie Club. Minnesota area.
Western Reserve Bearded Collie Club. Ohio area.

Bearded Collie Club. (England.) For address of current secretary, contact Miss Carol Gold, 580 Woburn Avenue, Toronto, Ontario M5M 1L9, Canada.

American Dog Owners Association. 1628 Columbia Turnpike, Castleton, New York 12033. ADOA is concerned with protecting the rights of responsible dog owners and promotion fair dog legislation nationwide. This group has been instrumental in prosecuting individuals and corporations responsible for dog abuse. Dues go to further these causes.

National Dog Registry. 227 Stebbins Road, Carmel, New York 10512. Telephone: 914-277-4485. NDR promotes tattooing dogs for identification, and assists in returning lost and stolen dogs to owners.

Stock Dog Fanciers of Colorado. Contact Mrs. Lu Kamber, 1208 Wabash Street, Denver, Colorado 80220. Promotes all breeds of stock dogs used for working livestock and encourages beginning trainers in herding.

MAGAZINES AND BOOKS ON BEARDED COLLIES

The Beardie Bulletin. Marcia Holava, Editor. 34613 Butternut Ridge Road, No. Ridgeville, OH 44039. Official publication of BCCA.

Bearded Collie Gazette. 47 Deerfoot Dr., East Longmeadow, MA 01028. Monthly magazine.

The Bearded Collie Club Year Book. (English) Jenny Osborne, Editor. Osmart Kennels, Bacup, Lancashire OL13 8ND England. (Published by English parent club. Several volumes available.)

Collis, Joyce. **All About the Bearded Collie.** London: Pelham Books Ltd. 1979.

Willison, Mrs. G.O. **The Bearded Collie.** London: W. and G. Foyle, Ltd. 1971. (Small booklet covering the history and revival of the breed.)

Index

205

About the Authors

A longstanding friendship between the authors began in the late 1960's, at which time Barbara was already an established breeder and B.J. was just getting started in Shelties. What began as a teacher-learner relationship eventually blossomed into a friendship and partnership.

The authors' first book, *Sheltie Talk*, published in 1967, was conceived because they wanted to give the Sheltie fancier a badly needed source of basic information specific to the breed—information which the authors had difficulty obtaining during their early years as breeders. The book has since become the most widely recommended work on the Shetland Sheepdog. Barbara and B.J. hope that *Beardie Basics* will provide equally valuable information for breeders and owners in this early stage of the Bearded Collie in America.

The authors worked closely, each writing approximately one-half of the chapters while the other critiqued and contributed further information. Therefore, readers will benefit from the knowledge and experience of not one, but two, experienced breeders. The use of "I" throughout the book was chosen to avoid incorrect connotations by the use of "we," as well as to avoid the awkwardness of identifying the writer in each instance.

Barbara Hagen began breeding Shelties in 1961, at the age of fourteen. Over the next sixteen years she bred or owned a dozen champions in Shelties and various other working breeds. In 1970, Barbara married Freedo Rieseberg, who previously had been involved in breeding German Shepherd dogs, and the two continued breeding and showing under her kennel name, Silverleaf. They obtained their first Bearded Collies from England in 1973, with the help of international judge Margaret Osborne.

B.J. McKinney began breeding and showing Shelties in 1966, under the name Kinni Kennels. Her interest in publications dates back to her twelfth year of age when, with camera and pen, she put together her first "book," a story about a litter of Sheltie puppies. Professionally, she has freelanced for a number of major metropolitan newspapers, and for over fifteen years she was involved in writing, planning, and producing publications for colleges and universities.

In April of 1980, Barbara Rieseberg died—a great loss not only to Freedo, but to the Beardie world as well. Silverleaf Kennel has remained as Barbara would have wanted, as Freedo is still involved with the showing and breeding to top quality puppies. Freedo has since married Betty "A Beardie person" and former friend of both Barbara and Freedo who shares the love and interest in the Beardies. They have continued with breedings planned before Barbara died to carry on the Silverleaf line.